ESSENTIAL READING SKILLS

ESSENTIAL READING SKILLS

John W. Presley
William M. Dodd

Augusta College

HOLT, RINEHART AND WINSTON New York Chicago San Francisco Philadelphia
Montreal Toronto London Sydney Tokyo Mexico City Rio de Janeiro Madrid

Library of Congress Cataloging in Publication Data

Presley, John W.
  Essential reading skills.
  1. College readers.   2. Developmental reading.
3. Reading comprehension.   I. Dodd, William, date.
II. Title.
PE1122.P7   428.4'3   81-4268
ISBN 0-03-058001-3   AACR 2

Copyright © 1982 by CBS College Publishing
Address correspondence to:
383 Madison Avenue
New York, N.Y. 10017
All rights reserved
Printed in the United States of America
Published simultaneously in Canada
2 3 4 5   039   9 8 7 6 5 4 3 2 1

CBS COLLEGE PUBLISHING
Holt, Rinehart and Winston
The Dryden Press
Saunders College Publishing

Instructor's Preface

Each year more and more students at both the senior high school and the college level are finding their way into developmental reading classes. Some come voluntarily, but most are placed there according to the results of standardized tests they have taken. Their instructors find themselves faced with students who must learn to deal with complex materials. These students need vocabulary and comprehension skills that are far more complex than the skills taught at the elementary and junior high school levels. To compound the problem, time is limited; reading instructors, in many cases, have only ten or twelve weeks to identify and remediate the students' reading problems. *Essential Reading Skills* is designed to aid these instructors. It provides both subject matter and comprehension skills exercises at the complex levels required in these courses. It also provides the reading instructor with a diagnostic tool for the identification of reading problems, along with a well-planned prescriptive text for remediation.

The text consists of more than ninety reading passages divided into four sections. Each of the first three sections contains twenty passages; the last section contains thirty-seven passages. Each section of passages has been number-coded by grade level, using the Fry Readability Scale.

The facts for the passages came from newspapers, encyclopedias, almanacs, and other reference works, but each passage was rewritten to a specific reading level. With one author, much closer control over progressively more difficult reading levels is possible, and the level is not sampled at several points in the passage and then averaged. The reading level is the same throughout the passage, no matter what is being discussed. In addition, the questions are more reliable because the passages were designed for the accompanying questions. The style of the passages is uniform throughout the text, so students aren't distracted by several different styles while developing their own vocabulary and reading skills.

Finally, these are high-interest passages, chosen for their ability both to interest and to inform students using the text. Students will pick up a wealth of specific information from these passages, discovering that informing can be a form of entertaining.

Each passage is accompanied by comprehension questions that help reinforce the following skills:

1. Understanding the main idea.
2. Recalling the facts.
3. Drawing conclusions.
4. Making inferences.
5. Defining vocabulary from context.

The numbering of the comprehension questions has been kept uniform throughout the text. All questions numbered #1 deal with the main idea of the passage. All questions numbered #2 deal with recalling factual material, and so forth. If a particular passage supports the inclusion of more than one question on any one of the five skills, the additional questions are included within the appropriate number by the use of subnumbering, as 3a, 3b, 3c, and so forth.

A pretest and a posttest have been included in the text. These tests are designed to give the instructor a means of evaluating the initial needs of the students, as well as providing a means of spot-checking improvement in the skills being taught. The design of the text and the detailed information provided by the pretest and posttest allow the instructor to assign practice in one particular skill at a time or in several particular skills at a time or to assign practice in all of the skills at different grade levels. The *Instructor's Manual* provides a detailed discussion on how to administer the tests, grade the tests, and make use of the data provided. Sample score sheets guide the instructor in making placement assignments that will most benefit the students.

In addition, the *Instructor's Manual* provides the following:

1. A guide to the "Developing the Skills" section of the students' text.
2. Suggestions for the use of the posttest.
3. Suggestions for managing the daily use of the text.
4. An alphabetical list of the vocabulary items taught in each section.
5. Suggestions for alternative uses of the text.
6. A grouping of the passages by subject matter.
7. Answer keys for the pretest and posttest and for all the reading passages.

The *Instructor's Manual* is available from your local Holt, Rinehart and Winston representative or by writing to the English Editor, Holt, Rinehart and Winston, 383 Madison Avenue, New York, NY 10017.

We wish to thank the following reviewers:
W. Royce Adams, Santa Barbara City College; Betty Bamberg, University of Southern California; D. W. Cummings, Central Washington University; Elizabeth Gibson, Pikes

Peak Community College; Louise S. Haugh, Pima Community College; Lee Kolzow, William Rainey Harper College; Cheryl McKernan, Central Washington University; Kathy Knowles Plummer, Northeast Louisiana University; Michael Policastro, Ramapo College; Barbara Reale, Aims Community College; Carol Sweedler, San Diego State University; Audrey Williams, Baruch College; Nancy Wood, University of Texas at El Paso. We also wish to thank Anne Boynton-Trigg and Lester A. Sheinis of Holt, Rinehart and Winston for their work on this book.

Augusta, Georgia

J.W.P.
W.M.D.

Contents

Instructor's Preface   v
Developing the Skills   1
    DESCRIPTION OF THE TEXT   1
    SAMPLE PASSAGES   2
    USING THE STUDENT PROGRESS CHART   12
    CONCLUSION   13

DIAGNOSTIC PRETEST   15
    OPTIONAL STUDENT ANSWER SHEET   16
    PARAGRAPHS 1-1 to 4-4   17
    STUDENT SCORE SHEET   37

Section 1   **READING PASSAGES**   39
    Passage 1-1   Subject: MANUEL THE MECHANIC   40
    Passage 1-2   Subject: COWBOY BOOTS   42
    Passage 1-3   Subject: LAZINESS   44
    Passage 1-4   Subject: WILD FOODS   46
    Passage 1-5   Subject: DENTISTS' OFFICES   48
    Passage 1-6   Subject: NITINOL, A SPACE AGE METAL   51
    Passage 1-7   Subject: RUGBY   53
    Passage 1-8   Subject: BLUEBIRDS   55
    Passage 1-9   Subject: PALM SPRINGS AND THE AGUA CALIENTE
                                INDIANS   57

Passage 1-10   Subject: THE OCTOPUS   60
Passage 1-11   Subject: DYE MAKING   62
Passage 1-12   Subject: RACEHORSES   65
Passage 1-13   Subject: WILD SEABIRDS AND OIL POLLUTION   68
Passage 1-14   Subject: THE INDY 500   71
Passage 1-15   Subject: CANOEING AND KAYAKING   74
Passage 1-16   Subject: PELÉ   77
Passage 1-17   Subject: JOHN REED   80
Passage 1-18   Subject: THE ART OF CHINESE PAINTING   83
Passage 1-19   Subject: IMMORTALITY   87
Passage 1-20   Subject: VIDEO DISCS   91

Section 2   READING PASSAGES   95

Passage 2-1   Subject: PURPLE MARTINS   96
Passage 2-2   Subject: HUMAN ALLERGIES   98
Passage 2-3   Subject: THE BRAIN   100
Passage 2-4   Subject: CRABBING   103
Passage 2-5   Subject: JOGGING   105
Passage 2-6   Subject: BLACK NEWSPAPERS   107
Passage 2-7   Subject: FRISBEE THROWING AND ORIENTEERING   110
Passage 2-8   Subject: VITAMINS   113
Passage 2-9   Subject: NORMAN ROCKWELL   116
Passage 2-10   Subject: THE MILGRAM EXPERIMENT   119
Passage 2-11   Subject: THE PILGRIMS   122
Passage 2-12   Subject: HIGHER EDUCATION FOR WOMEN   125
Passage 2-13   Subject: THE TINY ISLAND OF NAURU   128
Passage 2-14   Subject: INSOMNIA   131
Passage 2-15   Subject: FLEXIBLE WORK SCHEDULES   134
Passage 2-16   Subject: BULLFIGHTING   137
Passage 2-17   Subject: FORT KNOX   141
Passage 2-18   Subject: COMMON FOOT AND LEG INJURIES TO
                        EXERCISERS   144
Passage 2-19   Subject: CHINESE BRONZES   148
Passage 2-20   Subject: FIRST AID   152

Section 3   READING PASSAGES   157

Passage 3-1   Subject: OPERATION RED FLAG   158
Passage 3-2   Subject: McDONALD'S   160
Passage 3-3   Subject: THE MADRID FAULT   162
Passage 3-4   Subject: OPINION POLLS   164
Passage 3-5   Subject: CHEATING ON JOB APPLICATIONS   166
Passage 3-6   Subject: VITAMIN C   168
Passage 3-7   Subject: MATINICUS ISLAND   170
Passage 3-8   Subject: HENRY KISSINGER   172
Passage 3-9   Subject: WOMEN PILOTS   175
Passage 3-10   Subject: QUARTER HORSES   177
Passage 3-11   Subject: ROBERT E. LEE   179
Passage 3-12   Subject: BRASS RUBBING   182

Passage 3-13 Subject: SALMON 185
Passage 3-14 Subject: ROCK CONCERTS 188
Passage 3-15 Subject: DINOSAURS 191
Passage 3-16 Subject: SCIENCE FICTION WRITERS 194
Passage 3-17 Subject: ROLLER SKATING 197
Passage 3-18 Subject: MORMONISM 200
Passage 3-19 Subject: OBESITY 204
Passage 3-20 Subject: DEFINITIONS OF LOVE 208

Section 4 READING PASSAGES 211

Passage 4-1 Subject: THE WESTERN 212
Passage 4-2 Subject: *FOXFIRE* 214
Passage 4-3 Subject: GAME RANCHES 216
Passage 4-4 Subject: ISABELLA STEWART GARDNER 218
Passage 4-5 Subject: TENNESSEE VALLEY AUTHORITY 221
Passage 4-6 Subject: MARY CHURCH TERRELL AND RALPH BUNCHE 224
Passage 4-7 Subject: BLACK AMERICANS IN THE MILITARY 227
Passage 4-8 Subject: SUPERMAN 230
Passage 4-9 Subject: PASSPORTS AND VISAS 233
Passage 4-10 Subject: MICROWAVES 235
Passage 4-11 Subject: GEORGE AND JOHN JOHNSON 238
Passage 4-12 Subject: SUGAR 241
Passage 4-13 Subject: VITAMIN E 244
Passage 4-14 Subject: THE POLES AND AMERICAN HISTORY 247
Passage 4-15 Subject: ROY WILKINS 250
Passage 4-16 Subject: ORGANIC FOODS 253
Passage 4-17 Subject: HEALTH RISKS 256
Passage 4-18 Subject: NINETEENTH- AND TWENTIETH-CENTURY EATING HABITS 259
Passage 4-19 Subject: AGORAPHOBIA 262
Passage 4-20 Subject: ADJUSTING TO COLD WEATHER 265
Passage 4-21 Subject: ELIZABETH BLACKWELL 268
Passage 4-22 Subject: AMERICAN CLERICAL WORKERS 271
Passage 4-23 Subject: VEGETARIANISM 274
Passage 4-24 Subject: ANDREI GROMYKO 277
Passage 4-25 Subject: STRESS 280
Passage 4-26 Subject: UNDERGROUND HOMES 283
Passage 4-27 Subject: "FISH SNIFFING" 286
Passage 4-28 Subject: INSURANCE RISKS 290
Passage 4-29 Subject: GALILEO 293
Passage 4-30 Subject: MUHAMMAD ALI 297
Passage 4-31 Subject: BATTERIES 300
Passage 4-32 Subject: THE TELEVISION INDUSTRY 303
Passage 4-33 Subject: CONFUCIUS 307
Passage 4-34 Subject: BLACK TUESDAY 311
Passage 4-35 Subject: WOOD BURNING 314
Passage 4-36 Subject: THOMAS A. EDISON 318
Passage 4-37 Subject: OKEFENOKEE SWAMP 322

DIAGNOSTIC POSTTEST   **327**
    OPTIONAL STUDENT ANSWER SHEET   328
    PARAGRAPHS 1-1 to 4-4   329
    STUDENT SCORE SHEET   349

Student Progress Chart   **350**

Developing the Skills

DESCRIPTION OF THE TEXT

Essential Reading Skills is designed to help you prepare yourself for college-placement reading tests or for course-exit exams if you are already involved in a developmental reading program. The last section of the text is written at the level of these tests, and the first three sections gradually build up to that level. The questions at the end of the reading passages also become more complex as you work through the text. A pretest will help you and your instructor decide where to start in the book and how to plan your work most efficiently.

The Pretest and Posttest

The pretest serves as a miniature version of the text, with short paragraphs rather than longer passages. You will not be timed on the pretest, so you should read as thoroughly as possible and make every effort to answer all the questions; refer to the paragraph as often as you need to. The Student Score Sheet at the end of the pretest will be completed by either you or your instructor and will indicate your strengths and weaknesses for you. It will also provide your instructor with information for determining your placement in the text. The posttest at the end of the text is similar to the pretest and will be used by your instructor to determine how successful your practice in the textbook has been and to assign additional passages in the text.

Using the Text

As you work in the textbook and read each passage your instructor has assigned, you should underline main ideas, pay close attention to factual information, and notice the sequence in which the author develops the main ideas, even numbering each new detail. Think beyond the passage: consider what the author has omitted, as well as what has been included. What other kinds of information might have been useful to you, the reader? What other conclusions can be drawn from the information given? As you read, use a dictionary to determine the meaning of any word you do not recognize or for which the passage does not suggest a meaning. As you work through the comprehension questions, be sure to check your conclusions. After you have chosen an answer, reread the other possible answers, and make sure the passage eliminates them as possibilities.

SAMPLE PASSAGES

Read the following passage closely. Be sure to follow the advice you were given in "Using the Text" by underlining main ideas, paying close attention to factual information, and noticing the sequence in which the author develops the main ideas, even numbering each new detail. Use a dictionary to determine the meaning of any word you cannot define from the context.

In the upper right corner of each passage you will find a generalization about the subject of the passage. Before you read the passage, formulate some questions in your mind that you would like to have answered by the passage or that you would expect to have answered about the generalization. For example, the subject of the following passage is "nearsightedness." Here are some questions you might need answered about such a subject

—What is *nearsightedness?*
—What causes it?
—What problems can it cause?
—How can *nearsightedness* be corrected?

Now read the passage:

PASSAGE 1-0   SUBJECT: Nearsightedness

Weak eyesight is a term that generally is used to refer to nearsighted eyes. People who are nearsighted can see well at a short range, but anything very far away at all is likely to be a dull blur. The term *weak eyesight* is misleading, for in nearsighted eyes the lens of the eye is actually too strong. The nearsighted lens is so powerful that it focuses the light coming into the eye too quickly. The image is formed in front of the retina, which contains the optical nerves. *Nearsightedness* is common, and its growth may be gradual; often the blurring of distant objects is so slight at first that a person may not recognize the condition. Nearsightedness is frequently discovered first at school. It is here that a student first realizes the difficulty of seeing work on the blackboard, whereas others in the class have no trouble reading the board at all. After discovery, nearsightedness can easily be corrected. A concave lens called a "minus" lens because it decreases the power of the lens of the eye itself is the prescription.

▲ (182 WORDS) ▲

After you have read the passage, you can prepare yourself for the comprehension questions that follow by answering the following questions mentally:

—Have I identified the main idea or ideas?
—Have I noted the significant details given about the main idea or ideas?
—What other kinds of information might have been useful to me, the reader?
—What other conclusions can be drawn from the information given?
—What is implied by the passage?
   What statements can be made based on the material presented, even though they are not included in the passage?
—Do I understand all of the vocabulary in the passage? Have I defined unknown words either from the context or by using my dictionary?

Now answer question 1(a). Refer to the passage as you consider your answer. Circle the correct answer:

1(a) The main idea of this passage is that
   a. lens strength affects eyesight.
   b. *nearsightedness* causes difficulty for schoolchildren.
   c. *nearsightedness* is a visual problem caused by an abnormally strong eye lens but may be easily corrected.
   d. "minus" lenses correct *nearsightedness*.

This question tests your ability to identify the principal thought or concept of an entire passage. This text—and most standardized reading tests—asks this question in several different ways:

—The main idea of this passage is that . . .
—The main purpose of this passage is to . . .
—This passage is mainly about . . .
—This passage is primarily a discussion of . . .

All of the preceding test items ask you to apply your knowledge of the same skill—can you identify the principal thought or concept? Your answer must be a sentence or phrase that is broad or general enough to include every significant detail in the passage. On the other hand, your choice must also be narrow or specific enough to include *only* the details that are given in the passage.

In question 1(a) you should have circled answer *c*. It is the only answer that is broad enough to include all the significant details of the passage. At the same time, it is narrow enough to exclude details that are not included in the passage. Answer *a* is *too broad*. It does not specify that lens strength causes nearsightedness. It leaves open a discussion of lens strength as it affects *all* visual problems. Answer *b* is *too narrow*. It expresses a detail from the passage but excludes discussion of the cause and correction of nearsightedness. Answer *d* is also *too narrow*. It expresses a detail from the passage but excludes discussion of the cause and problems of nearsightedness.

Now answer question 1(b), another question about the main idea of the passage. Refer to the passage as you consider your answers. Circle the correct answer:

1(b) The best title for this passage is
    a. Diagnosing *Nearsightedness*
    b. The Cause and Correction of *Nearsightedness*
    c. The Amazing "Minus" Lens
    d. The Workings of the Eye

This question tests your ability to pick a short phrase that best sums up the main idea or principal thought of a passage. It is usually helpful to refer to the question that has asked you to identify the main idea. In this case, that would be question 1(a), where *c* was the correct answer; so as you consider your choices, look for the phrase that best sums up answer *c*.

In question 1(b) you should have chosen answer *b*. It is the only answer that is broad enough to include every significant detail that was mentioned in answer *c* for question 1(a). Answer *a* is *too narrow*; it does not include all the significant details included in the passage. In another sense, answer *a* is really *not discussed*. The passage does mention diagnosis of *nearsightedness*, but it does *not* discuss the procedure of diagnosis. Answer *c* is *too narrow*; it would not include a definition of nearsightedness or any of the problems associated with the ailment. Notice the word *Amazing*. Does the passage imply that the lens is "amazing?" No. The author uses the word to "dress up" the title and make it appealing. In doing so, he provides a title that is *not accurate*. Answer *d* is *too broad*. It would open a discussion of the physical functioning of the eye. The passage discusses only part, the lens; it does not discuss the *working* of the lens. Therefore, answer *d* is also *not accurate* because it implies information that isn't included in the passage. The workings of the eye are *not discussed*.

Remember that when you consider the choice of titles for a passage, you must examine each choice to see if it is:

  —*too narrow*
  —*too broad*
  —*not accurate*
  —*not discussed*

Also remember that a title can be an incorrect choice because of a combination of these items!

Now answer question 2. Refer to the passage as you consider your answers. Circle the correct answer:

2. According to the passage, which of the following statements is not true?
    a. Nearsighted people have little trouble seeing things close to them.
    b. *Nearsightedness* is usually a progressive visual problem.
    c. *Nearsightedness* is often found in school-age children.
    d. The "minus" lens cures the lens problem in nearsighted people.

This question tests your ability to identify major details in a passage. Choosing the correct answer is usually a simple matter if you check each choice by referring to the passage. However, there are several pitfalls you may encounter in the text and on standardized reading tests. First, be sure you read the question carefully and understand what it's asking! Notice in question 2 that you are asked to identify the statement that is *not* true. If you read over the word *not*, you will probably miss the question! Remember, also, that the word *except* is a form of *not*. It asks you to eliminate the one answer the could not be included with the other three choices. Second, double-check the answer you choose to be sure that it is not a misquote. Many times tests will quote an entire sentence from the passage, changing only one word. If you are looking for the one answer that is true among the choices, that one word may eliminate the answer as a correct choice. In other words, do *exactly* what the question is asking you to do—read closely, refer to the passage often, and pay close attention to the wording of your choices.

In question 2 you should have chosen answer *d*. Notice that the sentence comes very close to being accurate. However, the author changes one word—*cure*. The passage states that the "minus" lens *corrects* nearsightedness. It does not, in fact, alter the structure of the lens; it simply compensates for the abnormal structure. Answer *a* is a true statement; it is simply a rewording of the first part of sentence 2. Answer *b* is a true statement; the passage states that the "growth may be gradual." In this passage "gradual" and "progressive" mean basically the same thing. Answer *c* is also true. It is a rephrasing of sentences 7 and 8 in the passage.

Now answer question 3. Refer to the passage as you consider your answers. Circle the correct answer:

3. We can conclude from the passage that
    a. the number of nearsighted people in the world is probably greater than the number of diagnosed cases.
    b. the brain is incapable of picking up images that form in front of the retina.
    c. eventually, nearsighted people lose the ability to see at close distances.
    d. the "minus" lens is very expensive.

This question tests your ability to interpret or analyze the passage you read. Every passage has a main idea; otherwise, there would be no reason for the passage. A well-written passage has sufficient supporting details to make an assertion about the main idea. The supporting details expand or explain the main idea. These supporting details

5

or thoughts do not exist in a vacuum. Because you are a thinking, reasoning human being, the supporting details will always bring to mind *other* thoughts that complement or contradict the details of the passage. This question requires you to utilize *your* thoughts. It requires you to organize the thoughts in the passage in a logical manner and to predict other details that might have been included. Each of us does this daily in our normal routines. If you awake to cloudy skies, thunder, and lightning, you probably carry an umbrella to work because you *predict* that the logical extension or outcome of these events will be rain. If your math teacher writes the numbers 3, 5, 7, 9, ——, —— on the board, you immediately predict that the numbers 11 and 13 could be included in this sequence. Why? Because you study the relationship among the numbers. You notice that all of the numbers are odd and that they are increasing by two each time. Based on the evidence given, the only conclusion that is *justified* is that 11 and 13 go in the two blanks. The word *justified* is very important here. When you choose an answer for this type of question, you must always refer to the passage to be sure the facts "justify" the conclusion. You may only work with facts that are presented in the passage. Do *not* let your own personal knowledge of a subject or your own personal opinions about a subject sway your decision.

In question 3 you should have chosen answer *a*. The passage states (1) that *nearsightedness* is common, (2) that its growth may be gradual, and (3) that at first a person may not recognize the condition. The logical outcome is that many people don't realize that their eyesight is deteriorating until it becomes quite severe. Answer *b* is not an accurate representation of information presented in the passage. Obviously, the brain can pick up these images because the images appear as a "dull blur" to the nearsighted person. The image is not absent, but the clear focus is. Answer *c* would have to be based on your personal knowledge of the subject or your personal opinion based on experience. You may know of cases in which nearsighted people have lost all vision, but the passage does not discuss that possibility. Like answer *c*, answer *d* would have to be a conclusion based on information *outside* the passage. The passage does not *justify* either answer *c* or *d*.

Now answer question 4(a). Refer to the passage as you consider your answers. Circle the correct answer:

4(a) The passage suggests that
    a. if *nearsightedness* is left uncorrected, it can cause blindness.
    b. nearsighted students are often embarrassed by their inability to see as well as other students.
    c. the average person doesn't understand what causes *nearsightedness*.
    d. because of their particular lens abnormality, nearsighted people see better at close range than do other people.

This question tests your ability to use hints that the author provides to add additional information to the passage. What you are required to do here is to "read between the lines." This common phrase suggests that there are things written into a message that aren't explicitly stated. Each of us, at one time or another, has received a written communication that has been worded in such a way as to make a message that is not on the written page quite clear. If you receive a note from your boss that states, "Late yet again today, huh?" his or her intent is clear to you. The boss is not simply trying to impress you with heightened power of observation. Likewise, if you suddenly get a letter from your boyfriend or girlfriend that is signed "Your Affectionate Friend," you assume that the relationship has changed.

In addition, a lot of our everyday interaction with people depends on inference. If you pass a friend in the hall and he[1] doesn't speak, what happens immediately? You begin to analyze your friend's behavior to try to understand his reaction. Depending on your particular personality, you will probably make one of several inferences:

1. Your friend didn't see you.
2. Your friend was engrossed in thought.
3. Your friend was trying to avoid you.
4. Your friend is angry with you.

As you apply this same skill to a reading passage, you are somewhat more limited in the inferences you can make. You can only use hints that are given in the passage. Do *not* allow your opinions to cause you to read into the passage more than is there. Your response must be an objective one, based on information the author has provided.

In question 4(a) you should have chosen answer c. The passage states that the term *weak eyesight* is misleading. The reason it is misleading is explained in the second part of sentence 3. This sentence implies that the average person has a misconception of *nearsightedness* because he doesn't understand what *nearsightedness* is. Answer *a* is not discussed in the passage. The author states that nearsightedness is easily corrected when diagnosed, but it does not discuss the other alternative—not having it diagnosed or corrected. Answer *b* would have to be based on your own personal knowledge or opinions. The author is very objective in his mention of school-associated problems because of nearsightedness. He includes the information to point out *one* way in which nearsightedness is often detected—that's all. Answer *d*, at a glance, seems to be the logical deduction from the information given in sentence 3. That deduction is not, however, supported by the further discussion of lens strength.

Now answer question 4(b). Refer to the passage as you consider your answer. Circle the correct answer:

4(b) The author's tone is
   a. sarcastic
   b. critical
   c. subjective
   d. objective

This question tests your ability to judge the author's tone. Every author has feelings about his subject, and his manner of writing will usually reflect his attitude. An author's tone may be *sarcastic* (if the author is bitter about a subject), *satirical* (if the

---

[1] The generic *he* is idiomatic in English and is not to be considered as sexist. In fact, in the writing of this book, the authors have paid considerable attention to the breaking of stereotyped sex roles in the discussions of careers, education, and so on.

author uses ridicule to expose someone or something), *subjective* (if the author includes personal feelings about the subject), *objective* (if the author reports information in an unemotional, unbiased manner), *humorous* (if the author is consciously making light of the subject), *positive* (if the author supports or admires the subject), *negative* (if the author doesn't support or admire the subject), or *ironical* (if the author says one thing but means another). Many synonyms are used for these differing attitudes or tones, but these are the essential labels you will encounter in the text and on most standardized reading tests. To decide on the tone of a passage, ask yourself the following questions:

—Does the author make bitter remarks about the subject? (sarcastic)
—Is the author purposely ridiculing the subject? (satirical)
—Is the author giving his or her own ideas for the most part? (subjective)
—Is the author simply providing information about the subject? (objective)
—Is the author purposely making light of the subject, with no obvious attempt to ridicule? (humorous)
—Does the author support or admire the subject? (positive)
—Does the author obviously disagree with or dislike the subject? (negative)
—Is the author purposely stating one thing, when it is obvious that he or she means something else? (ironical)

Some of these tones can overlap in a passage. For example, an author can be both *subjective* and *positive* about a subject. An author can also be *humorous* but *negative* about a subject. With passages like this, you must weigh your choices carefully and decide on the one that best sums up one or both of these tones.

In question 4(b) you should have chosen answer *d*. The author is merely reporting information in this passage. Actually, it is very much like an article you might read in a newspaper. Answer *a* is incorrect because the author does not have any negative things to say about the subject. Answer *b* is incorrect for the same reason. The author is not trying to pass judgment on his or her subject (not even the people who are misinformed about the cause of nearsightedness). Answer *c* is incorrect because the author does not give personal ideas or opinions about *nearsightedness*.

Now answer question 5. Refer to the passage as you consider your answer. Circle the correct answer:

5. As used in this passage, the word *prescription* means
   a. suggestion
   b. treatment
   c. cure
   d. useless

This question tests your ability to define words from their surroundings. All of us use this skill in our daily reading. Read the following sentence:

John is the only *truculent* student in the class; the others are easily controlled.

What does the word *truculent* mean in this sentence? It means something like "defiant" or "argumentative," right? How do we know? The sentence states that John is the *only* "truculent" student in the class; he differs in some way from the rest of the class. What is stated about the rest of the class? They are easy to control. So John is the opposite or something different from "easily controlled."

When you apply this skill to the reading passages, you should first read the sentence that contains the vocabulary item. Does it suggest a meaning for the word, as in the preceding example? If not, read the sentences that come before and after the sentence that contains the vocabulary item. Do they suggest the meaning of the word? As a last resort you should try each of the four choices in question 5 in place of the underlined word. Choose the one that seems to fit best in the sentence.

In question 5 you should have chosen answer *b*. A *prescription* is the "treatment" that a doctor orders for a particular ailment. Answer *a* is incorrect because the doctor does not give you a *prescription* as a "suggestion" for you to follow. He expects you to follow his directions, and he is confident that the medicine he prescribes will help you. Answer *c* is incorrect because a concave, or "minus," lens will not "cure" the problem; it will "correct" the problem. Answer *d* is an obviously incorrect choice. A "minus" lens is "useful" to the nearsighted person, not "use*less*." The problem with this choice lies in the use of the suffix *-less* instead of *-ful*.

As you work through the text, use index cards like the ones below to keep your own personal vocabulary list of words you miss:

Side 1

truculent

(trŭk′yə lənt)

Adj.

Side 2

1. savage and cruel; fierce. 2. pugnacious; defiant

Review the words often; discard the index card only after you are sure you know the word. Keep adding to your list daily, using not only words from the text, but also words you find in your everyday reading. This may seem a tedious, time-consuming way to develop your vocabulary—but it works!

Now read the following passage closely. Analyze it as you read, exactly as you did passage 1-0. After you have read the passage, answer the five comprehension questions. Check your answers with the annotated key at the end. Check with your instructor on any answer you do not understand.

PASSAGE 4-0

SUBJECT:
Alcoholism

Misconceptions about alcoholism are common. Many people, for example, think that alcoholics are careless, pleasure-seeking people who have moral problems that make them easier prey for liquor. Actually, alcoholics often feel guilty about their drinking and are very self-conscious around other people. Alcoholics quite often have a low self-esteem and are too sensitive about what people may think of them. Another common myth is that the alcoholic is always drunk, but experts say this is not so. In truth, there are three types of alcoholics. <u>Episodic</u> drinkers, for example, drink only now and then, but each of their drinking episodes ends in overindulgence. Habitual excess drinkers are also only occasionally drunk, but their episodes are much more frequent than those of the episodic drinker. The addict is a person who must drink continually simply in order to function. It is the addict who needs medical assistance to withdraw from the support of alcohol.

▲ (155 WORDS) ▲

Circle the correct answer:

1(a) This passage is mainly about
   a. therapy for alcoholics.
   b. alcoholism.
   c. common misconceptions about alcoholism.
   d. three types of alcoholics.

1(b) The best title for this passage is
   a. What About the Habitual Drinker?
   b. Alcoholism: Fact and Fiction
   c. Curing the Alcoholic
   d. Alcoholism in America

2. According to the passage, which of the following statements is not true?
   a. Many alcoholics feel guilty about their drinking.
   b. The habitual drinker is only occasionally drunk.
   c. The addict needs medical help with his problem.
   d. Episodic drinkers never overindulge.

3. We can conclude from the passage that
   a. few alcoholics are episodic drinkers.
   b. episodic drinkers' "bouts" are worse than those of habitual drinkers.
   c. most alcoholics are emotionally disturbed people.
   d. the addict-type alcoholic is always drunk.

4(a) The passage suggests that
   a. the addict has an emotional *and* physical dependence on alcohol.
   b. more habitual drinkers become addicts than do episodic drinkers.
   c. addicts can be helped by chemical control of their drinking urges.
   d. alcoholics are basically immoral.

4(b) The author's tone is
   a. ironical
   b. sarcastic
   c. subjective
   d. objective

5. As used in this passage, the word *episodic* means
   a. constant
   b. periodic
   c. suicidal
   d. uncontrollable

ANNOTATED ANSWER KEY

1(a)
   a. not discussed
   b. too broad
   c. *correct*
   d. too narrow

1(b)
   a. too narrow
   b. *correct*
   c. not discussed
   d. too broad

2.
   a. sentence 3
   b. sentence 7
   c. sentence 8
   d. *correct* (sentence 6)

3.
   a. not discussed
   b. not discussed

11

    c. *correct* (sentences 3 and 4)
    d. not true. He "must drink . . . in order . . . to function . . ." normally.

4(a)
    a. *correct* (sentences 8 and 9)
    b. not discussed
    c. not discussed
    d. The passage states the opposite.

4(b)
    a. There is no indication that the author means anything except what he or she is stating.
    b. The author isn't bitter about the subject.
    c. The author doesn't provide any information about his or her own opinions or experiences.
    d. *correct*

5.
    a. Sentences 6 and 7 compare the episodic drinker to the constant (habitual) drinker.
    b. *correct*. Sentence 6—"The episodic drinker . . . drinks only now and then . . ."
    c. This does not make sense in the context of the passage.
    d. The comparison of "episodic" and "habitual" drinkers in sentences 6 and 7 negates this answer. The "episodic" drinker drinks only now and then; it is only when he *does* drink that his drinking becomes uncontrollable.

USING THE STUDENT PROGRESS CHART

As you work through the text, you should record your progress on the Student Progress Chart in the back of the book. This will indicate to you and your instructor where your strengths and weaknesses are at any point in the text. It will show those skills that you are improving, as well as those skills still needing work.

    On the following sample chart, the errors for an imaginary student have been recorded for the two sample passages that you just completed. These two samples do not appear in your Student Progress Chart in the text, but they will allow us to study what the chart can mean to you and to your instructor.

    Notice the entries under question #1 for both passages. The student has indicated which part of the question he missed by placing an *X* in the box with the question number (1a or 1b) beside it. The same is true for the entry for question #4, Passage 4-0. The student missed both parts of the question, so he recorded two *X*'s, with the question numbers (4a or 4b) beside each *X*. You should record your answers in the same manner, so that your Student Progress Chart truly reflects your progress.

    Now notice that the student missed some part of question #1 on both Passage 1-0 and Passage 4-0. Question #1 tests the student's ability to identify the main idea

	#1	#2	#3	#4	#5	Total
Passage 1–0	X 1a		X		X	3
Passage 4–0	X 1b	X		X 4a X 4b		4

Student Progress Chart

Record your progress by placing an X in the box beneath each item you answered incorrectly for a particular passage. Total your number of *incorrect* answers, and record them in the box marked *TOTAL*.

of a reading passage. If this pattern held true in several more passages, it would indicate to you and to your instructor that you really don't understand this skill. Your instructor could then work with you individually or assign you supplemental exercises to improve your understanding of the skill. Also notice that the student missed three questions on Passage 1-0, and four on Passage 4-0. The first number of each passage indicates its reading level. If this pattern held true in several more passages, it would indicate that you understand most of the skills, but that you are having trouble applying them to more difficult reading material. Again, your instructor would have to assist you.

CONCLUSION

The skills you will be practicing in this text, as well as the good habits you will be developing, will make you a more proficient reader and will prepare you for the demands of college reading. This text will help you develop an analytical approach to your reading, which will be invaluable to you as a student.

DIAGNOSTIC PRETEST

DIRECTIONS: Wait until your instructor has reviewed the pretest with you and has indicated how your answers are to be recorded. During the test, be sure to read each paragraph carefully and to check your answer on each item by referring to the paragraph and by eliminating the other choices as possible answers before moving on to the next paragraph.

OPTIONAL STUDENT ANSWER SHEET

Circle the correct answer:

PARAGRAPH 1-1
1. a. b. c. d.
2. a. b. c. d.
3. a. b. c. d.
4. a. b. c. d.
5. a. b. c. d.

PARAGRAPH 1-2
1. a. b. c. d.
2. a. b. c. d.
3. a. b. c. d.
4. a. b. c. d.
5. a. b. c. d.

PARAGRAPH 2-1
1. a. b. c. d.
2. a. b. c. d.
3. a. b. c. d.
4. a. b. c. d.
5. a. b. c. d.

PARAGRAPH 2-2
1. a. b. c. d.
2. a. b. c. d.
3. a. b. c. d.
4. a. b. c. d.
5. a. b. c. d.

PARAGRAPH 3-1
1. a. b. c. d.
2. a. b. c. d.
3. a. b. c. d.
4. a. b. c. d.
5. a. b. c. d.

PARAGRAPH 3-2
1. a. b. c. d.
2. a. b. c. d.
3. a. b. c. d.
4. a. b. c. d.
5. a. b. c. d.

PARAGRAPH 4-1
1. a. b. c. d.
2. a. b. c. d.
3. a. b. c. d.
4. a. b. c. d.
5. a. b. c. d.

PARAGRAPH 4-2
1. a. b. c. d.
2. a. b. c. d.
3. a. b. c. d.
4. a. b. c. d.
5. a. b. c. d.

PARAGRAPH 4-3
1. a. b. c. d.
2. a. b. c. d.
3. a. b. c. d.
4. a. b. c. d.
5. a. b. c. d.

PARAGRAPH 4-4
1. a. b. c. d.
2. a. b. c. d.
3. a. b. c. d.
4. a. b. c. d.
5. a. b. c. d.

PARAGRAPH 1-1

SUBJECT:
Babe Ruth

Babe Ruth was born in Baltimore, February 6, 1895, in a working class section, where his father was a saloonkeeper. Babe's early life was wild; he was eventually placed in St. Mary's Industrial School for boys, but baseball changed his life, as everyone knows—he led the American League in home runs 12 years, hitting a total of 714 homers in his career. For four seasons, he hit over 50 homers each year for the New York Yankees. Before he became the "Home Run King" or the "Sultan of Swat," though, he was a 23-game-winning pitcher for the Red Sox. In 1947, Ruth was diagnosed as a throat cancer patient and made his final appearance at Yankee Stadium. Today the diminutive brick row house at 216 Emory Street in Baltimore is a museum. The Babe Ruth Foundation and the city rescued the little house from the wreckers and gathered Ruth <u>mementos</u> from all over the country.

▲ (156 WORDS) ▲

PARAGRAPH 1-1

Circle the correct answer:

1. The main purpose of this paragraph is to
   a. provide a short biography of Babe Ruth.
   b. describe Ruth's early childhood.
   c. describe Ruth's baseball career.
   d. describe the Ruth museum.

2. Before becoming a leading home-run hitter, Ruth was
   a. the "Home Run King."
   b. a pitcher.
   c. the "Sultan of Swat."
   d. all of the above.

3. We can conclude from the paragraph that
   a. Ruth never forgot his early childhood.
   b. Ruth enjoyed pitching more than hitting.

c. baseball provided direction for Ruth's life.
   d. Ruth was ashamed of his background.

4. The paragraph suggests that
   a. Ruth became egotistical about his success.
   b. Ruth has become a national hero.
   c. Ruth was the greatest pitcher to ever play baseball.
   d. Ruth's final appearance at Yankee Stadium was emotional.

5. As used in this paragraph, the word *mementos* means
   a. trinkets
   b. antiques
   c. souvenirs
   d. relatives

GO ON TO THE NEXT PAGE ───────────────────────▶

PARAGRAPH 1-2   SUBJECT:
Altered Odometers

A 1972 law passed by the federal government makes it illegal to tamper with a car's odometer. Nothing can be done that would change the mileage shown on the car. Anyone who sells a car must sign a statement that lists the mileage on that car. If the mileage is incorrect because the odometer is not working, the seller must sign a statement saying that the mileage is unknown. No one except a repairman is allowed to do anything that would alter the mileage shown on the odometer. This is an important safeguard for the buyer of a used car, for an automobile may look in much better shape than its true mileage would indicate. A buyer should examine a used car carefully, ask to be shown the mileage statement, and contact previous owners. You can sue any seller who misrepresents the mileage on a car, but the best protection against this sort of fraud is a close inspection of the car before buying.

▲ (164 WORDS) ▲

PARAGRAPH 1-2

Circle the correct answer:

1. The main idea of this paragraph is that
   a. auto dealers make a habit of misrepresenting the mileage of cars.
   b. the auto industry can not be trusted to treat the public fairly.
   c. the federal government now protects consumers against the unfair practice of altering odometers.
   d. auto dealers can now be sued for unfair practices.

2. A prospective car buyer should
   a. examine a used car carefully.
   b. ask to be shown the mileage statement.
   c. contact the previous owner.
   d. all of the above.

3. We can conclude from the paragraph that
   a. high mileage cars are better buys than low mileage cars.
   b. changing the mileage on used cars had become common practice among dealers.

c. fraud is a common practice among new auto dealers.
   d. the federal government has made it impossible to alter odometers.

4. The paragraph suggests that
   a. the average buyer is gullible.
   b. consumer advocates were not pleased with the 1972 law.
   c. suing a dealer for altering an odometer won't do any good.
   d. the buyer will be better off buying a new car because all used cars are worn out.

5. As used in this paragraph, the word *tamper* means
   a. move forward
   b. replace
   c. repair
   d. alter

GO ON TO THE NEXT PAGE ─────────────▶

PARAGRAPH 2-1

SUBJECT:
Superplants

Few people realize that, starting in the 1920s, scientists began to develop "superplants." Unlike "natural" plants, these plants were developed to withstand pollution, drought, dirty soil, and poor light. Superplants were first created with chemical changes in the plants, then with genetic changes. Some plants created this way include most new roses, the new elm, and some new cotton and corn species. Giant pumpkins, radishes, tomatoes, and strawberries are being developed now, as well as new violets and other flowers. These superplants were designed to thrive in home gardens and households, but the techniques have created plants that resist disease, require less special care, and, more importantly, grow larger seeds and fruits on fewer nutrients and less water. So what began as an effort to make stronger houseplants may end up as a major way to increase the yields of farms and garden crops.

▲ (144 WORDS) ▲

PARAGRAPH 2-1

Circle the correct answer:

1. This paragraph is mainly about
    a. superplants that grow in gardens.
    b. developing hardier houseplants.
    c. the development of superplants.
    d. techniques of growing superplants.

2. Superplants were developed to withstand all of the following except
    a. pollution
    b. drought
    c. disease
    d. poor light

3. We can conclude from the paragraph that
    a. scientists did not fully anticipate the results of their initial experiments.
    b. superplants pose a problem because they are resistant to disease.
    c. superplants reproduce more quickly than natural ones.
    d. genetic engineering could also work on people.

4. The paragraph suggests that
   a. superplants are more nutritious than natural ones.
   b. consumers prefer superplants for their gardens.
   c. superplants have one drawback in that the chemicals used to develop them are dangerous.
   d. superplants may be a way of meeting the world food shortage.

5. As used in this paragraph, the word *withstand* means
   a. require
   b. tolerate
   c. eliminate
   d. fight against

GO ON TO THE NEXT PAGE ⎯⎯⎯⎯⎯⎯⎯⎯⎯⎯⎯⎯⎯⎯⎯⎯⎯⎯▶

PARAGRAPH 2-2   SUBJECT:
Recreational Vehicles

Americans are buying recreational vehicles for traveling, for vacations, and for camping. More leisure time and more available money mean that these vehicles will be on the highways in greater numbers this summer. If you are considering the purchase of an "RV," you should know that there are several types. A "slide-in" camper is designed to slide into the bed of a pickup truck. When the living facilities are not needed, the unit can be quickly removed. A van conversion is a <u>conventional</u> van that an RV dealer has altered by installing living quarters in the rear. Sometimes extra windows and a raised roof are added. A mini-motorhome is built on the frame of a van or pickup that has been cut behind the cab. A conventional motorhome is usually built on a larger truck chassis. These are the large, plush, self-powered units. They have complete facilities for cooking, sleeping, and bathing.

▲ (150 WORDS) ▲

PARAGRAPH 2-2

Circle the correct answer:

1. The main idea of this paragraph is that
    a. a "slide-in" camper is more useful than a van conversion.
    b. most RVs are conversions of regular vehicles.
    c. mini-motorhomes are the plushest of the RVs.
    d. there are several different kinds of RVs.

2. Conventional motorhomes are not
    a. large
    b. plush
    c. van conversions
    d. self-powered units

3. We can conclude from this paragraph that
    a. "slide-in" units are the most inexpensive RVs.
    b. van conversions of vehicles are ways to defraud the consumer.
    c. too many RVs are on the road in the summer.
    d. the RV industry has a variety of vehicles to suit most anyone.

4. The paragraph suggests that
   a. there is a large market for RVs in America.
   b. the consumer could make his own home cheaper.
   c. RVs are dangerous on the highway.
   d. RVs don't get good gas mileage.

5. As used in this paragraph, the word *conventional* means
   a. traditional
   b. convenience-equipped
   c. converted
   d. expensive

GO ON TO THE NEXT PAGE

PARAGRAPH 3-1 SUBJECT:
Tension and Anxiety

Tension and anxiety are obstacles to effective learning. The ability to relax is just as important to success in school as the ability to read. Anxiety can cause students to forget chapters that they may have read, to "go blank" at quiz time, or to fail to meet deadlines and to complete assignments on schedule. Anyone can learn to rid himself or herself of tension by resting the body, breathing deeply, and relaxing for three to four minutes before a test. Attention to details such as outlining, note-taking, and time scheduling will help free mental energy to work on the tasks of learning. Planning one day ahead on a pocket calendar has done as much to improve the grades of some students as memory or speed-reading courses.

▲ (127 WORDS) ▲

PARAGRAPH 3-1

Circle the correct answer:

1. The main idea of this paragraph is that
    a. the ability to relax is *most* important to success.
    b. tension and anxiety are obstacles to learning.
    c. anyone can learn to rid himself or herself of tension.
    d. planning ahead will help ward off anxiety attacks.

2. All of the following are recommended to rid the body of tension except
    a. vigorous exercise.
    b. relaxing three to four minutes before a test.
    c. breathing deeply.
    d. resting the body.

3. We can conclude from the paragraph that
    a. tension is more dangerous than anxiety.
    b. memory is a function of anxiety.
    c. anxiety and tension seldom affect test grades.
    d. students are often tense and anxious because they are unorganized.

4. The paragraph suggests that
    a. learning how to prepare for tests is as important as learning the material for the test.
    b. tests shouldn't be *so* important to a student that they make him or her anxious and tense.
    c. vigorous exercise increases mental energy.
    d. anxiety is more dangerous than tension.

5. As used in this paragraph, the word *anxiety* means
    a. grades
    b. migraine
    c. indecision
    d. apprehension

GO ON TO THE NEXT PAGE ─────────────────────▶

PARAGRAPH 3-2   SUBJECT:
Blood Pressure

Blood pressure is created by the heart as it pumps the blood through the circulatory system. The pressure is not constant but varies with the action of the heart. The higher pressure, called the systolic (sĭs tŏl′ ĭk), occurs when the heart contracts; and the lower pressure, called the diastolic (dī ə stŏl′ ĭk), is the pressure remaining in the veins when the heart relaxes. Both pressures are measured, which is why blood pressures are given in two figures; a pressure of 120/80 is normal for adults up to the mid-forties. A systolic pressure over 165 or a diastolic pressure over 95 is considered "high blood pressure." Because the blood pressure can vary as a result of excitement, stress, or sleep, most doctors will measure blood pressure several times before deciding that a patient is suffering from high blood pressure. Unless the pressure remains at high levels, there is no cause for alarm. Everyone's blood pressure "goes up" sometimes.

▲ (153 WORDS) ▲

PARAGRAPH 3-2

Circle the correct answer:

1. The main purpose of this paragraph is to
   a. define blood pressure.
   b. indicate that everyone's blood pressure varies.
   c. define high blood pressure.
   d. indicate the dangers of high blood pressure.

2. Diastolic pressure measures
   a. the heart rate.
   b. pressure as the heart contracts.
   c. the pressure left in the veins when the heart relaxes.
   d. constant vein pressure.

3. We can conclude from the paragraph that
   a. "normal" blood pressure drops as we grow older.
   b. blood pressure is affected by heart rate.

    c. "normal" blood pressure rises as we grow older.
    d. high diastolic pressure indicates arterial disease.
4. The paragraph suggests that
    a. a high diastolic reading is more dangerous than a high systolic reading.
    b. stress and excitement are the causes of high blood pressure.
    c. it is not particularly important to check blood pressure until the mid-forties.
    d. the most accurate reading of blood pressure would probably be an average of several readings.
5. As used in this paragraph, the word *stress* means
    a. strength
    b. tension
    c. emphasis
    d. physical condition

GO ON TO THE NEXT PAGE ⎯⎯⎯⎯⎯⎯⎯⎯⎯⎯⎯⎯⎯⎯⎯⎯⎯⎯▶

PARAGRAPH 4-1   SUBJECT:
Zinc Oxide (ŏx′ īd) Batteries

Before the American auto industry can develop electric cars for daily use, someone has to invent a better battery. The lead-acid batteries used in autos since 1900 are too heavy and cannot store enough electricity to allow an electric car to travel very far from home without recharging. This sad fact has given rise to hundreds of "extension-cord" jokes and jibes. At least one manufacturer, GM, foresaw the problem as early as 1960. GM has spent $33 million since then developing a zinc oxide battery that can store two and a half times as much energy as the old batteries. Zinc oxide batteries will work for 30,000 to 40,000 miles, and they should be available in 1985 or 1986 to carry millions of commuters and shoppers in efficient, nonpolluting electric cars.

▲ (133 WORDS) ▲

PARAGRAPH 4-1

Circle the correct answer:

1. This paragraph is mainly about
    a. GM's development of a better battery than the lead-acid one.
    b. the development of zinc oxide batteries.
    c. the ineffectiveness of lead-acid batteries.
    d. the need for nonpolluting electric cars.

2. Zinc oxide batteries can store
    a. 2.2 times as much energy as lead-acid batteries.
    b. 2.5 times as much energy as lead-acid batteries.
    c. 2.6 times as much energy as lead-acid batteries.
    d. 25 times as much energy as lead-acid batteries.

3. We can conclude from the paragraph that
    a. electric cars will replace fuel-driven cars in the eighties.
    b. zinc oxide batteries are more energy-efficient than lead-acid batteries.
    c. electric cars will be more energy-efficient than fuel-driven cars.
    d. the auto industry will begin producing electric cars immediately, now that they have the zinc oxide batteries.

4. The paragraph suggests that
   a. zinc oxide batteries are very expensive.
   b. consumers will be able to travel great distances using zinc oxide batteries.
   c. GM had the foresight to prepare for an emerging market.
   d. GM stalled the introduction of zinc oxide batteries until it became profitable for them.

5. As used in this paragraph, the word *jibe* means
   a. an insult
   b. a compliment
   c. a mocking remark
   d. arguments

GO ON TO THE NEXT PAGE ⟶

PARAGRAPH 4-2   SUBJECT:
Polio (pō′ lē ō) Vaccine

Years ago, polio was a common disease among young children and often left its victims with paralysis. In 1954 the first vaccine was developed, and, in the years since, widespread use of the vaccine has almost eliminated the disease. In 1977 only nine cases were reported. Two kinds of vaccine are available; the newest vaccine is an oral vaccine made from weakened, but live, polio viruses. The older vaccine type is made from dead viruses and is given in a series of injections. Most doctors agree that the oral vaccine is far more effective. The vaccines are easily available now; but because polio seems to be less threatening, almost nineteen million children, 36 percent of the population under fourteen, have not been <u>immunized</u>. This may allow yet another outbreak of this horrible disease. All children between six weeks and eighteen years of age should be immunized.

▲ (145 WORDS) ▲

PARAGRAPH 4-2

Circle the correct answer:

1. The main idea of this paragraph is that
   a. polio is a common childhood disease.
   b. polio has been eliminated in the twentieth century.
   c. there are two types of vaccine.
   d. although polio has been practically eradicated, there is now the possibility of an epidemic.

2. The paragraph states that
   a. oral vaccine is made from dead viruses.
   b. oral vaccine is considered more effective.
   c. the older vaccine type is made from live viruses.
   d. all of the above.

3. We can conclude from the paragraph that
   a. oral vaccines have to be reintroduced to the body regularly.
   b. people over eighteen never contract polio.

    c. the earlier vaccine is no longer effective.
    d. Americans have become lax in seeking immunization against polio.

4. The paragraph suggests that
    a. the introduction of polio virus in vaccine form can be harmful.
    b. parents aren't as conscientious about their children's health as they used to be.
    c. the American public needs reeducating about the dangers of polio.
    d. the oral vaccine is more expensive than the older vaccine.

5. As used in this paragraph, the word *immunized* means
    a. injected
    b. inoculated
    c. exposed
    d. examined

GO ON TO THE NEXT PAGE ───────────────▶

PARAGRAPH 4-3

SUBJECT:
Carville Hospital

Leprosy, or Hansen's disease, has the worst reputation of any disease. It affects startingly large numbers of people to varying degrees even in the modern era, so the U.S. Public Health Service operates a leprosarium (lĕp rə sâr′ ē əm) in Carville, Louisiana, one of two in the United States. The disease does not cause <u>disfigurement</u> in most cases, nor is it highly communicable after initial treatment. The Carville hospital provides treatment, but it is operated mainly as a research and training hospital. Seminars are held in its clinics, and a newsletter originates there. Carville has its own golf course, its own churches, and its own library. The hospital also has on its grounds a twenty-acre lake for boating and fishing. Many of the three hundred or so patients at Carville have made the hospital their home. Research on Hansen's disease is moving rapidly, and facilities like Carville are helping to make the disease better understood.

▲ (158 WORDS) ▲

PARAGRAPH 4-3

Circle the correct answer:

1. The main purpose of this paragraph is to
    a. explain Hansen's disease.
    b. discuss the rapid progress that is being made in research on Hansen's disease.
    c. describe the facilities available at the Carville hospital.
    d. distinguish between Hansen's disease and leprosy.

2. The Carville hospital does not provide
    a. plastic surgery for patients disfigured by leprosy.
    b. treatment for Hansen's disease.
    c. research facilities for the study of leprosy.
    d. seminars and a newsletter to provide information about Hansen's disease.

3. We can conclude from the paragraph that
    a. the U.S. government wants to separate leprosy patients from the general populace because of the stigma of the disease.
    b. hospital care at Carville is very expensive.

c. many patients with leprosy feel more comfortable staying at Carville than returning home.
   d. leprosy is eventually fatal.

4. The paragraph suggests that
   a. leprosy causes a lot of emotional problems in patients.
   b. Carville serves primarily as a recreational facility for leprosy patients.
   c. Carville is not as concerned about patient treatment as it is about research.
   d. the Carville hospital attempts to provide its patients with a normal social environment.

5. As used in this paragraph, the word *disfigurement* means
   a. scarring or skin lesions
   b. death
   c. brain damage
   d. paralysis

GO ON TO THE NEXT PAGE ──────────────────────▶

PARAGRAPH 4-4 SUBJECT:
Capitol Hill News Service

Local newspapers find reporting national news too expensive, and so far efforts to solve their problems have failed. Only 27 percent of the nation's 1,200 daily newspapers actually have a reporter in Washington. To make it look as if they have a "man in Washington," many small-town papers reprint press releases. They seldom edit or check these press releases, and they always caption them "Washington, D.C." Very often the papers finally present only one side of the issue—the side they are handed by the people they are supposed to be watching over. In 1972 a Ralph Nader grant helped found Capitol Hill News Service, a cheap subscription service that supported ten reporters who reported to client newspapers. Ironically—and unfortunately—CHNS was too successful. Reports about graft and lists of ineffective congressmen were among stories that drew the wrath of government officials. In 1975 the director of CHNS resigned, and the list of subscribers began to dwindle.

▲ (158 WORDS) ▲

PARAGRAPH 4-4

Circle the correct answer:

1. The main idea of this paragraph is that
   a. no effort to make covering news in Washington affordable has yet proved successful.
   b. Capitol Hill News Service offered newspapers up-to-date Washington news.
   c. CHNS failed because its number of clients dwindled.
   d. news that comes from press releases is not accurate.

2. Capitol Hill News Service was successful because it carried
   a. stories of graft.
   b. lists of least-effective legislators.
   c. reports on the achievements of each senator.
   d. all of the above.

3. We can conclude from this paragraph that
   a. Ralph Nader wanted to use the CHNS for his own personal crusades.
   b. CHNS offended the philosophies of many local papers.

c. local news is usually biased owing to the paper's philosophy.
  d. some 73 percent of the nation's newspapers rely on press releases for their Washington news.

4. The paragraph suggests that
   a. CHNS failed because of the heavy work load on the director.
   b. CHNS failed because too few people used their services.
   c. accurate news can only be obtained from a national newspaper.
   d. CHNS failed because of congressional pressure.

5. As used in this paragraph, the word *dwindle* means
   a. change.
   b. become more prestigious
   c. grow smaller
   d. grow larger

STOP ▲

You have now completed the diagnostic test. Await further instructions from the teacher.

STUDENT SCORE SHEET

	QUESTION NUMBER					
	1	2	3	4	5	TOTAL
PARAGRAPH 1-1						
PARAGRAPH 1-2						
PARAGRAPH 2-1						
PARAGRAPH 2-2						
PARAGRAPH 3-1						
PARAGRAPH 3-2						
PARAGRAPH 4-1						
PARAGRAPH 4-2						
PARAGRAPH 4-3						
PARAGRAPH 4-4						
TOTALS						

ASSIGNMENT: Begin work in Section _____, passage _____, and work through Section _____, passage _____. Answer all of the test items numbered (circle all items assigned) #1, #2, #3, #4, #5.

SECTION 1 | READING PASSAGES

DIRECTIONS: Read all of the passages that your instructor has assigned in this section. Answer the comprehension items that have been assigned on your Student Score Sheet. Be sure to read each passage carefully and to refer to the passage to check your answers to the comprehension questions.

PASSAGE 1-1   SUBJECT:
Manuel the Mechanic

You should see Manuel when he works on a car down at his father's garage. He picks out a wrench or a screwdriver the way an artist would choose a brush to use on his masterpiece. He turns the tool over carefully in his hands, assuring himself that it's the right size and type of tool for the job at hand. He is also as particular with his tools as an artist might be with his brushes. Manuel will not use a rusty or broken wrench; when he finishes a job, he protects the tool with a slight film of oil and replaces it on his shelves, carefully arranging his tools so that he can easily and quickly find the tool he wants.

   When he has finally selected the tool he needs, Manual moves to the ailing car confidently like a surgeon in an operating room. He is quiet; he carefully touches the engine with his delicate hands. He may reach into the car's inner <u>recesses</u> and move a lever or connection, testing its tension, its range of movement, or its <u>lubrication</u> and adjustment. Once he has made the diagnosis, he arranges his tools like scalpels and clamps in a tray. The power and confidence he has are obvious when he leans over into the engine compartment and makes the repair he has chosen. Manuel is a true genius, born to work with machines.

▲ (235 WORDS) ▲

PASSAGE 1-1

Circle the correct answer:

1. The main idea of this passage is that
   a. Manuel is as skilled as a surgeon.
   b. Manuel takes good care of his tools.
   c. Manuel always studies his work carefully.
   d. Manuel is a highly skilled mechanic.

2. Manuel moves to the ailing car confidently like a(n)
   a. electrician
   b. artist
   c. genius
   d. surgeon

3. We can conclude from this passage that
    a. Manuel should be a doctor.
    b. Manuel takes his work seriously.
    c. Manuel charges high prices.
    d. Manuel should be an artist.

4. The passage suggests that
    a. Manuel is as good at his job as surgeons and artists are at theirs.
    b. Manuel should go to medical school.
    c. artists and surgeons know little about mechanics.
    d. a good set of tools is essential to becoming a good mechanic.

5. As used in this passage, the word *recesses* means
    a. adjournments
    b. cylinders
    c. depths
    d. processes

PASSAGE 1-2

SUBJECT:
Cowboy Boots

"Cowboy" boots were originally made to be walked in, so the heels were flatter than the heels we now associate with these boots. As it became obvious that working around a ranch required more and more riding, a boot with much higher stacked leather heel was designed for a riding boot. The higher heel is also slanted forward to keep a rider's foot in the stirrup. This design was necessary because the American cowboy rode fast and hard, making short, abrupt turns as he herded cows. The top of cowboy boots was tall to protect a rider's legs as he rode through brush and cactus country.

Boots designed for rough ranch work are usually made of tough hides like bull hide, water buffalo, or elk hide. Standard boots are usually sold in simple colors like brown and black, but now the boot business has gotten rather showy. High fashion designers have discovered the cowboy boot, and the boot has suddenly become a status symbol. First of all, there are a lot of new bright colors available, like red, green, blue, and orange, even purple.

Demand among Westerners is strong for boots made from exotic hides, and Easterners are beginning to demand the exotic leathers as well. Suede (swād) is old-fashioned now; lizard, snake, and alligator are becoming common themselves. Caribou (kăr′ ə boo) is a favorite just now, a subtle material that looks like many other leathers but has a more interesting texture. Among reptile skins, eel is considered a status item, for it too has a subtle texture lacking in other reptile skins. Among ranchers in Texas, the highest status boot is a pair of ostrich skin boots, about $500. Add a fancy "toe bug," the little silver covers for the toe, and you've outstepped your competition completely.

▲ (294 WORDS) ▲

PASSAGE 1-2

Circle the correct answer:

1. The purpose of this passage is to
    a. discuss the new materials used in producing cowboy boots.
    (b.) compare the different types of cowboy boots.

c. discuss the current demand for cowboy boots.
   d. describe the boot industry.

2. Which of the following leathers is currently considered old-fashioned?
   a. suede
   b. caribou
   c. eel
   d. ostrich

3. We can conclude from the passage that
   a. cowboy boots have always been short.
   b. Texas ranchers don't like expensive boots.
   c. lizard skin boots are more popular than snakeskin boots.
   d. cowboy boots have changed drastically over the years.

4. The passage suggests that
   a. cowboy boots are more popular in the West than in the East.
   b. caribou are becoming extinct.
   c. brightly colored boots are not popular in the West.
   d. the cowboy boot is no longer bought just for ranching or riding.

5(a) As used in this passage, the word *exotic* means
   a. colorless
   b. useless
   c. common
   d. unusual

5(b) As used in this passage, the word *subtle* means
   a. slightly noticeable
   b. dark
   c. shiny
   d. quiet

PASSAGE 1-3

SUBJECT: Laziness

Laziness is a sin; everyone knows that. We've probably all had lectures pointing out that laziness is immoral, that it is wasteful, and that lazy people will never amount to anything in life.

But laziness can be more harmful than that, and it is often caused by more complex reasons than the simple wish to avoid work. Some people who appear to be lazy are suffering from much more serious problems. They may be so distrustful of their fellow workers that they are unable to join in any group task for fear of ridicule or fear of having their ideas stolen. These people who seem lazy may be paralyzed by a fear of failure that prevents fruitful work. Or other sorts of fantasies may prevent work: some people are so busy planning, sometimes planning great deals or fantastic achievements, that they are unable to deal with whatever "lesser" work is on hand. Still other people are not avoiding work, strictly speaking; they are merely procrastinating—rescheduling their day.

Laziness can actually be helpful. Like procrastinators, some people may look lazy when they are really thinking, planning, contemplating, researching. We should all remember that some great scienic discoveries occurred by chance or while someone was "goofing off." Newton wasn't working in the orchard when the apple hit him and he devised the theory of gravity. All of us would like to have someone "lazy" build the car or stove we buy, particularly if that "laziness" were caused by the worker's taking time to check each step of his work and to do his job right. And sometimes, being "lazy"—that is, taking time off for a rest—is good for the overworked student or executive. Taking a rest can be particularly helpful to the athlete who is trying too hard or the doctor who's simply working himself overtime too many evenings at the clinic.

So be careful when you're tempted to call someone lazy. That person may be thinking, resting, or planning his or her next book.

▲ (336 WORDS) ▲

PASSAGE 1-3

Circle the correct answer:

1. The main idea of this passage is that
   a. laziness is a moral sin.

b. there are advantages and disadvantages in being lazy.
   c. laziness is the sign of deep-seated emotional problems.
   d. lazy people do more careful work.

2. The passage states that
   a. laziness is a disease.
   b. some people appear lazy because they are insecure.
   c. laziness is more beneficial than harmful.
   d. a good definition of laziness is emotional illness.

3. Which of the following conclusions does the passage support?
   a. The word *laziness* is sometimes applied incorrectly.
   b. Most of the time laziness is a virtue.
   c. Most assembly line workers are lazy.
   d. Most insecure people are lazy.

4. The first paragraph is
   a. somber
   b. humorous
   c. serious
   d. trite

5(a) As used in this passage, the word *fantasies* means
   a. fears
   b. anxieties
   c. ailments
   d. delusions

5(b) As used in this passage, the word *procrastinating* means
   a. overworked
   b. putting things off
   c. setting priorities
   d. supervising

5(c) As used in this passage, the word *devised* means
   a. formulated
   b. understood
   c. wrote
   d. proved

PASSAGE 1-4

SUBJECT: Wild Foods

Wild foods grow in almost every lawn, roadside strip, or park in America. In marshes or at the edge of lakes, cattails can be discovered and are easily recognized by everyone. The <u>bulbous</u>, fibrous top of the plant can be eaten either raw or cooked; it actually tastes like potatoes, and it can be prepared in any way that potatoes can be prepared. The roots of the cattail can be ground into flour and can be used as a flour substitute.

The wisteria vine, often used as a decorative plant around older homes, is edible. Dandelions, the enemy of the suburban lawn, are also a delicious wild food. The leaves are delicious in salads; and the roots cooked in an oven and grated, will serve as an excellent coffeelike drink. Dock, chives, onion, garlic—all these and other spices and herbs, including wild asparagus, grow in or at the edges of our lawns.

Many salad plants, such as mustard, shepherd's purse, or winter cress, grow along roadways or in parks. These add very interesting tastes to salads, particularly in winter. Even flowers can be eaten. Violets are a rich source of vitamins and can be eaten in salads or dried as a candy.

If you venture just a little way into the woods, your menu can become even more varied. The roots of Jerusalem (jə rōō′ sə ləm) artichokes are often dug in spring and fall at the edges of woods, where the ground may once have been <u>tilled</u> or farmed. Many wild berries or fruits like black cherry can be spotted deeper in the woods. Raspberries, blueberries, and huckleberries are all common, but the most common berry is the blackberry, which grows almost anywhere, even in towns; the blackberry, like all other berries, can be eaten by itself or in pies and breads, preserved, jellied, or dried.

Many of these wild foods are actually tastier than their domestic or commercial counterparts. Wild strawberries are much smaller than the strawberries you might buy in your grocery store, but they are much, much sweeter; no one need ever add sugar to wild strawberries.

▲ (349 WORDS) ▲

PASSAGE 1-4

Circle the correct answer:

1. The main idea of this passage is that
   a. people aren't very aware of their surroundings.

b. wild foods are better than commercial foods.
   c. many things that grow around us are edible.
   d. farmers never want for edible plants.

2. Mustard, shepherd's purse, and winter cress are all
   a. salad plants
   b. herbs
   c. spices
   d. flowers

3. We can conclude from this passage that
   a. grocers probably gather food in the woods.
   b. we can gather all our food near our home.
   c. we buy a lot of foods we could gather around our homes.
   d. buying commercial foods is unhealthy.

4. The passage suggests that
   a. the author is a farmer.
   b. the author gathers and eats wild foods.
   c. people are being cheated by grocers.
   d. people should become vegetarians.

5(a) As used in this passage, the word *bulbous* means
   a. bulb-shaped
   b. textured
   c. bitter
   d. misshapen

5(b) As used in this passage, the word *tilled* means
   a. watered
   b. fertilized
   c. paved
   d. plowed

PASSAGE 1-5

SUBJECT:
Dentists' Offices

More people than ever before are now going to dentist's offices, but fully one half of the United States population will not see a dentist. The reason is quite simple, believe most dentists: they're scared.

And, really, what experience is worse than seeing a traditional dentist? You wait in silence, thumbing through old magazines, in a sterile white waiting room in which no one ever speaks. All is silent until an assistant calls your name and leads you back to another white room, this one filled with machinery to frighten you still further.

At the Medical College of Georgia, dentists are taught principles of behavior and techniques of office design that should help reduce the patient's anxiety and tension. Assistants and receptionists are taught to smile and speak to the patient; this helps create an atmosphere of trust. Dentists themselves are being taught to communicate more fully with the patient. A phrase such as "You're doing fine" tells the patient that the dentist is <u>appreciative</u> of the patient's predicament. These phrases also help by rewarding the <u>tolerance</u> of pain.

Dentists' offices are being repainted in "earth tones," brown, green, tan, and other soothing colors. A startling color such as red should be avoided at all costs; red brings to mind blood and pain. Paintings and other distractions are <u>strategically</u> located; music is piped in to help the patient ignore his or her pain.

Until recently, dentists had ignored the fact that most patients never see much more than the ceiling of the practice room. Most of the time, patients are lying flat on their backs with little to busy their minds other than their pain. Now dentists are not only building ceilings with fancy patterns, but also distracting their patients with ceiling TV sets, computer games and mazes, and mobile sculptures. One quick technique involves placing mirrors so patients can distract themselves by watching fish in a tank located near the ceiling.

Less drastic changes include redoing the practice rooms to include less of the sterile color white and redesigning the machinery a dentist must use to make it appear less frightening. Uniforms are also being made in pastel and earth colors, no longer in white.

Some dentists go much further. They take an active role in teaching their patients to relax; some are teaching their patients deep muscle relaxation and breathing control. Some use advanced techniques such as hypnosis and biofeedback to help their patients relax in the chair. Drugs and painkillers may still be used to ease physical pain, but all these techniques of relaxation help the patient relax and avoid anxiety over their pain.

▲ (437 WORDS) ▲

PASSAGE 1-5

Circle the correct answer:

1. The main idea of this passage is that
   a. physical surroundings affect people's emotional reactions.
   b. decoration is the primary factor in relieving patients' fears.
   c. "earth tones" are soothing colors.
   d. most people feel anxious about physical pain.

2. Some dentists distract their patients with
   a. mobiles
   b. televisions
   c. computer games
   d. all of the above.

3. We can conclude from the passage that
   a. relaxation blocks out all pain.
   b. patients feel more pain if they think the dentist is unconcerned with their feelings.
   c. being anxious and tense exaggerates the pain a patient feels.
   d. being anxious and tense causes the pain a patient feels.

4(a) The passage suggests that
   a. dentists' offices are usually painted white because they must be kept sterile.
   b. warm colors ease physical pain.
   c. most pain associated with dentistry is caused by unprofessional dentists.
   d. some of the pain felt by patients may be psychological.

4(b) The passage suggests that dentists should
   a. learn to communicate with their patients.
   b. use hypnosis on most patients.
   c. constantly console their patients.
   d. also be psychiatrists.

5(a) As used in this passage, the word *appreciative* means
   a. indifferent to
   b. thankful
   c. understanding
   d. fearful

5(b) As used in this passage, the word *tolerance* means
   a. acceptance
   b. level
   c. degree
   d. denial

5(c) As used in this passage, the word *strategically* means
- a. dramatically
- b. systematically
- c. randomly
- d. artistically

PASSAGE 1-6   SUBJECT:
Nitinol, a Space Age Metal

A metal with a built-in memory is one of the very useful discoveries made during America's space program. Nitinol (ni′ ti nōl) was discovered by scientists working at the Naval Surface Weapons Center. They were looking for heat-shield metals for missiles and satellites, but what they found was nitinol. This alloy can be formed into shapes just like any other metal, but it returns to its original form at a certain temperature.

When this alloy of nickel and titanium is first formed, it is shaped into ingots, brick-shaped masses of the metal. Then it is drawn out into a wire of varying thickness, depending on the job it is destined to do. It is set into its desired curve or shape and heated briefly. It is then cooled off by dipping the wire in cold water. This "sets" its memory. The metal can then be formed into any desired shape, but whenever its temperature exceeds room temperature, it returns to the shape it has memorized.

This makes nitinol perfect, of course, for spacecrafts, for antennas, probes, shields, and folding "arms" made of nitinol can be stored safely inside a spacecraft, protecting them from damage during the launching. Then, once safe in orbit, the spacecraft would suddenly "grow" antennas and other structures. The sun's rays would have warmed up the folded and coiled nitinol, and it would have returned to its original shape.

But scientists have found a more down-to-earth use for this wire: they now use it to straighten teeth. Before nitinol, teeth that needed straightening had brackets attached to them; wires were attached to these to exert a pull in the right direction. But this pull must be constant, and the stainless steel arch wire can't exert the correct force if it has been bent several times or if the tooth has actually moved toward it as planned. As a result, many people with dental braces must have the wire replaced monthly, tightened every few weeks, or adjusted painfully tight at the beginning of the treatment.

But nitinol wires can be formed to exert force in a certain direction, cooled off, and then reformed to fit the patient's mouth. As the mouth warms the nitinol, it begins to try to assume its preset shape. This exerts a steadier, more constant pull on the tooth than could ever be achieved with stainless steel wire. Nitinol can be bent into such intricate shapes—while maintaining its pull—that very difficult treatments, such as moving one tooth from behind another, can be done now without the expense or pain of constant adjustment. Nitinol has cut the time needed for these treatments by almost half, a real benefit for both patient and dentist.

▲ (448 WORDS) ▲

PASSAGE 1-6

Circle the correct answer:

1. The main idea of this passage is that
   a. nitinol is a highly versatile metal.
   b. nitinol helped make the space program a success.
   c. nitinol has revolutionized dental care.
   d. most alloys have "memories."

2. Which of the following is not a step in forming nitinol for space use?
   a. The metal is shaped into ingots.
   b. The metal is separated into nickel and titanium.
   c. The metal is drawn into a wire.
   d. The metal is set in its desired curve or shape and heated briefly.

3. We can conclude from this passage that
   a. nitinol has its "memory" function because it is an alloy.
   b. the sun's rays are necessary to trigger the metal's "memory."
   c. people have only begun to discover the many uses of nitinol.
   d. one of the problems with nitinol is that it often returns to its original shape at inopportune times.

4. The passage suggests that
   a. nitinol is an organic metal.
   b. nitinol is stronger than any metal.
   c. nitinol's sensitivity to temperature changes makes it impractical for most uses.
   d. nitinol is better than stainless steel in jobs that require constant stress on the metal.

5(a) As used in this passage, the word *alloy* means
   a. base
   b. competitor
   c. mixture
   d. predecessor

5(b) As used in this passage, the word *exert* means
   a. stretch out
   b. put into vigorous action
   c. bring to bear
   d. serve the purpose of

5(c) As used in this passage, the word *intricate* means
   a. abnormal
   b. complex
   c. regular
   d. perfect

PASSAGE 1-7

SUBJECT: Rugby

Rugby has the reputation of being one of the roughest sports in the world. Outside the British Isles, rugby is little known and, in fact, is often confused with soccer. But in England, an old sports saying serves to point out the differences between the two games; soccer is supposedly a gentlemen's game played by ruffians, whereas rugby is a ruffian's game played by gentlemen.

The game begins with a kickoff from one end of a 100-yard field. The receiving ruggers, as a rugby team is called, attempt to move the ball down the field; the opposing team attempts to stop the man with the ball.

The rules are quite simple. You cannot tackle anyone but the man who is carrying the ball, and once the ball carrier is tackled, he must give up the ball. Obviously, a good strategy for moving the ball downfield is to carry it as far as possible, then pass the ball before being tackled.

If the ball carrier can travel the length of the field, his team is awarded four points, and another two points are won by kicking the ball over the goalpost after the score. Penalties are equally simple: tackling a player who isn't carrying the ball carries a ten-yard penalty.

Much of rugby's reputation for roughness stems from the fact that the players wear no pads. To Americans accustomed to seeing professional football players in suits and helmets like armor, a rugby player's uniform seems suicidally simple. Most ruggers wear a very thick jersey, heavy gymnasium shorts, heavy socks, rugby shoes, and a mouthpiece. Ruggers use other equipment or pads only when an injury requires protection. But even with this mimimal equipment, the game is apparently not as brutal as it might seem. The players are quite satisfied with the lack of padding and helmets and actually think the game might be too rough if players used more equipment. "Human nature is not to hit as hard if no one is wearing pads," one rugger explains.

Rugby games are played in two halves, each lasting forty minutes. Teams always meet to play two games consecutively, back-to-back. Again, playing a demanding, physical sport like rugby for more than 160 minutes seems like an impossible task, but the ruggers love this idea. "It gives everyone on the team a chance to get into the game," they say.

Rugby is slowly catching on in America. The sport is gaining an enthusiastic following among college teams and in independent rugby "unions," organized on the British model. It has all the appeal of football, but it is simpler and requires much less costly equipment. Rugby is ready to be rediscovered.

▲ (446 WORDS) ▲

PASSAGE 1-7

Circle the correct answer:

1. The main purpose of this passage is to
    a. compare English and American sports.
    b. compare rugby to football.
    c. discuss the brutality of rugby.
    d. provide a brief introduction to rugby.

2. According to the passage, which of the following statements is true?
    a. Tackling a player who isn't carrying the ball is a ten-yard penalty.
    b. It is legal to pass the ball in rugby if you are already down.
    c. Only the offensive team in rugby can be called "ruggers."
    d. all of the above.

3. We can conclude from the passage that
    a. basketball was derived from rugby.
    b. rugby is most closely identifiable with our American sport of football.
    c. soccer and rugby are essentially the same game.
    d. rugby is the roughest of all contact sports.

4. The passage suggests that
    a. there is seldom an injury in rugby.
    b. scoring points in rugby is easier than in most sports.
    c. padding may make contact sports rougher.
    d. all rugby players are superb athletes.

5(a) As used in this passage, the word *strategy* means
    a. deception
    b. method
    c. defense
    d. rule

5(b) As used in this passage, the word *accustomed* means
    a. in the habit of
    b. wishing to
    c. not used to
    d. conscious of

PASSAGE 1-8

SUBJECT:
Bluebirds

Bluebirds, the little birds celebrated in song and poetry as symbols of happiness, are becoming <u>extinct</u>. They were once one of the most common birds in America; early settlers <u>called them</u> "the blue robins." But in the last thirty-five years, particularly in the eastern United States, there are many people who have never seen a bluebird.

There are several reasons why the bluebird is fighting for survival. First, their nesting areas are disappearing. Bluebirds like to nest in the edges of woods, in hedgerows, and in hollow trees. They prefer an enclosure of some sort rather than an open nest on a branch. More and more, the sort of environment bluebirds like is being covered with parking lots, shopping centers, and housing developments.

Chemicals such as pesticides used to control insects are also causing problems for the bluebird. Bluebirds are ground feeders; they cannot feed in flight as some other birds do. Bluebirds live on insects, and pesticides are killing off their food source; worse, the chemicals in some of the insects the birds eat are killing the bluebirds themselves. Add to this problem the effects of the last few extremely cold winters on both the birds and their food supply.

The bluebird's most serious problems, though, are two other birds with which the bluebirds must <u>contend</u> for nesting sites. And man may actually be to blame for these problems, too. In the middle of the nineteenth century, house sparrows were brought to America from England. In 1890, eighty starlings were released in New York's Central Park; both species adapted well to America and thrived.

Unfortunately, both of these newcomers like the same sort of nesting sites that bluebirds like. Bluebirds are meek little birds; they fight only to defend their nest. Starlings and sparrows, on the other hand, are strong and aggressive. They soon moved into the available nesting holes, sometimes breaking bluebird eggs or shoving baby bluebirds out of the nest.

A group of bird lovers, the <u>N</u>orth <u>A</u>merican <u>B</u>luebird <u>S</u>ociety, is trying to help; they're making bluebird nesting boxes and explaining to other bird lovers how to place them and <u>monitor</u> them. A small box with an entrance exactly one and a half inches round will <u>let</u> bluebirds in while keeping starlings out; the boxes should be mounted five feet off the ground in low brush. If you have plenty of space, the NABS urges you to build as many nesting boxes as possible. The boxes must be checked during the nesting season and cleaned and repaired once a year.

The effort is well worth it if the bluebird can be saved. Most people find the bluebird, its song, and its gentle nature delightful. It is the single bird most often mentioned in poetry and in song; it would be a shame if this bird disappeared.

▲ (470 WORDS) ▲

PASSAGE 1-8

Circle the correct answer:

1. The main purpose of this passage is to
   a. discuss the bluebird's feeding problems.
   b. discuss the bluebird's nesting problems.
   (c.) discuss the problems facing the bluebird in its fight for survival.
   d. discuss the operations that are being undertaken to try to save the bluebirds.

2. Which of the following statements is not true?
   a. Bluebirds are meek birds.
   b. Pesticides cause problems for the bluebirds.
   (c.) Starlings destroy the nests of bluebirds.
   d. Bluebirds prefer enclosed nesting sites.

3. We can conclude from the passage that
   a. pesticides are the most threatening problem the bluebird faces.
   (b.) most of the problems that threaten the bluebird are man-made.
   c. the starling preys on the bluebird as a food source.
   d. pesticide poisoning weakens the bluebird so much that it is unable to adjust to extremely cold weather.

4. The passage suggests that
   (a.) if enough people take an interest in the bluebird, it may be saved.
   b. because of the NABS, the bluebird is in little danger today.
   c. unless starlings are controlled, the bluebird faces extinction.
   d. as long as pesticides are used, the bluebirds will continue to diminish in number.

5(a) As used in this passage, the word *extinct* means
   a. famous
   b. strange
   c. plentiful
   (d.) uncommon

5(b) As used in this passage, the word *contend* means
   (a.) share
   b. defer
   c. compute
   d. agonize

5(c) As used in this passage, the word *monitor* means
   a. heat
   (b.) design
   c. bait
   d. watch over

PASSAGE 1-9   SUBJECT:
Palm Springs and the Agua Caliente Indians

Ask anyone which is the richest town in America; high on the list of answers will be Palm Springs, the desert resort in California.

Within a few square miles in this desert city live two presidents and two vice-presidents. There is a Bob Hope Drive; there is a Frank Sinatra Drive. Few houses ever sell for less than one third of a million dollars. The Rolls-Royce dealer is quite accustomed to customers writing checks for the full price of $70,000 cars and not even driving them around the block first.

Politicians, movie stars, athletes, even royalty come here to relax. To keep them happy and to keep Palm Springs looking as wealthy as it does, things are strictly regulated. There are no motels in Palm Springs; everything is called "a resort." Billboards and flashing neon signs are outlawed, and no sign can quote a price for anything; the dimensions of signs are strictly controlled, as is the height of every building. Even the color of homes is regulated; everything must be painted in a pastel color. If one of Palm Springs' wealthy citizens installs a lighting fixture that is visible from the street, the fixture has to be approved by a review group.

The result is one of the most beautiful cities in America, as well as one of the richest. The visitor sees only white stucco walls, red Spanish tiled roofs, million-dollar lawns, Rolls-Royces, and the occasional Mercedes.

Except for downtown, that is. Here among the famous stores, boutiques, and discos, there is a startling number of empty lots. These lots are the most valuable land in Palm Springs, worth around one-third of a million per acre. These lots and another few thousand acres inside the city limits are all owned by 107 Agua Caliente (äg' wä kä lĭ ĕn' tā) Indians.

The Agua Caliente Indians originally owned all the land in and around Palm Springs. When the Southern Pacific Railway went through, President Grant gave the Indians 32,000 acres of sand in exchange for the rail right of way. In 1959 the Indians were given the right to sell or lease the land to white businessmen, mainly hotel and homeowners. That's why a lot of the Mercedes and Rolls-Royce cars belong to these Indians.

These 107 Aguas are without doubt the single richest minority group in the United States. The original treaty promised the Indians that their land would be "without encumbrance." Recent court decisions have ruled that taxes and zoning laws are "encumbrances." So the Agua Calientes pay no property or income taxes; they're also the only people in Palm Springs who can do whatever they want with their land.

Right now the Indians are letting their land remain empty. The city government is testing the treaty one more time to see if the Agua Calientes can really do anything they want with their $300 million empty lots. The Agua Calientes ride around in their Rolls-Royces right along with the movie stars while the city worries about becoming ugly.

▲ (497 WORDS) ▲

PASSAGE 1-9

Circle the correct answer:

1. The main purpose of this passage is to
   a. discuss Palm Springs and the Indians who own a large part of it.
   b. discuss the resort town of Palm Springs.
   c. discuss the Agua Caliente Indians.
   d. discuss the wealth of Palm Springs.

2. Which of the following items is not regulated by the Palm Springs review group?
   a. types of cars
   b. light fixtures
   c. billboards
   d. building heights

3. We can conclude from the passage that
   a. President Grant paid a fair price for the Indians' land.
   b. the Indians aren't aware of how much their land is worth.
   c. President Grant did not intend to give the Agua Caliente Indians anything of value for the right to cross their land.
   d. the Agua Caliente Indians are ill-educated.

4. The passage suggests that
   a. the Indians are fully accepted by the residents of Palm Springs.
   b. the treaty with the Indians is a forgery.
   c. the residents of Palm Springs are worried that the Indians will not share their concern over the beauty of their community.
   d. all of the Indians combined aren't as wealthy as one or two of the other residents of Palm Springs.

5(a) As used in this passage, the word *regulated* means
   a. impersonal
   b. financial
   c. controlled
   d. reactionary

5(b) As used in this passage, the word *startling* means
 a. abounding
 b. amazing
 c. unrecorded
 d. ugly

5(c) As used in this passage, the word *encumbrance* means
 a. benefit
 b. wealth
 c. impediment
 d. worth

PASSAGE 1-10

SUBJECT:
The Octopus

For hundreds of years, people have feared the octopus as a monster of the deep. Legends of sailors slowly squeezed to death by huge tentacles or watchmen snatched off a deck by one long, snaky arm have presented a picture of the octopus that is designed to cause terror. Scientists are now beginning to learn more about this creature; and, as with most mysteries, the more we know, the less there is to fear.

The octopus is found in almost every ocean and sea, even in the Antarctic, and there are around one hundred different species. Their size ranges from over thirty feet in diameter to some very small species that are less than an inch around, but of all these sizes and types, only one species, a four-inch variety found in Australia, is poisonous to man. And this poisonous species has caused only three deaths in recorded history.

The octopus has a beak—very much like the beak of a parrot or parakeet—and it manufactures venom in its salivary glands, but all this is only for catching and eating its food, fish and shellfish. It is very difficult to provoke an octopus enough to make it bite a human. An octopus will sometimes use the suckers on its tentacles to stick to a human, but even this is only an effort on the part of the octopus to hide itself. Most often, the reaction of the octopus is fear.

The frightened octopus has several devices it may use to protect itself. It may change color to blend in with its background and camouflage itself; it may even change from the white of fright to a fiery, angry red in order to frighten its attacker. It also is able to squirt a black ink to confuse an attacker, but the octopus's most common method of defense is flight. It runs away either to its den or to a crack or indentation in a rock where it can hide or change its color.

When an octopus is captured, it becomes very tame; some even allow their keepers to pet them. The octopus is so intelligent, though, that keeping one in captivity is difficult. They can pull the plug out of some types of tanks, and they can lift the top off a tank with their very strong tentacles, or they can shrink until even a very large octopus can slide through a tiny hole. In fact, their behavior in captivity has prompted many marine scientists to claim that the octopus is one of the most intelligent creatures in the world. Some even claim that octopuses each have individual, distinct personalities. They play tricks on their keepers and are able to learn. Some octopuses are shy, and others are quite aggressive, even raiding neighboring tanks for food and then returning to their own tank to hide. An octopus may live up to six years of age, depending on its species and on its personality. The more aggressive it is, the more it eats and the bigger it may eventually grow to be.

▲ (511 WORDS) ▲

PASSAGE 1-10

Circle the correct answer:

1. The main purpose of this passage is to
   a. discuss the myths surrounding the octopus.
   b. describe the behavior of the octopus in captivity.
   c. discuss the different species of octopuses.
   d. present current scientific knowledge about the octopus.

2. Which of the following statements about the octopus is true?
   a. Only two species of octopuses are poisonous to man.
   b. Octopuses are found in the Antarctic.
   c. Octopuses turn white to frighten their attackers.
   d. Most octopuses are over thirty feet in diameter.

3. We can conclude from the passage that
   a. octopuses are complex animals that man has only begun to understand.
   b. the octopus is dangerous only if attacked.
   c. the octopus will flee only if it is outnumbered.
   d. octopuses may provide a valuable food source in the future.

4. The passage suggests that
   a. most myths about octopuses are founded on scientific evidence.
   b. the tentacles of the octopus are harmful to man.
   c. the octopus's intelligence is the major reason for so much current scientific investigation.
   d. the octopus is only ferocious if attacked.

5(a) As used in this passage, the word *indentation* means
   a. bulge
   b. plant growth
   c. shallow place
   d. other animal's den

5(b) As used in the passage, the word *distinct* means
   a. tame
   b. ferocious
   c. gregarious
   d. different

PASSAGE 1-11

SUBJECT:
Dye Making

As more people become interested in the arts of spinning and weaving, it is only natural that they should want to pursue the art of dyeing their own wool as well. In colonial days, when spinning and weaving in the home were an economic necessity, housewifes used natural objects to make their dyes.

To make dye from a natural source, one has to soak the object in water from one to eight days. The water is strained, and the liquid is then a pure dye. And interestingly the color of the object is not necessarily the color of the dye it will produce. In fact, one batch of dye can produce a variety of colors, depending upon the mordant (môr′ dənt) that is used along with the dye.

A mordant is a metal or other chemical used to make the fiber being dyed more absorbent, making the color permanent. Some common mordants include tin, copper, iron, or cream of tartar. The mordant used to presoak the fiber determines the color the fiber will become once it soaks in the dye.

Depending on the mordant used beforehand, marigolds can dye wool any color from bright yellow to pale green. Dried insects can dye wool any shade from maroon to pink. Without the use of a mordant, apple bark and beets produce a yellow dye; with alum as a mordant, these same substances produce a red dye. Blueberries and elderberries make a blue dye; reds and blues are the dyes hardest to make, and yellows are the easiest. Most fibers have to be dyed twice to obtain a green or orange color.

Indigo is the one dye that does not require a mordant to make it a permanent stain. The precise shade of blue produced with indigo is determined by the length of time the fiber remains in the dye; as long as the fiber remains in dye vat, it will appear to be green; but as soon as the yarn is removed, the air causes the indigo to oxidize, and the fiber turns blue.

Other things that affect the color obtained by natural dyeing include the mineral content of the water, the type of pots and stirrers used (because all metals are mordants), and even the geographical location. For example, dandelion roots from North America make a yellow dye, but those from Scotland yield a bright purple.

Natural dyeing is a long process. The yarn is first washed carefully, then simmered in the mordant mixture for an hour or so, and then rinsed very carefully. Next the yarn is lowered into the dye and simmered for an hour or so, depending on the shade the wearer wants. Then the yarn is rinsed in cooler and cooler water until the water is finally clear.

Because almost anything affects the color results from natural dyeing, many hobbyists attempt to be as authentic as possible. They try to duplicate the original colonial practice as much as possible, even to the point of simmering the dye over a wood fire outdoors. And they have a point—even heat and smoke alter the results. The fascinating thing about natural dyeing is that you can never be sure what color you may end up wearing next year.

▲ (539 WORDS) ▲

PASSAGE 1-11

Circle the correct answer:

1. The main purpose of this passage is to
   a. discuss the different colors that can be achieved in home dyeing.
   b. show how people dyed their wool in the colonial days.
   c. provide fairly detailed information about the art of dyeing.
   d. discuss the effects of mordants on the dyeing process.

2(a) Which of the following is not a mordant?
   a. tin
   b. cedar
   c. copper
   d. iron

2(b) According to the passage, which of the following statements is not true?
   a. Most fibers have to be dyed twice to obtain a green or orange color.
   b. Apple bark and beets produce a yellow dye.
   c. Marigolds can dye wool pale green.
   d. Articles being dyed with indigo will appear purple in the vat.

3. We can conclude from the passage that
   a. smoke and heat are the most important factors in dye color.
   b. natural dyeing is at least a six-step process.
   c. the color of the object used for making dye always approximates the color of the dye produced.
   d. the dye coloring has more effect on the final color of an object than does the mordant used.

4. The passage suggests that
   a. alloys make better mordants than pure metals.
   b. indigo dye is harder to make than yellow dyes.
   c. plastic pots are the best containers to use for natural dyeing.
   d. only a few dyes require the use of a mordant.

5(a) As used in this passage, the word *mordant* means
   a. a collective name for the several processes in natural dyeing.
   b. a chemical used to tint neutral colored dyes.
   c. a substance used to insure quality in natural dye.
   d. a metal or other chemical used to make fiber more absorbent.

5(b) As used in this passage, the word *oxidize* means
   a. to combine with oxygen
   b. darken
   c. lighten
   d. become wetter

PASSAGE 1-12   SUBJECT: Racehorses

Racing thoroughbred horses may be a romantic way of life for some people. But for others, it is a business, complete with its own rigid rules and its own social classes.

Most racing horses are still bred and raised in Kentucky. Huge farms in Kentucky are the breeding grounds for future Derby winners. On these rolling acres of bluegrass, horses worth hundreds of thousands of dollars receive the best of care. These farms are beginning to resemble genetics laboratories more than working ranches. Racing is a fragile, expensive business, and no effort is spared when owners try to breed the best stock.

But the farms in Kentucky are too cold in the winter, when serious training begins. Most owners have training grounds in Florida, where winter days are mild enough to let the horses train all day; some train halfway between Kentucky and Florida, in towns like Aiken, South Carolina, where old polo grounds have been converted for training racers. At these halfway farms, the mornings are chilly enough to train longer, and the afternoons are mild.

These farms are a world apart; almost everyone who works on the farm is, has been, or wants to be a jockey. Everyone weighs around one hundred pounds, even the older trainers.

The social order begins with stable boys and stable girls; slightly above these are the "hot walkers," who walk the horses to cool them after their morning training, and the grooms. All of these workers clean stalls, groom and rub the horses, and bandage leg joints; all of them are waiting for the opportunity to get into the saddle.

The jockeys and exercise riders are the next class up in the social scale. Most outsiders think that the jockeys are the highest step in the social ladder here, but they're incorrect. The king of the hill is the trainer, the man who runs the entire farm.

Millions of dollars may ride on the trainer's every decision. The entire business of horse racing finally depends on only the trainer's experience; only the trainer has the <u>intuition</u> to know how to train each fragile horse—a <u>potential</u> gold mine or a potential disaster. Only the trainer knows when each nervous thoroughbred is ready to race. Most trainers have spent their lives around horses, learning to care for them and to "bring them along."

The horses are broken to the saddle on the Kentucky farms. At the breeding farms, they are left alone a great deal. At the training farms, however, they are gradually introduced to larger groups of horses and people. They are exercised in a daily routine, fed differently, and groomed more often. The horses are slowly accustomed to the pressure of the racetrack. Trainers actually prepare the horses mentally as well as physically for the competition they face at the track.

The training farms are also a halfway stop to calm down older horses after a season of racing. They are brought back to the farms almost like vacationers escaping the pressure of a city job. Trainers say the horses return very nervous from the city and the racing circuit. Sometimes, they say, the horses run around for a week or longer before they realize that they have no audience; then they calm down.

Only a trainer could describe the way a horse thinks.

▲ (558 WORDS) ▲

PASSAGE 1-12

Circle the correct answer:

1. This passage is mainly about
   a. training farms for thoroughbred racing horses.
   b. breeding farms for thoroughbred racing horses.
   c. Kentucky thoroughbred racing horses.
   d. the social order on a training farm.

2. Which of the following statements is not true?
   a. Most racing horses are still bred and raised in Kentucky.
   b. At breeding farms the horses are left alone a great deal.
   c. Training farms are a halfway stop to calm down older horses after a season of racing.
   d. Jockeys are at the highest step in the social order of a training farm.

3. We can conclude from the passage that
   a. racehorses perform best in very humid climates.
   b. mild temperatures increase a horse's lung power.
   c. cold climates are best for young thoroughbreds.
   d. racehorses don't train well in extremely cold climates.

4(a) The passage suggests that
   a. only a jockey can get the "best" from a horse.
   b. trainers are the elite of the training farm workers.
   c. a thoroughbred forms close attachments with the stable hands.
   d. owners dictate the development of a thoroughbred racehorse.

4(b) The author discusses the social order on a training farm to
   a. show the importance of the trainer.
   b. put the different jobs in order of descending importance.
   c. differentiate jockeys from trainers.
   d. separate the workers from the ownership of the farm.

5(a) As used in this passage, the word *intuition* means
   a. right
   b. insight
   c. training
   d. freedom

5(b) As used in this passage, the word *potential* means
   a. certain
   b. undiscovered
   c. possible
   d. demonstrative

PASSAGE 1-13 SUBJECT:
Wild Seabirds and Oil Pollution

The most visible damage done by oil slicks at sea is the damage done to wild seabirds. Fish, scallops, oysters, and other sea creatures are damaged, of course, but the evidence of this is hard to find. However, by now almost all Americans are familiar with the image of oil-soaked birds struggling to live through their ordeal.

In late 1976 four tankers went down just off the Nantucket coast; these wrecks spewed millions of gallons of crude oil into the sea, endangering the Georges Bank, one of the world's greatest fishing grounds. Scores of scientists came to the area to study the effects of the oil spill on the seabirds. They also wanted to rescue as many of the birds as possible.

The texture of heavy crude oil once it has been discharged into the ocean has been described in different ways. Observers have described it as feeling like chocolate pudding, like Vaseline, or like Jell-O, but everyone agrees, though, that it's thick and sticky. As long as the oil is floating in a slick offshore, it is particularly dangerous to birds for two reasons. First, the petroleum is heavy, and it is inclined to calm the water and slow down any wave action. This attracts the birds because a calm patch of water is a natural place for a tired bird to rest. Secondly, the petroleum darkens the waters, and the birds seem to think the darkened water means large predators are feeding in the slick. They land, anticipating to feed off the remains; thus, diving birds, such as the auk and the loon, are damaged most.

Once a bird has dived into an oil slick, it rapidly becomes coated with oil, and oil can kill a bird in several different ways.

Seabirds depend upon their feathers for insulation and protection from the cold temperatures. The cores of a seabird's feathers are hollow, so they can trap more air inside their layer of feathers. The hollow cores contact the bird's skin and remain at body temperature. When the feathers are coated with crude oil, they lose their protective insulating layer. The feathers can no longer trap air, so the hollow interiors of the feathers become cold, and then the bird's skin temperature begins to drop; many of the birds simply develop pneumonia and die.

Other birds are killed when they swallow the crude oil. They might swallow it at sea while feeding or while attempting to clean themselves. Others, perhaps sensing the danger of the oil, attempt to clean themselves for hours and eventually starve to death; they are simply too tired to feed.

Science is still searching for help for these birds. At Nantucket a detergent was employed to help clean the oil from the birds, but only about half of the birds treated ever lived. The detergent was intended to clean tankers, so it washed all the oil, including the bird's own natural oils, from the feathers. Without these natural oils, the birds cannot fly, and they thus are helpless.

Many of the birds must remain in pens for up to a year until their natural molting cycle can replace the feathers ruined first by the oil and then by the detergent. The cost is incredible, but the scientists are learning a great deal about the birds.

Of all the seabird species in oil spill areas, ducks and gulls have suffered least, for ducks do not fly far out to sea, and gulls have wide ranges of flight, but do not dive. Spills must be blown or carried ashore before these species are affected.

▲ (597 WORDS) ▲

PASSAGE 1-13

Circle the correct answer:

1. The main purpose of this passage is to
   a. discuss the damage that is being done to wild fowl by oil spillage.
   b. discuss the rescue efforts of the inhabitants of Nantucket.
   c. discuss the advances science is making in finding ways of removing oil from birds.
   d. discuss the ecological effects of oil spills.

2. The texture of heavy crude oil, once it has been spilled into the sea, has been described as feeling like
   a. chocolate pudding
   b. Vaseline
   c. Jell-O
   d. all of the above

3(a) We can conclude from the passage that
   a. birds rely on the heat of the sun to warm their bodies, like reptiles.
   b. birds must rely on regulating their internal body heat for survival.
   c. crude oil on the feathers of birds acts as insulation, trapping in body heat.
   d. crude oil causes the feathers to trap body fluids in their hollow cores.

3(b) Which of the following conclusions does the passage support?
   a. Current detergents clog the skin pores when used on oil-soaked birds.
   b. Current detergents soften the hollow cores of the feathers of oil-soaked birds.
   c. Current detergents are an excellent solution for oil-soaked birds if applied immediately.
   d. Current detergents wash off the bird's natural oils from the feathers.

69

4. With which of the following statements would the author probably agree?
   a. Scientists are making some progress in designing ways to help oil-soaked birds.
   b. Scientists are not sufficiently concerned with the ecological effects of oil spills.
   c. It is better to allow an oil-soaked bird to die than have it suffer the side effects of detergent usage.
   d. The damage to wildlife caused by oil spills is a "necessary evil" if we are to have adequate energy supplies.

5(a) As used in this passage, the word *texture* means
   a. smell
   b. appearance and feel
   c. taste
   d. ingredients

5(b) As used in this passage, the word *predators* means
   a. preying animals
   b. victims
   c. mammals
   d. seals

PASSAGE 1-14

SUBJECT:
The Indy 500

Watching the Indy 500 on TV gives you only a general idea of the size of this spectacle. Cameras simply cannot do justice to an auto race. If the car is moving toward the camera and the camera is mounted at track level, all you see is a blur. If the camera is farther away, mounted on the scoring tower or circling on a blimp, the distance seems to make the cars move slowly. Most importantly of all, though, most televisions simply cannot reproduce the sound of thirty engines thundering by, strained to the limit. The high-pitched whine of a well-tuned racing engine blasting by at two hundred miles an hour is enough to make your scalp crawl and your flesh creep. The only place you can hear that sound is at the track itself.

The track isn't really in Indianapolis at all. The Indianapolis 500 is run in a suburb called Speedway, Indiana. Each year since 1911, the endurance race has been held at a huge oval track here. First the track was covered with paving brick, so one of its nicknames is "the old brickyard." But as cars became faster and a greater emphasis was placed on safety, the brick was covered over with smoother asphalt, except for one strip of bricks left exposed for history's sake. The race was once held on Monday, after a weekend of parades and parties, but it has since been moved to Sunday in order to capture a larger television audience. Once the race itself was billed as "the largest single-day sporting event in the world," but now with the modern Indy cars approaching average speeds of two hundred for the entire race, the race only lasts about three hours. Still, over three hundred thousand people routinely show up to watch the most famous automobile race in the world.

But even at the track, it's difficult to decide how to watch the race. No one can see the entire track except the track officials in the three-story-high scoring tower, who must judge the conduct of the race. The main grandstands line the two straightaways on either side of the oval track. Most enthusiasts who return to the Indianapolis 500 every year sit somewhere in these grandstands, but the choice is a difficult one. As tickets for these seats cost anywhere from $20 to $50, the choice is made as carefully as possible, too. Many fans believe that all the action takes place in the turns, where the drivers are fighting to brake their cars and where most of the passing takes place. Other fans prefer to sit along one of the long straightaways to watch the cars streak by at peak speeds. If your seat is along the main straightaway, you also are given the chance to watch the cars pull into the pits for repairs and changes. Some fans are experts on pit stops, bringing along their stopwatches to check each team's performance. Watching five mechanics change four tires and refuel a car in about twenty seconds is exciting, to say the least, particularly when winning the race may depend on their efforts.

For a slightly lower price, the Indy 500 can be seen from the infield, the huge area inside the track itself. On race day, the infield becomes an enormous parking lot and picnic area. But even here, a fan cannot see the entire track; at one time fans used to build temporary towers and sell space on them for viewing the track, but in 1960 two people were killed when their scaffold collapsed. So there is no one way to see the entire track at once and to see it satisfactorily. Maybe that's why fans return every year—the 500 simply cannot be taken in at one visit.

▲ (631 WORDS) ▲

PASSAGE 1-14

Circle the correct answer:

1. The main idea of this passage is that
   a. the pit is a good place to watch the race.
   b. the Indy 500 is held at Speedway, Indiana.
   c. the size of the Indy 500 is difficult to grasp.
   d. the current cars that run at Indy are faster than the cars of the past.

2. According to the passage, which of the following statements is true?
   a. Only the turns are exciting viewing points at Indy.
   b. The Indy 500 was first run in 1911.
   c. The best seats at Indy provide the fan with a view of the whole racetrack.
   d. Some people still watch the race from towers they build in the infield.

3(a) We can conclude from the passage that
   a. the infield is too dangerous for spectators.
   b. the track officials at Indy are very safety-conscious.
   c. the officials in the scoring tower cannot see the entire racetrack.
   d. the Indy 500 is not as famous as it used to be.

3(b) Which of the following conclusions does the passage support?
   a. Fans enjoy different aspects of the Indy 500.
   b. Most fans enjoy sitting near the curves at Indy.
   c. Most fans enjoy sitting on the straightaways at Indy.
   d. Most fans enjoy sitting in the infield at Indy.

4. The author's tone is
   a. negative
   b. admiring
   c. cynical
   d. satirical

5(a) As used in this passage, the word *suburb* means
   a. state
   b. racetrack
   c. area outside the city
   d. area inside the city

5(b) As used in this passage, the word *routinely* means
   a. boringly
   b. repeatedly
   c. occasionally
   d. scarcely

PASSAGE 1-15　　　　SUBJECT:
Canoeing and Kayaking

A major new sport in America, white water boating, involves the use of two boats with <u>uniquely</u> American histories.

The canoe was first developed by the Indians of the Great Lakes, the Northeast, and neighboring regions in Canada. This long, sleek boat with its deep, V-shaped hull was first made of wood. Later thin, scraped bark was stretched over wooden ribs to make an even more lightweight canoe. Modern canoes are made from aluminum and fiberglass. Recreational boaters have used the canoe to make trips down Arctic rivers and to cross the Atlantic Ocean, but the <u>basic</u> design has changed very little. Modern materials and production techniques have made the canoe slightly better, but the original design continues to perform the job it was designed for.

A canoe doesn't require the perfect skill and balance demanded by sailboats, nor does canoeing require expensive outboard motors and gasoline; a canoe's hull carries mountains of equipment and supplies for exploring, fishing, or camping, yet the canoe itself is light enough to allow carrying from one body of water to another by one or two people. A canoe can be carried on a cartop for longer trips; no trailer is necessary. Most importantly, a canoe is easy to paddle, and it is extremely <u>versatile</u>. A canoe gives as much enjoyment on a still, glassy lake as it gives on a rolling, roaring mountain stream.

The kayak (kī′ ăk), on the other hand, is more at home on rough and dangerous mountain rivers. Its unique design has made it the recognized, <u>ultimate</u> craft for white water boating. The original kayaks were built by the Eskimos of northern Canada and Greenland of sealskin stretched over wooden or bone framing. Like the canoe, the kayak may now be made of plastic, aluminum, or fiberglass, but it is made only to hold one person—or at the most, two. The passenger or passengers sit flat on the bottom of the kayak, with a watertight flap around the waist, sealing them into the craft.

Kayak fans are interested in only one kind of water condition—the rapids found in mountain rivers. No other boat is as well-suited as the kayak is for <u>negotiating</u> rapids. Because the boat is watertight, it's almost impossible to sink; if it turns upside down, the pilot of a kayak can turn the boat back up with a simple twist of the hips or by using his two-bladed paddle as a lever. This <u>maneuver</u> is called "the Eskimo roll."

Anyone who wants to try the sports of white water canoeing or kayaking should first try to find a white water club. The sport has plenty of hazards, and they should not be ignored. Many canoers or kayakers have been killed or seriously hurt when they tried rapids too fast for their skills or when they tried to ride down a new river. White water clubs require safety and knowledge. Clubs teach new members all the skills, such as the Eskimo roll, needed for taking on a rough river, as well as the teamwork needed for groups of canoers to negotiate a river successfully. A good club will organize white water expeditions—no one should attempt a river alone—and provide books and experience to help people new to the sport prepare for trips.

But clubs are necessary only for people who want to attempt mountain rivers and rapids. There are other things to do with canoes and kayaks—and generally close to home—making the hobby even more inexpensive. Few cities aren't within driving distance of rivers and lakes for fishing, camping, or just paddling around for relaxation. And the ease of transporting a canoe or kayak makes these weekend trips even more tempting. Throw the boat on top of the car, pitch in some food and your gear, and you're ready for one of North America's oldest sports.

▲ (645 WORDS) ▲

PASSAGE 1-15

Circle the correct answer:

1. The purpose of this passage is to
    a. discuss the benefit of the kayak in white water boating.
    b. discuss the many enjoyments of the canoe.
    c. discuss white water boating safety.
    d. discuss canoeing and kayaking.

2. According to the passage, which of the following statements is not true?
    a. The canoe was first developed by the Indians.
    b. A canoe requires more skill and balance than a sailboat.
    c. The kayak is at home on rough and dangerous mountain rivers.
    d. White water clubs teach safety.

3. We can conclude from the passage that
    a. canoes are safer than kayaks.
    b. only kayaks should be used for negotiating rapids.
    c. canoes and kayaks can be fun on most any kind of water.
    d. kayaks don't handle well on still water.

4. The passage suggests that
    a. the Eskimo roll can only be done by the very best kayakers.
    b. modern canoes are not as good as those made by the Indians.
    c. kayaking is a less popular sport than canoeing.
    d. the canoe and the kayak appeal to a broad group of fans.

5(a) As used in this passage, the word *uniquely* means
    a. little
    b. particularly

75

    c. strangely
    d. embarrassing

5(b) As used in this passage, the word *basic* means
    a. fundamental
    b. new
    c. modern
    d. unusual

5(c) As used in this passage, the word *versatile* means
    a. unstable
    b. dangerous
    c. adaptable
    d. inexpensive

5(d) As used in this passage, the word *ultimate* means
    a. useless
    b. unsafe
    c. best
    d. expensive

5(e) As used in this passage, the word *negotiating* means
    a. handling
    b. capturing
    c. buying
    d. swimming

5(f) As used in this passage, the word *maneuver* means
    a. paddle
    b. kayak
    c. position
    d. move

PASSAGE 1-16

SUBJECT:
Pelé (pā′ lā)

The game of soccer was invented by the British in the 1800s and was introduced to Brazil in 1880 by English sailors on leave from their ships. Brazilians took to the game rapidly, but they did not become a <u>dominant</u> power in world soccer until the middle of this century. Before then, soccer players for the Brazilian national teams were recruited from the rich sports clubs in and around Rio (rē′ ō). Blacks barred from these clubs played the game on the beaches and on the sand in the countryside.

Most of these black players were from the northern Brazilian state of Minas (mē′ nŏs). The 32,000,000 people of Minas and other northern Brazilian states are among the poorest in Latin America. Most of these people are descended from black slaves who worked on the huge sugar cane farms there when Brazil was a colony of Portugal. The children in these areas play a game of street soccer called *pelada* (pā lŏ′ də), a word that gave a name to the greatest soccer player in the world, Pelé.

Pelé was born in Minas in 1940; his father was a soccer player, but in 1940 in Brazil there was no such thing as a professional soccer player. A man played any game then simply for the game itself. Pelé loved the game and played soccer in the streets continually. He had no interest in studying, though he performed odd jobs to help bring in money for the family. When he wasn't out in the street playing at a neighborhood *pelada,* Pelé was practicing kicking with his father.

Pelé gained the attention of coaches, first in the neighborhood contests and later as he led his team to win the junior league tournament two years in a row. At the age of fourteen, Pelé was playing for one of the first professional soccer teams in Brazil. As Pelé matured, in years and in <u>stature</u> as a player, the game of soccer grew. By 1950, soccer was the most popular game everywhere in the world, except for the United States; what had begun as a British sport became the favorite sport of the working classes all over the world. Soccer had become the one truly international sport.

Pelé was on the Brazilian team in the World Cup matches of 1958. The Brazilian team had failed in the finals for three years in a row. Some sports writers said the blacks, though gifted, had no discipline. In the 1958 finals against Sweden, Pelé kicked the winning goal, and he returned home to Brazil a hero and a rich man by way of his next contract with his professional team, Santos (sŏn′ tōs).

After a long career in which Pelé established the rights of the black athlete to play international games, Pelé found himself a wealthy man—in fact, he was a millionaire. He owned dozens of apartment houses, in which he often allowed poor families to live without paying rent. He bought his mother the mansion he had promised her when he signed his first professional contract. But the most telling moment of all was in

1969, when Pelé scored his thousandth goal. As flashbulbs fired and fans stormed onto the field and reporters begged for a speech, all he said was, "Remember the poor children."

The man who was the most famous black athlete in the world also became one of the richest in 1975. Pelé came out of retirement to play for three years with the New York team. He could not resist the challenge of trying to popularize soccer in the United States, one of the few countries in the world where soccer had not become the national sport; but in 1977, Pelé retired for good at the age of thirty-seven. As a poor boy in north Brazil he had played soccer for four and a half cents per game; his American contract was for a salary of millions. Pelé's growth as an athlete of world stature had followed the same course as the growth of soccer.

▲ (670 WORDS) ▲

PASSAGE 1-16

Circle the correct answer:

1. The main purpose of this passage is to
   a. trace the development of soccer.
   b. give a short biography of Pelé's soccer career.
   c. discuss discrimination in professional soccer.
   d. discuss Brazil's influence on international soccer.

2(a) According to the passage, which of the following statements about Pelé is not true?
   a. Pelé was born about the time World War II began.
   b. Pelé spent a lot of time playing street soccer.
   c. Pelé's father was a professional soccer player.
   d. Pelé was on the Brazilian team that won the World Cup matches of 1958.

2(b) Pelé
   a. became a professional at the age of fourteen.
   b. retired at the age of thirty-nine.
   c. played soccer as a child for two and a half cents per game.
   d. came out of retirement to play for four years with a New York soccer team.

3. We can conclude from the passage that
   a. Pelé never hoped to play soccer professionally.
   b. Pelé's father wanted him to get an education before turning professional.
   c. Pelé's involvement in soccer had a great effect on helping minorities receive equal rights in athletics.
   d. Brazil lost its prominence in world soccer after Pelé became a professional.

4. The passage suggests that
   a. Pelé quickly forgot his "roots" when he became a professional soccer player.
   b. Pelé helped make soccer America's favorite pastime.
   c. Pelé never felt accepted by his professional peers.
   d. Pelé received little formal education.

5(a) As used in this passage, the word *dominant* means
   a. controlling
   b. unimportant
   c. challenging
   d. novice

5(b) As used in this passage, the word *stature* means
   a. wealth
   b. law
   c. courage
   d. caliber

PASSAGE 1-17

SUBJECT:
John Reed

John Reed was about as American as it is possible for a person to be. The facts of his life, his early days in particular, have always surprised anyone who knows the course his later life took.

Reed was born in Portland, Oregon, in 1887. He was literally born in a mansion owned by his grandfather. His grandfather had made a fortune in the utilities business. He owned, among other things, the Portland gas works and waterworks. John Reed was given an extremely fine education, exactly the sort of education one would expect for a wealthy businessman's grandson. First, enrollment in a private school (the Portland Academy) where Reed excelled in swimming. Then Reed attended an exclusive Eastern prep school. Next he enrolled in Harvard. In 1911 he obtained his first job with a new magazine, *Masses,* published in New York by Lincoln Steffens, the famous crusading journalist and a friend of Reed's father. Up to this point, Reed's life was a model of success and privilege.

But John Reed never really felt a unity with all this because he constantly felt himself an outsider. His own father wasn't as wealthy as the rest of the Reeds, and John's expensive education was a financial struggle. Also, John was sickly as a child; his tendency to withdraw was reinforced by his love of books and his own writing. At Harvard he couldn't make the rowing team; he was in some clubs and held some offices, but the top posts and the top clubs were always just beyond his reach. His father probably had influenced him in the direction of rebellion. President Roosevelt had named his father as federal marshal to head the fight to save Oregon's forests from big business and the lumber companies, and in this fight he drew the hatred of Portland society.

After Harvard, working with Lincoln Steffens, John Reed gradually became a radical critic of America. He identified with the cause of organized labor in particular. The magazine for which he wrote, *Masses,* was a hodgepodge of radical opinions. Anarchism, socialism, feminism, all points of view critical of current society were encouraged. Steffens and Max Eastman, the editors, gave Reed more and better assignments, covering strikes and protests. In 1913, Reed went to cover the Mexican revolution, traveling with the fighting troops. His reports from Mexico and the book he wrote about the experience, *Insurgent Mexico,* are fine reading. Both mix Reed's reporting events and accounts of his own adventure. He was one of the first journalists to live by the idea that a journalist must participate in the events he writes about.

In 1914, Reed went to cover the war in Europe. By this time he had adopted the radical-socialist viewpoint. He found the war in Europe dull compared to his adventures riding with Pancho Villa (pŏn′ chō vē′ yɔ). He was pro-German and anti-English, claiming that World War I was being fought for commercial reasons, over trading rights. He returned home to America to work on his autobiography, *Almost Thirty,* disillusioned.

When Lenin came to Russia and started the Russian Revolution, though, Reed was there. Already sympathetic to Lenin's cause, Reed pushed his participating journalism to the limit. He attended every rally and meeting, saw every battle and every street fight. He visited the battlefront at Tsarskoe (zär' skō) and Gotchina (gŏt chēn' ə). He wound up addressing crowds. He posed as a spokesman for American socialists. He handed out leaflets. In fact, he took part in the Russian Revolution, and from the experience he wrote *Ten Days That Shook the World,* the only firsthand account of the revolution. Reed idealized the Russian working man, and he considered the leaders of the movement to be men beyond reproach.

Ten Days That Shook the World has been published in almost every language in the world. It has stayed in print since the day it was published. As Russian opinion changed about some leaders of the revolution, the Russian edition was banned or censored in that country, but Reed became almost a saint of the revolutionary movement. He died of typhus at the age of thirty-three while attending a Communist congress as a self-appointed American delegate. He is the only American whose ashes lie in the Kremlin Wall in Moscow.

▲ (705 WORDS) ▲

PASSAGE 1-17

Circle the correct answer:

1(a) The main purpose of this passage is to
    a. show how wealth can corrupt an individual.
    b. trace the financial factors that led to Reed's radicalism.
    c. provide a short history of John Reed's career as an activist.
    d. show how journalism can affect history.

1(b) A good title for this passage might be
    a. The Perils of Wealth
    b. John Reed, Activist
    c. John Reed
    d. An American Success Story

2. Which of the following statements about John Reed is not true?
    a. John Reed found the war in Europe more exciting than the Mexican revolution.
    b. John Reed's financial status was not as stable as that of his other relatives.

    c. After Harvard, Reed worked for *Masses*.
    d. John Reed is the only American whose ashes lie in the Kremlin Wall in Moscow.

3. We can conclude from the passage that
    a. John Reed became a socialist because of his abhorrence of his family's wealth.
    b. John Reed was emotionally immature.
    c. John Reed's liberal education influenced him to become a radical.
    d. John Reed never felt completely comfortable with his background.

4. With which one of the following movements would John Reed *most* probably have associated himself?
    a. the NAACP
    b. the student activists of the seventies
    c. the John Birch Society
    d. the Ku Klux Klan

5(a) As used in this passage, the word *exclusive* means
    a. foreign
    b. inexpensive
    c. selective
    d. parochial

5(b) As used in this passage, the word *unity* means
    a. conformity
    b. nonconformity
    c. oneness
    d. loneliness

5(c) As used in this passage, the word *identified* means
    a. sided
    b. disagreed
    c. fought
    d. named

5(d) As used in this passage, the word *hodgepodge* means
    a. forum
    b. concentration
    c. mixture
    d. magical effect

5(e) As used in this passage, the word *disillusioned* means
    a. angry
    b. disenchanted
    c. degraded
    d. revived

PASSAGE 1-18
The Art of Chinese Painting

SUBJECT:

Those of us raised in Western cultures tend to think of painters and artists as unique individuals, each of whom has a separate style, technique, and way of seeing a subject. In China, however, painting is governed by strict rules. It comes as a shock to many Westerners to realize how thoroughly ruled by tradition the Chinese artist may be.

Chinese painting must always be realistic; size and proportion of objects must always be natural. Color is always used to present the subject of the painting in its natural appearance. Artists may select the details that they wish to include in their paintings, but they must not ever become abstract. The Chinese consider artists truly creative when they can copy the ancient masters of the art or when the painter's own subjects seem to exist. Chinese folklore has many stories about paintings that come alive at night or painted birds that actually sang.

The Chinese art of painting is considered to be very closely related to the art of writing in Chinese characters. The setting is the same, inside a studio at a table or desk, for most Chinese artists work from memory. Very few sit in front of their subject at an easel, as do Western artists. Chinese artists must concentrate on their subjects very intensely, plan their composition, then draw it carefully and quickly. They cannot erase, cannot paint over a mistake, and cannot fill in details later. All these techniques are considered debasements of the painting and are forbidden.

Even the materials used are similar to the materials used by Chinese letterers. The painter draws on paper or silk, which is not stretched like a Western canvas. Instead, it is spread on the floor or on a table and held in place by the artist's left arm while the right hand holds the brush. In ancient China, paintings could be drawn on other types of cloth or cut into stone or walls, but silk became the material used for most paintings.

The brushes used in this art come in ten very precise sizes. The largest brush has a diameter of two inches. The smallest will have a diameter of one-third of an inch, still rather large by Western standards. Whereas the sizes of the brushes are regulated strictly, materials used in their construction vary greatly. Like all artists, a Chinese artist owns a set of brushes with which he is comfortable and whose characteristics in use he can become thoroughly familiar with. The brush collections may be very beautiful in themselves, for the handles may be intricately carved. Simple sets may have bamboo or wooden handles, and more highly valued brushes may have handles made of gold, quartz, or horn. The large brushes sometime have bristles made of sheep, goat, or pig hair to make wide, bold strokes. The brushes for very delicate work are often made of rabbit, weasel, sable, fox, or deer hair. Some famous Chinese artists have used highly individual materials for their brushes. One artist preferred wolf hair for bold work; for very delicate strokes, one artist actually had a set of brushes formed from mouse whiskers. Another's brush set included small brushes made from the discarded hair of human babies.

Chinese artists often use only one color in a painting, so their ink-mixing tools receive as much careful attention as their brushes. The ink is a compound of lampblack, or the soot from a particular species of pine, and glue, pressed into a cake. The artist grinds the ink on a stone slab and mixes it carefully with miniscule amounts of water to make a thick, thin, light, or dark ink. Ink-mixing secrets are highly valued, for very subtle shadings of ink can be used to create a sense of full, natural color. Some artists use watercolors, but ink is the more highly regarded form.

Chinese artists must practice their technique constantly, for even brush strokes are regulated by rules. The brush is held at a 90-degree angle to the silk, grasped by the thumb and first two fingers; the fingers do not move, and, for large figures, the arm is unsupported, though it may be rested on the left arm for drawing fine details. Only years of practice make smooth, even lines and strong but meaningful strokes possible. To have their work recognized as art—rather than a mistake—Chinese artists must practice constantly, study and copy the ancient traditions, and follow all the rules that govern their art.

▲ (753 WORDS) ▲

PASSAGE 1-18

Circle the correct answer:

1(a) The purpose of this passage is to
    a. explain why Chinese painting is so controlled.
    b. discuss several Chinese painters.
    c. describe the techniques of painting that must be followed by Chinese artists.
    d. discuss the training of Chinese painters.

1(b) A good title for this passage might be
    a. The Long Arm of Government
    b. China—Yesterday and Today
    c. The Ancient Art of Chinese Painting
    d. Chinese Art Schools

2(a) Brushes used for delicate work are often made of the hair of
    a. rabbits
    b. sables

c. foxes
  d. all of the above

2(b) According to the passage, which of the following statements is not true?
  a. Chinese art is not related to Chinese writing.
  b. Chinese artists don't sit in front of subjects at an easel.
  c. Chinese artists use brushes in one of ten different sizes.
  d. Chinese artists often use only one color in a painting.

3. We can conclude from the passage that
  a. government artists supervise all Chinese painting.
  b. the Chinese government licenses all artists.
  c. all Chinese paintings must pass a close inspection by art experts.
  d. Chinese artists adhere to the strict regulations because they want to be considered true artists.

4. The passage suggests that
  a. most Chinese painters don't go by the strict rules of the ancient tradition of painting.
  b. there are very few artists in modern China.
  c. the Chinese aren't interested in changing their style of painting.
  d. because of the extreme control over artists in China, many promising Chinese artists are moving to the West.

5(a) As used in this passage, the word *unique* means
  a. strange
  b. special
  c. neurotic
  d. average

5(b) As used in this passage, the word *composition* means
  a. painting
  b. day
  c. attack
  d. sculpture

5(c) As used in this passage, the word *debasements* means
  a. advantages
  b. errors
  c. degradations
  d. improvements

5(d) As used in this passage, the word *intricately* means
  a. barely
  b. uninterestingly
  c. terribly
  d. complicatedly

5(e) As used in this passage, the word *miniscule* means
   a. tiny
   b. large
   c. colored
   d. different

5(f) As used in this passage, the word *subtle* means
   a. dark
   b. obvious
   c. slight
   d. startling

PASSAGE 1-19   SUBJECT: Immortality

Death is now an "in" subject once more. Schools and colleges are offering courses in thanatology (thăn′ ə tŏ lə gē), the study of death and dying. Books and, oddly enough, movies are treating audiences to descriptions of the afterlife by people thought dead and then later revived. A book called *Life After Life* collected dozens of these descriptions. It spent months on the best-seller list. Dr. Elizabeth Kubler-Ross has written two successful books on dying and gives quite popular courses around this country and Europe. Not all the people interested in the subject are in the health field, though, of course, many are.

    Death, the afterlife, and the possible immortality of the soul are related parts of an unanswerable question that has fascinated all people. The Egyptian *Book of the Dead* is one of the earliest works of literature that we know. It is a collection of formal guidelines, virtually a rule book, to guide the soul through the next world; thus, the Egyptians were the first people to teach that the soul was immortal. They believed that the life of the soul in the next world would be similar to life in this world. The soul would live in the tomb, as living Egyptians lived in houses. Because the tomb was to be a home, its size was as much a status symbol as the home's size; this is why the Pharaohs built pyramids as tombs for themselves. The soul needed food, so food was left in Egyptian tombs, along with the dead person's clothing, jewelry, tools, and weapons. Apparently, the Egyptians believed that the soul would use the same body, which explains the careful preservation of the body as a mummy.

    The Tibetans (tĭ bĕt′ nz) had their own *Book of the Dead,* which was collected into book form in the eighth century A.D. The Tibetans believed that dying was an art that had to be learned before the soul's passage could be successful. After death, the soul separates from the body and takes on a new form. The first new sensation is that of watching friends and relatives prepare the old body for burial. But the new soul has a "shining" body that can travel through walls and closed doors. The soul passes through several stages, possibly meeting and learning from spirits. Eventually, the soul stands before "a clear light" to be judged for his or her actions during life.

    Among other ancient peoples, the Babylonians (băb′ ə lō′ nē ənz) and Persians (pûr′ zhənz) also believed in the immortality of the soul. Like the Egyptians, the Babylonians buried food, drink, tools, and weapons with their dead. Dead females were buried with jewelry, combs, and cosmetics. The Babylonians believed that individual souls would rise from the grave and face judgment for their lives, along with possible punishment if their lives had been less than pure. The Persians believed in a judgment of the soul, as well, but it was to happen in a unique way; when a Persian soul separated from the body, it passed over a bridge into the afterlife. For three days, the spirits of good and the spirits of evil fought for the soul. If the good spirits won, the soul was allowed to enter "the boat of song," a beautiful afterlife. If the evil spirits won the soul, it was thrown into a bottomless pit, "the house of hell."

The Greeks also considered the problem of the afterlife in their various philosophies. One poet, Pindar (pĭn′ dər), guessed that a wise man could return to the earth after death. (He didn't venture a guess as to what might happen to the souls of lesser men.) Plato (plā′ tō) believed that the soul was immortal and eventually faced a judgment in the afterlife; before facing this judgment, each soul saw all the past events of his or her life played out before him or her. Each soul also saw dead friends and relatives, as well as other spirits.

Plato describes this judgment of souls in detail in *The Republic.* He tells of the death of a soldier in a battle; the soldier sees his body prepared for burning on a funeral pyre. In the afterlife, the soldier found himself in a large place with openings leading to different afterlives for different kinds of souls. Each opening is guarded by a judge who questions the soul after reviewing each soul's life on earth. Spirits who had led good lives were led into a heaven by a column of light, but souls that had led corrupt or evil lives were sent to a place of punishment.

Only one Greek writer ever refers to any other kind of belief in the afterlife among the Greeks. This is Thucydides (thū′ sĭ dĭ dēz), the historian who wrote a history of the Greek wars. He includes in his book a speech delivered by Pericles (pĕ′ rĭ klēz) for the dead soldiers from Athens. He does not refer to the literal immortality of the soul. He says that man's hope for eternal life lies in allowing the state to exist forever.

The list of examples could be added to almost endlessly. African tribes, American Indians, Hindus, Buddhists, Muslims—all believe that the soul is immortal. Although an occasional person may believe that there is no afterlife, it is very difficult to cite an example of a whole culture that does not hope that the human soul lives on.

▲ (876 WORDS) ▲

PASSAGE 1-19

Circle the correct answer:

1. The purpose of this passage is to
    a. discuss the ancient Egyptians' outlook on immortality.
    b. argue the existence of the soul.
    c. discuss how different cultures have viewed the issue of immortality.
    d. compare the beliefs of the ancient Egyptians and the ancient Greeks.

2. According to the passage, which of the following statements is not true?
    a. The Egyptians believed that the soul lived on in its tomb.

b. The Babylonians and the Persians held exactly the same beliefs about the afterlife.
   c. The Tibetan equivalent of the *Book of the Dead* was collected into book form in the eighth century A.D.
   d. all of the above.

3(a) We can conclude from the passage that
   a. the Egyptian *Book of the Dead* was the earliest work of literature.
   b. the Tibetans were more afraid of death than the Greeks were.
   c. most cultures believe in the immortality of the soul.
   d. Pericles' beliefs about the immortality of the soul were the same as those of Plato.

3(b) Which of the following conclusions does the passage support?
   a. Pindar's views on immortality differed greatly from those of Plato.
   b. Pericles agreed more closely with Pindar than with Plato.
   c. Plato's and Pericles' beliefs about immortality were basically the same.
   d. Pericles' views on immortality differed greatly from those of Plato.

4. The passage suggests that
   a. the Persians believed the soul's destiny was based on chance.
   b. the Tibetans were atheistic.
   c. only the Babylonians and the Persians did not believe in the immortality of the soul.
   d. most Greek writers believed that man's hope for eternal life depended upon the eternal existence of the state.

5(a) As used in this passage, the word *immortality* means
   a. afterlife
   b. death
   c. sinfulness
   d. reincarnation

5(b) As used in this passage, the word *formal* means
   a. religious
   b. well-dressed
   c. essential
   d. fixed

5(c) As used in this passage, the word *preservation* means
   a. burial
   b. prediction
   c. protection
   d. destruction

5(d) As used in this passage, the word *venture* means
   a. advise
   b. offer

  c. oppose
  d. possess

5(e) As used in this passage, the word *cite* means
  a. mention
  b. place
  c. prove
  d. believe

PASSAGE 1-20 SUBJECT: Video Discs

An exciting new era in television recording is about to begin. For several years at least five different companies have been working quickly to perfect systems for recording video signals on discs rather than tape. Soon these systems will be released to the public.

Almost all of us have become familiar with video tape recorders. These have been available for use at home for some time now. Models are available that record programs from the home set, storing the programs on magnetic tape in cassettes. Some models are available with clocks and timers. These will even record a program for you if you can't be at home to watch it. There are, however, difficulties with recording on tape. The tape itself is expensive; a blank cassette may cost $20 to $25. The recording process is expensive, so commercially prepared cassettes are even more expensive. The tape deteriorates, stretches, or breaks; and, most annoyingly of all, you cannot start playing wherever you want. To see the end or middle of a video tape, you must sit through the beginning. And even if you speed the tape up, it is still being worn down. Most tapes only last about four hundred plays.

The video disc has none of these disadvantages. The disc is a thin, clear sheet of plastic that looks very much like a record album. Because it is so thin and made of Mylar (mī′ lär), a very common plastic, the disc can be produced cheaply. Because it can be pressed like a record album, the recording process does not figure as greatly in the cost of a disc. Some video discs may eventually sell for less than a dollar.

Two systems are currently being developed to play video discs. One system uses a needle, like a phonograph needle, to "read" the grooves in the disc. Electrical cells transform the movement of the needle into electronic signals, exactly like a record player. But the television set hooked to a video disc will play both sound and pictures from the information on the video disc.

The second system for playing video discs involves not a needle, but a laser. This concentrated beam of light is directed through the clear disc onto an electric cell beneath the disc. The bumps in the grooves of the disc change the intensity of the laser, and the cell beneath transforms the variation into electronic commands for a television. It is the laser method that makes discs so efficient. As nothing touches the disc, it cannot wear out; it should last forever.

In addition, each circle or groove around the disc is one full frame on a television. The laser can be made to ride one circle continuously so as to stop the action on the TV screen, just as a stuck needle replays the same music. But because the laser isn't touching the disc, nothing is harmed. When a video tape is stopped to "freeze" the picture, the tape overheats and deteriorates. The laser will, of course, follow grooves from start to finish, too, so the viewer watches an entire recorded program. Or—and here is another advantage—it can move from groove to groove if you prefer, without playing the intervening material.

The discs can play for exactly thirty minutes on each side. The video disc players are capable of playing forward or backward, fast or slow, or one picture at a time. Each side of the disc has 54,000 grooves—or 54,000 single frames. Thus, the disc can be used to store and record continuous material such as television or movies or material such as slides or the pages of books. Each groove or frame could be one page of a book, which could be displayed on your home television screen. With 108,000 frames on each disc, whole libraries could be contained in a filing cabinet. One disc could contain all the volumes of a major encyclopedia—and more. One expert has stated that a single video disc could contain 360 books of 300 pages each. One disc could hold, for an art teacher, for example, all the world's great paintings—everything needed to teach any art history course. The discs can record stereo, computer data, and multiple sound tracks, as well. A single disc of *Gone with the Wind* might allow the user to choose any of a dozen languages for the sound track.

Because the discs can store instructions for computers, educators see some interesting possible uses. Small computers can read information off the disc to direct the laser from groove to groove. Video courses can thus be tailored to a student's needs. The material can be slowed or speeded up, depending on the student's performance. (Some computers are being developed that respond to the student's touch on the screen or to oral answers). The computer might direct the laser to skip over some learning units or to "read" a review of material a slower student might spend weeks on. Several research centers are developing disc programming to use computers in this way.

It will be interesting to watch the development of versatile video disc players for the home and for education. Seeing their full potential for things other than entertainment may take decades, though.

▲ (867 WORDS) ▲

PASSAGE 1-20

Circle the correct answer:

1(a) The main idea of this passage is that
   a. video discs resist deterioration better than video tapes.
   b. video discs may be played by using a laser.
   c. video discs may greatly expand the use of video courses in American education.
   d. video discs are a versatile, new recording system that may revolutionize the video-recording industry.

1(b) A good title for this passage might be
   a. The Indestructible Video Disc
   b. Using the Miracle Laser
   c. The Revolutionary New Video Disc
   d. Video Discs and American Education

2. According to the passage, which of the following statements is not true?
   a. Video discs resist deterioration better than video tapes, but they stretch more easily.
   b. Video discs are made of Mylar.
   c. The laser method makes Video discs more efficient.
   d. Video discs can play for thirty minutes on each side.

3. We can conclude from the passage that
   a. only video tapes can store computer instructions.
   b. video discs can help solve the information storage problems of large libraries.
   c. the laser is less versatile than the needle.
   d. video discs are more expensive to produce than video tapes.

4(a) The passage suggests that
   a. video discs are more difficult to store than are video tapes.
   b. video discs will be used more in education than for simple home entertainment.
   c. the laser method is superior to a needle for playing video discs.
   d. lasers generate a great deal of heat.

4(b) The author's tone is
   a. ironic
   b. subjective
   c. negative
   d. positive

5(a) As used in this passage, the word *deteriorates* means
   a. burns
   b. improves
   c. wears out
   d. lasts

5(b) As used in this passage, the word *transform* means
   a. relay
   b. change
   c. adopt
   d. strengthen

5(c) As used in this passage, the word *intensity* means
   a. direction
   b. power
   c. color
   d. sound

5(d) As used in this passage, the word *variation* means
- a. sound
- b. direction
- c. power
- d. change

5(e) As used in this passage, the word *intervening* means
- a. in-between
- b. external
- c. loudest
- d. worst

5(f) As used in this passage, the word *versatile* means
- a. inexpensive
- b. adaptable
- c. larger
- d. laser-oriented

SECTION 2 | READING PASSAGES

DIRECTIONS: Read all of the passages that your instructor has assigned in this section. Answer the comprehension items that have been assigned on your Student Score Sheet. Be sure to read each passage carefully and to refer to the passage to check your answers to the comprehension questions.

PASSAGE 2-1

SUBJECT: Purple Martins

The swallows of Capistrano (kăp ĭ strŏ′ nō) may be famous for returning to the same nests each spring, but they have nothing on the purple martin. These beautiful birds spend each winter in the warm climate of South America, then return each spring to nesting sites in the Southeastern United States.

Purple martins are entertaining birds that are amusing to watch. Many people also like to have the martins around because the birds control insect pests, particularly mosquitoes. If <u>hollow</u> gourds with two-inch openings are hung out for them, martins are happy to move in. They require only the small openings, to discourage predators. The gourds should also be hung in an open space away from buildings or trees, so squirrels or cats can't disturb the birds.

Common, garden grown gourds sometimes rot in the <u>humid</u> climate of the Southeast, so many purple martin lovers have tried using different materials to create a more permanent nest. Lengths of plastic pipe have been used, along with old-fashioned wooden birdhouses with martin-sized entrance holes, but the birds clearly prefer the shape of a gourd—or maybe the way a gourd swings in even a slight breeze. One company is now marketing a plastic gourd, just the right size and shape, with a two-inch entrance hole for the martins. The hole is high enough to allow the martins about four inches of nesting space. The plastic gourd has three drainage holes and a rust-proof wire to allow it to be hung up easily; best of all, it's permanent.

Permanence is important for martin lovers because the birds can become almost like part of the family. Some families have had the same colonies of martins returning to their yards each year for sixty years.

▲ (289 WORDS) ▲

PASSAGE 2-1

Circle the correct answer:

1. The purpose of this passage is to
    a. discuss the swallows of Capistrano.
    b. describe homes for purple martins.
    c. to discuss the mating cycle of purple martins.
    d. discuss the uses of gourds.

2. According to the passage, which of the following statements is not true?
   a. Gourds should be hung in open spaces.
   b. Small openings in the gourds discourage predators.
   c. The swallows of Capistrano are actually purple martins.
   d. Plastic gourds are now being marketed as homes for purple martins.

3. We can conclude from the passage that
   a. purple martins require very little care besides housing.
   b. purple martins seldom nest in the same place two years in a row.
   c. too many purple martins nesting in one area can become a nuisance.
   d. plastic gourds are inferior to some types of martin houses.

4. The passage suggests that
   a. wooden birdhouses are too small for purple martins.
   b. purple martins refuse to live in anything but plastic gourds.
   c. purple martins are dangerous around small animals.
   d. purple martins can become like pets to some people.

5(a) As used in this passage, the word *hollow* means
   a. rotted
   b. empty
   c. ripe
   d. mature

5(b) As used in this passage, the word *humid* means
   a. unpredictable
   b. smelly
   c. cool
   d. damp

PASSAGE 2-2   SUBJECT:
Human Allergies

Four of the most common human allergies are directly caused by substances in the air we breathe. Asthma (ăz′ mə) is a lung condition that causes coughing, wheezing, and great difficulty in breathing; asthma may be made worse by the victim's inhaling cigarette smoke or by air pollution. Sinusitis (sī nə sī′ tis) is an <u>inflammation</u> of the <u>sinus cavities</u> in the skull around the nose and eyes. The <u>inflammation</u> is caused by inhaling dust, mold, or pollen, and the condition may last only a short while, or it may be <u>chronic</u>. Allergic eczema (ĕk′ sə mə) is an itching rash on the neck, legs, or arms; some people assume that these areas of the body have contacted a food or drug to become affected by allergic eczema, but very often the condition is caused by inhaling mold or pollen.

The most common of all allergies is, of course, hay fever. The running eyes and nose, itchy throat, sneezing, and coughing that we call hay fever are caused by inhaling <u>pollen</u> from trees, grasses, or weeds. The allergy is not really an allergy to hay, and sufferers from hay fever may not really have a fever, though often they are miserable enough to assume they have a fever. There is no season of the year that is "safe" for someone suffering from hay fever; early in the spring, most trees are producing <u>pollen</u>; in the early summer, pollen from grasses fills the air; in the fall, the air is full of pollen from weeds.

Nor is any part of the country safe for the allergy victim. Years ago, doctors prescribed moving to desert areas that were free of the pollen that caused these allergies. Now that prescription is ineffective. <u>Irrigation</u> has brought more plants to the deserts and, ironically, the allergy sufferers all planted lawns and trees and brought their houseplants with them.

▲ (305 WORDS) ▲

PASSAGE 2-2

Circle the correct answer:

1. The purpose of this passage is to
   a. discuss the causes of hay fever.
   b. discuss the process of pollination.
   c. compare hay fever to three other allergies.
   d. discuss briefly four of the most common human allergies.

2. According to the passage, which of the following allergies is not directly attributable to the inhaling of pollen?
   a. sinusitis
   b. asthma
   c. hay fever
   d. eczema

3. We can conclude from the passage that
   a. some allergies can be fatal.
   b. all allergies have basically the same symptoms.
   c. some people are more sensitive to irritants in the air than other people.
   d. hay fever is more dangerous than any of the other three allergies.

4. The passage suggests that
   a. some allergy victims help create situations that promote their symptoms.
   b. allergies can now be cured with antibiotics.
   c. the desert is now more dangerous for allergy victims than is the city.
   d. most allergies are the result of contact with certain foods and drugs.

5(a) As used in this passage, the word *inflammation* means
   a. activity
   b. destruction
   c. swelling
   d. shrinking

5(b) As used in this passage, the word *cavities* means
   a. decays
   b. hollow areas
   c. swellings
   d. vents

5(c) As used in this passage, the word *chronic* means
   a. abrupt
   b. short
   c. continuing
   d. mysterious

5(d) As used in this passage, the word *pollen* means
   a. limbs
   b. flowers
   c. sap
   d. seedlike dust

5(e) As used in this passage, the word *irrigation* means
   a. provided with water
   b. provided with pollen
   c. denied water
   d. transplanted

PASSAGE 2-3

SUBJECT:
The Brain

When you refer to your brain, you should probably say, "Brains." Most modern scientists studying the brain have concluded that there are three major parts of our brain, that each is separate from the others, and that each has its own functions and distinctive processes.

Brain 1 includes the spinal cord, the medulla (mə dŭl' lə)—which sits directly atop the cord—and the middle section of the brain. It includes the controls for involuntary functions like breathing and digestion, along with the nerves necessary for reproduction. The structure of the human brain 1 is little different from the structures of the brains of mammals and reptiles. Brain 1 is apparently responsible both for aggressive and social behavior.

Brain 2 is an area surrounding brain 1. In this "second brain" are the various glands located in the brain, such as the pituitary (pi tōō' ə tĕr ē) and amygdala (ə mĭg' də lə). Scientists studying brain 2 are convinced that human emotions such as excitement, fear, and love are centered here, as well as the senses of taste and smell. Memory and learning are also controlled by brain 2. Electrical charges applied to this section of the brain causes seizures and psychotic behavior.

Brain 3 is the neocortex (nē ō cōr' tĕx), the thick covering that surrounds the top and side portions of the brain. This is the "gray matter" we often think of when we speak of the brain. Only the higher orders of animals have brain 3, and none is as highly developed as the human neocortex. Brain 3 sends information from the other two brains to the body and receives data from the body. It is apparently brain 3 that makes us fully human: Brain 3 allows us to stand erect, to plan and anticipate the future, to see, to speak, to write, to use symbols and tools, and to remember. Brain 3 apparently also acts as a unifying control of the other two brains.

As scientists continue to study the brain, they discover specific areas that control particular functions of the body and particular emotions. It is interesting to speculate about the future of the old idea of "the mind." As we learn more about our three brains, will we be more or less awed by our own complexity?

▲ (367 WORDS) ▲

PASSAGE 2-3

Circle the correct answer:

1. This passage is mainly about
   a. the functions of the three sections of the brain.

b. the human brain.
   c. complexity of the human brain.
   d. the areas that control different kinds of behavior.

2(a) Excitement, fear, and love are centered in
   a. the neocortex
   b. the pituitary
   c. brain 2
   d. the medulla

2(b) "Gray matter" is a synonym for
   a. the amygdala
   b. the medulla
   c. the spinal cord
   d. the neocortex

3. We can conclude from this paragraph that
   a. only humans have the neocortex section of the brain.
   b. we know very little about the brain.
   c. brain 3 is all we need to survive.
   d. we still have a lot to learn about the brain.

4. The passage suggests
   a. the human being is the only animal that has emotions.
   b. "mind control" will be possible very soon.
   c. research on the human brain is one of the most important types of research scientists are engaged in.
   d. we have learned as much as we are capable of understanding about the human brain.

5(a) As used in this passage, the word *involuntary* means
   a. strained
   b. convulsive
   c. automatic
   d. abnormal

5(b) As used in this passage, the word *reproduction* means
   a. breathing
   b. generating offspring
   c. digestion
   d. speech

5(c) As used in this passage, the word *psychotic* means
   a. common
   b. friendly
   c. highly abnormal
   d. natural

5(d) As used in this passage, the word *data* means
   a. blood

     b. oxygen
     c. pleas
     d. information

5(e) As used in this passage, the word *symbols* means
     a. signs
     b. visions
     c. movement
     d. interjection

PASSAGE 2-4

SUBJECT:
Crabbing

Living a quiet, calm life is still possible today. And it's possible in the midst of heavily populated areas. For example, Salem County, on the Delaware Bay, has our country's largest chemical manufacturing companies located in its boundaries. There are plans to build a huge nuclear power reactor in Salem County soon. But the bay still affords about a dozen men a quiet, peaceful, independent way to earn their living.

These dozen men are crabbers; they gather wild crabs with traps that are called "pots," selling the fresh crabs to restaurants and commercial seafood packers in the area. Each crabber has about 150 pots. From July through October, the men work an eight-hour day, beginning very early each morning, going out in boats to check their pots.

Each pot has to be reeled in—and it is heavy. The crabber pours his catch into a trough, removes any old bait, then repacks fresh bait into the pot. After lowering the pot back into the water for another day's trapping, he moves on to the next pot.

It is very hard work. The pay isn't enough to make you rich, either. When there are plenty of crabs and good weather, a crabber can make around a hundred dollars a day during the limited season. So most of the crabbers have to work at another job on farms or in factories near the bay. So why do they continue this backbreaking work?

Most of the crabbers learned the skills as children; many of them are descended from families that produced their income from fishing and crabbing long before the industrial factories moved into the bay region. Crabbing is always a constant battle of intelligence with the crabs, for the crabber must move his pots as the crabs move; the crabber has to keep an eye out for patterns of empty pots and for changes in the bay's currents and conditions.

But most importantly the crabbers all love the work; they're independent. Each is his own boss, and the morning hours out on the bay, alone, with no hurry and no rush, have made addicts out of them all. It is the relaxed life-style, not the money or the challenge, that keeps them at their work.

▲ (372 WORDS) ▲

PASSAGE 2-4

Circle the correct answer:

1. This passage is mainly about
    a. Salem County, Delaware.

b. industrialism versus primitivism.
   c. how to run crab pots.
   d. crabbing as an alternate life-style in Salem County, Delaware.

2. Which of the following is not a step in handling crab pots?
   a. The crabber repacks fresh bait into the pots.
   b. The pots must be reeled in.
   c. The crabber removes any old bait.
   d. The elevation of the pots is changed.

3. We can conclude from this passage that
   a. the most a crabber could make in a good season is around $12,000.
   b. there is little market for crabs in New England because there are so many crabbers.
   c. crabbers don't mind the hard work because of the pay.
   d. most crabbers are unsuccessful because they can't outguess the crabs concerning their movement.

4. The passage suggests that
   a. many crabbers pursue crabbing as a hobby.
   b. money is not as important as independence to the crabbers of Salem County.
   c. factories don't pay enough for the crabbers to make a living.
   d. crabbers don't like challenges.

5. As used in this passage, the word *descended* means
   a. trained by
   b. to have as one's ancestors
   c. bought by
   d. hindered

PASSAGE 2-5

SUBJECT: Jogging

Jogging has become the most popular individual sport in America. It has become commonplace to see people of all ages running along city streets, in parks, and along special jogger's trails that have been built in some cities. Many theories, even some <u>mystical</u> ones, have been advanced to explain the popularity of jogging. The plain truth is that jogging is a cheap, quick, and efficient way to maintain (or achieve) physical fitness.

The most useful sort of exercise is exercise that develops the heart, lungs, and circulatory systems. If these systems are fit, the body is ready for almost any sport and for almost any sudden demand made by work or emergencies. One can train more specifically, as by developing strength for weight lifting or the ability to run straight ahead for short distances with great power as in football, but running trains your heart and lungs to deliver oxygen more efficiently to all parts of your body. It is worth noting that this sort of exercise is the only kind that can reduce heart disease, the number one cause of death in America.

Only one sort of equipment is needed—a good pair of shoes. Physicians advise beginning joggers not to try to run in a tennis or gym shoe. Many design advances have been made in only the last several years that make an excellent running shoe indispensable if a runner wishes to develop as quickly as possible, with as little chance of injury as possible. A good running shoe will have a soft pad for absorbing shock, as well as a slightly built-up heel and a full heel cup that will give the knee and ankle more <u>stability</u>. A wise investment in good shoes will prevent blisters and foot, ankle, and <u>knee</u> injuries and will also enable the wearer to run on paved or soft surfaces.

No other special equipment is needed; you can jog in any clothing you desire, even your street clothes. Many joggers wear expensive, flashy warm-up suits, but just as many wear a simple pair of gym shorts and a T-shirt; in fact, many people just jog in last year's clothes. In cold weather, several layers of clothing are better than one heavy sweater or coat. If joggers are wearing several layers of clothing, they can add or subtract layers as conditions change.

It takes surprisingly little time to develop the ability to run. The American Jogging Association has a twelve-week program designed to move from a fifteen-minute walk (which almost anyone can manage who is in reasonable health) to a thirty-minute run. A measure of common sense, a physical examination, and a planned schedule are all it takes.

▲ (447 WORDS) ▲

PASSAGE 2-5

Circle the correct answer:

1. The main purpose of this passage is to
   a. discuss jogging as a physical fitness program.
   b. describe the type of clothing needed for jogging.
   c. provide scientific evidence of the benefits of jogging.
   d. distinguish between jogging as a "commonsense" fitness program and a cult movement.

2. The most useful kind of exercise is exercise that
   a. trains the body for weight lifting.
   b. enables a person to run straight ahead for short distances with great power.
   c. is both beneficial and inexpensive.
   d. develops the heart, lungs, and circulatory systems.

3. We can conclude from this passage that
   a. because of jogging, heart disease is no longer an American problem.
   b. jogging can be harmful if the runner is not properly prepared.
   c. warm-up suits are preferable to gym shorts and T-shirts.
   d. jogging is bad for the ankles and knees.

4. The author's tone is
   a. skeptical
   b. belligerent
   c. approving
   d. purely objective

5(a) As used in this passage, the word *mystical* means
   a. awesome
   b. horrifying
   c. a spiritual discipline
   d. vicious

5(b) As used in this passage, the word *stability* means
   a. height
   b. support
   c. fluctuation
   d. agitation

PASSAGE 2-6

SUBJECT:
Black Newspapers

The first newspaper published by blacks in America was called *Freedom Journal*. The editors were J. B. Russwum, one of the first American blacks to earn a college degree, and Samuel Cornish of Delaware. Cornish was a freeborn black who also started the first Presbyterian church in the United States. *Freedom Journal* was first published in New York in 1827, just 123 years after the first newspaper was published in America.

Other New York papers of the time were all owned by whites. These papers were critical of freed slaves. They were particularly critical of the idea of allowing ex-slaves to vote. *Freedom Journal* was begun as a response to this issue, and the paper urged blacks to educate themselves.

Freedom Journal was forced to close within two years, though. The editors agreed on "schooling, training, and work" according to a March 1827 editorial. But they could not agree on the question of whether blacks should stay in America or return to help colonize Africa by settling in Liberia. Russwum and Cornish dissolved their partnership and closed the paper.

Most other black papers printed before the Civil War had equally short lives. There were forty black-owned newspapers printed between 1829 and 1860, but none lasted very long at all.

Since the Civil War, dozens of black newspapers have started up and closed down. Nearly all of these shared the same message as the *Freedom Journal*'s demand for equal rights. Many famous black Americans have been associated with these papers. Frederick Douglass published the *North Star* in New York; W. E. B. Du Bois, who helped found the NAACP, was editor of *The Crisis;* and Marcus Garvey was an editor of *Negro World*.

Despite sometimes suffering for their beliefs, these publishers can claim much of the credit for helping change minds in America. A black paper like the *Living Way* of Memphis might have its offices burned and sacked, but the messages of the black newspapers were heard.

Robert Abbott, a black man from Savannah, Georgia, left the South and used his paper, the *Chicago Defender,* to tell blacks of the need for labor in the North. Thousands of blacks moved North to work in industries at the start of World War I. In 1944 black publishers asked President Truman to integrate the armed forces. Truman ordered the integration of our armies immediately after World War II.

This was the work of the National Newspaper Publishers Association. This group was formed in 1940 to represent the 125 black-owned newspapers in the United States now. The group helps black newspapers with the problems shared by the white press—circulation, revenues, delivery. But despite these problems, the black press is now reaching twenty-five million readers in the thirty-eight states.

▲ (461 WORDS) ▲

PASSAGE 2-6

Circle the correct answer:

1. The main purpose of this passage is to
   a. discuss the history of the *Freedom Journal.*
   b. trace the development of black-owned newspapers in America.
   c. show how black-owned papers differed from white-owned papers.
   d. show how the *Chicago Defender* changed history.

2. Frederick Douglass was publisher of
   a. the *North Star*
   b. *The Crisis*
   c. the *Negro World*
   d. the *Living Way*

3. We can conclude from this passage that
   a. black-owned papers often failed for the same reasons that white-owned papers failed.
   b. black-owned papers failed because they offended readers.
   c. many papers closed up in fear after having their offices ransacked.
   d. black-owned papers have declined in numbers recently.

4. The passage suggests that
   a. black newspapers have been unsuccessful because they don't reach enough readers.
   b. black newspapers have been successful because they were backed by white liberals.
   c. black newspapers have been successful because they persevered in the face of hardship.
   d. black newspapers have been unsuccessful because they are too sensitive to criticism.

5(a) As used in this passage, the word *colonize* means
   a. defend
   b. restore
   c. reclaim
   d. settle

108

5(b) As used in this passage, the word *dissolved* means
- a. strengthened
- b. financed
- c. ended
- d. reinstated

PASSAGE 2-7   SUBJECT: Frisbee Throwing and Orienteering

In the last few years, America's college campuses have been the birthplaces of at least two new sports, Frisbee throwing and orienteering.

In a period when budget figures were making big-time sports such as college football absorb cuts in financing, students on lawns after classes and on breaks were developing Frisbee throwing to a fine art. Beginners can casually toss the plastic disks back and forth, idly entertaining themselves, but the Frisbee also offers the chance to compete.

One variation is Frisbee golf, which is now played in hundreds of towns on special courses. For Frisbee golf, special wire cages take the place of the hole. As in regular golf, a Frisbee golfer begins at a tee and tries to move the Frisbee into the wire cage with the fewest strokes possible. The game is complicated by varied designs for each "hole" and by difficult obstacles the disk must clear. Each hole is up to two hundred yards long, so a Frisbee golfer must develop a strong arm for long throws, as well as accurate aim for the final approaches to the cage.

Another Frisbee variation on an older game is Frisbee tennis, or "Double Disk," in which two players toss two Frisbees against another team on a regular tennis court. If a toss is missed or if both disks wind up on one side of the net at the same time, points are scored. The most competitive of the Frisbee sports is "Ultimate Frisbee," a variation on soccer; each game of Ultimate lasts forty minutes and is played by two seven-member teams. There are no referees because the players call their own fouls (no contact is allowed), but the object of Ultimate Frisbee is to pass the disk into the opposing team's end zone. Fans love show-off catches, and school officials love the low cost of Ultimate Frisbee leagues.

Orienteering (or′ ē ən tir′ ing) is another sport that only recently became popular. The sport combines cross-country running or hiking with map reading. At orienteering meets, each contestant receives a map of the course marked with a series of checkpoints. The object of orienteering competition is to use your map and compass to locate each checkpoint and to travel from one to the next in the least time possible, which takes brains, experience, and stamina. Courses range from an easy three-mile jaunt through lightly wooded plains or hills to ten-mile monster runs through swamps or cliffs.

Orienteering meets are friendly gatherings, as much like picnics as athletic events. Many people are turning to the sport as a natural extension of hiking or camping. Over ten thousand people took part in meets last year. The U.S. Orienteering Federation has over three thousand members and hopes to make orienteering an Olympic sport.

Ironically, these two sports, which were invented as a protest against high pressure, competition sports, have become this organized—complete with leagues, teams, championships, and, inevitably, winners and losers.

▲ (485 WORDS) ▲

PASSAGE 2-7

Circle the correct answer:

1. The main idea of this passage is that
   a. Frisbee throwing and orienteering are taking the place of more traditional college sports on some college campuses.
   b. Frisbee golf is the most popular new game on college campuses.
   c. orienteering is becoming so popular that it may soon become part of the Olympics.
   d. Frisbee throwing is more popular than orienteering on today's college campuses.

2. According to the passage, which of the following statements is not true?
   a. Frisbee tennis is a variation of Frisbee golf.
   b. Frisbee throwing is done with plastic disks.
   c. Holes are placed as much as two hundred yards apart in Frisbee golf.
   d. all of the above.

3. We can conclude from the passage that
   a. Frisbee throwing is more popular than orienteering because it requires less physical stress.
   b. both of the new sports discussed appeal to basically outdoors-type people.
   c. "Double Disk" is replacing traditional tennis on most campuses.
   d. "Ultimate Frisbee" is the most popular of all the new Frisbee games.

4. The passage suggests that
   a. Frisbee throwing can be dangerous for beginners.
   b. Frisbee throwing and orienteering are in danger of becoming as competitive and controlled as the games they are supposed to replace.
   c. orienteering is a rigorous dangerous sport that is not recommended for anyone but the most physically fit.
   d. the U.S. Orienteering Federation controls the selection of games for the Olympics.

5(a) As used in this passage, the word *casually* means
   a. frantically
   b. barely
   c. expertly
   d. informally

5(b) As used in this passage, the word *varied* means
   a. differing
   b. similar
   c. the same
   d. impossible

5(c) As used in this passage, the word *object* means
   a. loss
   b. goal
   c. thing
   d. height

5(d) As used in this passage, the word *stamina* means
   a. expense
   b. endurance
   c. fear
   d. equipment

5(e) As used in this passage, the word *jaunt* means
   a. ride
   b. labor
   c. trip
   d. appearance

5(f) As used in this passage, the word *extension* means
   a. diversion
   b. escape
   c. requirement
   d. outgrowth

PASSAGE 2-8

SUBJECT: Vitamins

Vitamin research may be the fastest growing area of research in medicine. Despite the fact that the public apparently trusts vitamins to do exactly what their manufacturers say they will do and rushes to buy vitamins, there are a great many misunderstandings and myths about what vitamins are and how consumers should use them. And research is consistently proving these myths wrong.

First of all, many vitamins simply will not do what is often claimed. Vitamin C has never been proven to aid in the prevention of colds. B vitamins do not get rid of "the rundown feeling"; any effect a person feels when taking a B-12 capsule, for example, is purely a psychological effect. B-12 deficiencies are rare, and even in cases where B-12 treatment is necessary, the vitamin must be injected because it is ineffective when taken orally.

Vitamin E is often said to prevent heart disease, improve virility, and slow the aging process, but there has been no experimental proof of any of these claims. The fact that male rats become sterile when deprived of vitamin E does not mean that the same thing happens to humans who are deprived of E. In fact, it is nearly impossible to study vitamin E deprivation in human beings because vitamin E is present in almost all sources of human food.

The same is true of almost every other vitamin. They are abundantly present in a balanced diet. The most common vitamins are A, B-1, B-2, C, and D; and if a person eats a balanced diet that provides these vitamins, all the other vitamins will be present in enough quantity. Though many people claim that vitamins are rare and that you should eat special foods or take vitamin pills daily to make sure you are getting the correct quantity, this is simply not true. In fact, you can overdo vitamin supplements. Some vitamins are toxic if you take in too much of them. Vitamin C overdose can cause diarrhea and kidney stones. Large amounts of A can cause pressure to build up in the brain or cause dryness in the skin, headaches, general pains. Vitamin D overdoses can cause mental and physical retardation, nausea, and high blood pressure. In fact, vitamin overdose is often more severe than vitamin deficiency and is becoming more common.

Another myth about vitamins is that "natural" ones are superior to those produced in the lab. People will often pay high prices for vitamins made up of natural ingredients—such as C from rose hips—when synthetic, lab-produced vitamins are available at much cheaper prices. In fact, a vitamin always has exactly the same molecular structure, whether its source is a plant, animal, or test tube; any change in its structure would make it a different substance altogether. There is not any difference between a synthetic and a "natural" vitamin, so the body cannot possibly make a distinction between the two.

▲ (492 WORDS) ▲

PASSAGE 2-8

Circle the correct answer:

1(a) A good title for this passage might be
- a. The Dangers of Vitamin Overdose
- b. Vitamins
- c. Myths About Vitamin Supplements
- d. Natural and Synthetic Vitamins

1(b) The main idea of this passage is that
- a. vitamins aren't "miracle" drugs and can be harmful.
- b. vitamin supplements are dangerous.
- c. natural vitamins are no better than synthetic ones.
- d. vitamin overdose can cause serious problems.

2(a) The passage states that
- a. most vitamins are not effective when taken orally.
- b. vitamin E can be toxic.
- c. synthetic vitamins are better than natural ones.
- d. all the vitamins we need are present in a balanced diet.

2(b) Slowing the "aging process" has been associated with
- a. vitamin C
- b. vitamin E
- c. vitamin B-12
- d. vitamin D

3. Which of the following conclusions does the passage support?
- a. Vitamin supplements need to be controlled by law.
- b. If you take vitamin supplements, you should take natural ones.
- c. "Junk" foods do not provide enough vitamins.
- d. People should try to eat balanced diets instead of taking vitamin supplements.

4. The author probably
- a. is a vegetarian.
- b. doesn't take vitamin supplements.
- c. uses only natural vitamins.
- d. avoids taking vitamins A and D.

5(a) As used in this passage, the word *virility* means
   a. emotions
   b. life
   c. good health
   d. potency

5(b) As used in this passage, the word *sterile* means
   a. stronger
   b. impotent
   c. female
   d. clean

5(c) As used in this passage, the word *toxic* means
   a. poisonous
   b. deadly
   c. harmful
   d. useless

5(d) As used in this passage, the word *synthetic* means
   a. artificial
   b. natural
   c. expensive
   d. useless

PASSAGE 2-9

SUBJECT: Norman Rockwell

Norman Rockwell is probably America's best-known painter. His very popular scenes of home and small-town life have been used as illustrations for some of America's most widely sold magazines. As his illustrations were often used for the covers of these magazines, his style of drawing has become as familiar to most readers as the names of these magazines themselves—*Saturday Evening Post, McCall's, Look, Boy's Life.* In fact, as he sometimes painted himself into paintings and illustrations, his is probably the only painter's face that is as well known as his work.

Rockwell's early training had an enormous influence on his style and popularity. The son of an artistic father, Rockwell was uninterested in most boyish pursuits. But even as a very young child he was interested in drawing and painting. At the age of fifteen, he attended the Chase School and the National Academy School in New York City. He later studied at the Art Students League, where he was taught by the eccentric and fiery George Bridgman, one of the century's finest draftsmen, who used skeletons to teach anatomy to his students and who would spit tobacco juice on any drawing he thought a failure. At the Art Students League, Rockwell also studied under Thomas Fogarty, who insisted that artists use real costumes and settings for models and who also helped his students land real work assignments.

After leaving school, Rockwell earned a living by drawing for boys' adventure magazines. In addition to this sort of work, he began to pick up assignments to illustrate books and novels. He was paid the princely sum of $150 for his first set of twelve illustrations for a book. But his biggest break came in 1915, when he was appointed art director for *Boy's Life* magazine. For $50 each month, he painted a cover for that month's issue, and he was obliged to illustrate at least one of the stories carried in an issue.

In his first year with *Boy's Life,* Rockwell painted over seventy illustrations, but the important point was that the position of art director paid steadily, and he could do all the *Boy's Life* work at his own studio—he had to travel to the magazine's office only once a week. This relative freedom allowed Rockwell to take on other jobs, and the title of art director gave him a professional status he would not have had otherwise. And the job with the Boy Scouts' magazine gave him a great deal of regular, monthly exposure in a popular, high-quality publication.

Rockwell never forgot this early kindness. He knew what *Boy's Life* had meant to his own career. Even after he left the magazine for greener pastures and greater fame, Rockwell continued his relationship with the Boy Scouts organization. He received the Boy Scouts' Golden Eagle award and was an honored guest at many national "jamborees." He returned this kindness and the organization's earlier kindness by always managing to paint at least a picture a year for the Boy Scouts.

▲ (500 WORDS) ▲

PASSAGE 2-9

Circle the correct answer:

1(a) A good title for this passage might be
   a. Young Rockwell
   b. Rockwell and *Boy's Life*
   c. Rockwell's Training and Early Career
   d. Norman Rockwell, Artist

1(b) This passage is *mainly* about
   a. the schools Rockwell attended.
   b. Rockwell's training and early career.
   c. Rockwell's association with *Boy's Life*.
   d. Rockwell's artistic debt to the Boy Scouts of America.

2. Rockwell was paid $50 a month by *Boy's Life* for
   a. a cover painting and illustration for one article.
   b. twelve illustrations.
   c. designing their monthly cover.
   d. editing their magazine.

3. We can conclude from this passage that
   a. Rockwell felt indebted to the Boy Scouts of America.
   b. Rockwell's artistic talents weren't challenged by the work he did for *Boy's Life*.
   c. Rockwell never made much money.
   d. Rockwell is only interested in making money.

4. The passage suggests that
   a. Rockwell left *Boy's Life* out of boredom.
   b. the steady pay provided by his job at *Boy's Life* helped Rockwell develop as an artist because it provided him with free time.
   c. Rockwell was egotistical.
   d. most Americans like Rockwell.

5(a) As used in this passage, the word *pursuits* means
   a. interests
   b. chases

c. races
   d. stupidity

5(b) As used in this passage, the word *eccentric* means
   a. calm
   b. gentle
   c. boring
   d. unconventional

5(c) As used in this passage, the word *status* means
   a. ranking
   b. height
   c. title
   d. feeling

PASSAGE 2-10   SUBJECT:
The Milgram Experiment

Think of all the criminals who have killed, all the soldiers who have killed; consider the mass murder of Jews in Nazi (nät′ sē) Germany. Is there something inside human beings that allows us to take part in this sort of violence, or were these people swept along by the situation?

Stanley Milgram, a New York psychologist, designed an experiment to find answers to this question, paying adult males four and a half dollars to act the role of "teacher" in a complicated experiment. The "teachers" were to ask questions of a "learner," a middle-aged man in another room. If the learner gave an incorrect answer, the teacher was instructed to turn a knob to send an electric current to the learner's chair. There were thirty positions on the control knob, with the shocks ranging from 15 to 450 volts, the last position marked "Danger: Severe Shock." The teachers were told to increase the severity of the shock with each incorrect response.

With the first few shocks, the learner could be heard over the intercom, grunting and moaning. When the dial reached 150, he demanded that the experiment be ended; shortly afterwards, at 180 volts, he began to complain of the pain. At 300 volts, he complained about his heart condition, screamed, and no longer responded to the questions; but the teachers who complained about their roles in the experiment were told the experiment had to continue. According to the rules, the learner's failure to respond was an "error," so he must be shocked.

A group of psychiatrists was asked for predictions. Certainly, they said, most people would not punish the victim beyond 150 volts. Furthermore, they predicted fewer than 4 percent would persist up to 300 volts; only abnormal individuals—less than one-tenth of a percent—would proceed to 450 volts.

And, in fact, nearly every "teacher" did protest—each became concerned that he might injure the learner, and many said they could not continue to follow instructions. At 180 volts, one "teacher" said, "He's hollering. He can't stand it; what if anything happens to him? I mean who is going to take responsibility if anything happens to that gentleman?"

When the experimenter said he would accept responsibility, the teacher meekly responded, "All right."

Some teachers, alarmed by the silence in the next room, called out to the learner to answer so they wouldn't have to continue shocking him. In fact, most of the teachers protested, but the important thing is that they did not disobey their instructions. Sixty-two percent of all the subjects delivered shocks all the way up to 450 volts—the average highest shock was 370 volts.

Of course, the learner was not being shocked. Even his screams were tape-recorded. But this experiment and similar variations of it have been repeated several times, and the results are invariably the same: in the presence of authority, in a situation governed by rules, most of us follow the rules. Personality tests given to the subjects who delivered the shocks of 450 volts show that they are not abnormal or sick in any way. They're exactly like the rest of us.

▲ (519 WORDS) ▲

PASSAGE 2-10

Circle the correct answer:

1. The main purpose of this passage is to
    a. prove that all men are violent.
    b. discuss historical incidences of violence.
    c. describe the Milgram experiment.
    d. show how shock affects the ability to learn.

2. Which of the following statements is true?
    a. At 150 volts, the learner began to complain about the pain.
    b. At 300 volts, the learner complained about his heart condition.
    c. At 180 volts, the learner demanded that the experiment be halted.
    d. The position of 370 volts had been marked "Danger: Severe Shock."

3(a) We can conclude from the passage that
    a. most teachers complained after the initial shock.
    b. 4 percent of the teachers went up to 300 volts.
    c. the majority of teachers did not deliver shocks above 150 volts.
    d. thirty-eight percent of all the subjects did not deliver shock all the way up to 450 volts.

3(b) Which of the following conclusions is supported by the passage?
    a. People feel no compunction about inflicting pain.
    b. People enjoy inflicting pain on others.
    c. People are easily influenced by structure.
    d. People are becoming more violent and aggressive.

4. From the results of the Milgram experiment, we can infer that
    a. violent or sadistic actions may not really be "abnormal" human behavior.
    b. adult males are more violent than adult females.
    c. psychiatrists are fairly accurate in their predictions about human behavior.
    d. only the abnormal individuals in the study delivered shocks all the way up to 450 volts.

5(a) As used in this passage, the word *severity* means
   a. intensity
   b. austerity
   c. pleasure
   d. strictness

5(b) As used in this passage, the word *abnormal* means
   a. regimented
   b. dedicated
   c. deviant
   d. dictatorial

PASSAGE 2-11

SUBJECT:
The Pilgrims

Because of the usual image of the Pilgrims taught in schools, we tend to think of them as very religious people in the modern sense. Not so, say researchers at Plimoth Plantation, a historical recreation of the original settlement.

The Pilgrims might best be described as radicals. They separated from the Church of England, wanting to enjoy a simpler worship. Some had lived in Holland, where they enjoyed religious freedom, but they wanted their children to grow up English, not Dutch.

But only about one-third of the 102 passengers on the *Mayflower* were actually Pilgrims. The rest of the passengers were volunteers or recruits. A group of merchants provided money for the trip; the Pilgrims and other settlers had agreed to send back goods the merchants could sell at a profit in England.

The Pilgrims called themselves "Saints"; the other settlers they called "Strangers." The two groups actually had very little in common at first. Some of the Strangers missed England terribly; imagine the shock of leaving London for a wilderness settlement. Most were illiterate, of course, because most people in 1620 could neither read nor write.

Along with the Bradfords, future governors of the little colony, were families of drunkards and criminals; both men and women were often placed in the stocks for public drunkenness. Two Stranger children caused early problems for the Pilgrims. One child almost blew up the *Mayflower* while playing near the powder supply; this child's brother caused an uproar in the colony by managing to get himself lost for several days. Their mother was charged with being "a common gossip," and ten years after the landing, their father was hanged for murder. Thus, there were whole families of rather unwholesome people along with the Pilgrims.

Some of the Strangers, though, were honest, hardworking people; they had come to the New World, where there was more opportunity. Servants could work themselves free, marry other freed servants, and thus rise in social position. Such opportunity did not exist in Holland or England.

The opportunity must have been great to tempt people to make the voyage; because one ship was lost in port owing to leaking, twice as many people had to huddle in the *Mayflower* for nine weeks. One sailor was killed during the crossing (the Pilgrims took this as a sign from God because the sailor had been less than sympathetic to their cause). After the landing at Plymouth, nearly half the settlers died during the first winter; only a successful crop of corn the next year saved the colony.

Even the first Thanksgiving wasn't really a religious festival as we sometimes think. The settlers were celebrating a harvest festival called a "harvest home," an old English custom, which wasn't really a time for prayers but a celebration of games, dancing, singing, feasting, and beer drinking—the settlers drank more beer per person than any other group for whom we have figures.

But the Pilgrims' beer consumption is an unreliable gauge of their religious feeling. Many things in the New World they assumed were dangerous. The night air, the hot sun—all were dangerous; but nothing was more dangerous than the water, so all they drank was beer. Logical, but certainly not part of the usual image of the Pilgrims.

▲ (545 WORDS) ▲

PASSAGE 2-11

Circle the correct answer:

1. The main idea of this passage is that
   a. only one-third of the passengers on the *Mayflower* were actually Pilgrims.
   b. the majority of settlers were drunkards and criminals.
   c. most of the Strangers were honest, hardworking people.
   d. history has provided us with a distorted view of the true character of the Pilgrims.

2. Which of the following statements is true?
   a. More Pilgrims than Strangers were illiterate.
   b. Most of the Pilgrims came from Holland.
   c. About two-thirds of the passengers on the *Mayflower* were not Pilgrims.
   d. One of the Bradford children almost blew up the *Mayflower*.

3. We can conclude from the passage that
   a. the Pilgrims were more motivated by financial opportunities than religious zeal.
   b. mass education was not prevalent in the seventeenth century.
   c. the Pilgrims felt comfortable in the New World.
   d. the first Thanksgiving was a traditional religious festival.

4. The passage suggests that
   a. the Pilgrims were a group made up largely of drunkards and criminals.
   b. the Strangers were primarily responsible for the defense of the colony.
   c. the Pilgrims were not very tolerant of the Strangers.
   d. the Strangers caused most of the problems in the colonies.

5(a) As used in this passage, the word *radicals* means
   a. atheists
   b. obedient servants
   c. sympathizers
   d. revolutionaries

5(b) As used in this passage, the word *illiterate* means
- a. born out of wedlock
- b. the inability to read and write
- c. educated
- d. intellectually inferior

5(c) As used in this passage, the word *unwholesome* means
- a. degenerate
- b. diseased
- c. proper
- d. educated

5(d) As used in this passage, the word *gauge* means
- a. demonstration
- b. attack
- c. defense
- d. indication

PASSAGE 2-12   SUBJECT:
Higher Education for Women

In 1804, Blount College admitted a very small group of women as students. These students did not attend classes with males, and their courses were simpler. In fact, their study may have been similar to that done in finishing schools. And the fact that one of the students was named Blount might explain the school's early interest in women's education. Whatever the reason, Blount College, which is now the University of Tennessee, admitted no more women until the 1860s.

Other women's colleges were founded only slightly later. Wesleyan in Macon, Georgia, was the first women's college to offer a full course of study leading to degrees. Sharp College in Tennessee was the first women's college to require the same course of study as men's colleges.

Not many people at the time thought women should attend college. Colleges of that era prepared men to be ministers, lawyers, and teachers, and few women entered these fields. Some people thought education would make a woman unfit to be a wife or might make her aggressive and ambitious.

Few women in early America finished high school, so the early women's colleges had serious problems; the age of the students coming to college was low, and the students were often poorly prepared. There were shortages of students because many parents feared that a college education would make their daughter an "old maid."

The first college for both men and women, Oberlin, opened its doors in 1833. Other co-ed colleges soon followed, but the greatest advance in American higher education for women came in 1862. In that year, the Morrill Act established a system of land grant colleges. The law required that these state colleges teach practical subjects (such as farming) to both men and women. By 1900, all but three of the large state schools accepted women as students.

In the western United States, women were much more involved in social life and in work. There were fewer customs than in the East. In Wyoming and Utah, women could vote and could thus demand the chance for higher education. In the West, there were no particularly rich states with huge populations that could support separate colleges for men and women, so there were few arguments over men and women attending the same college.

In the East, though, change came much more slowly. The "Seven Sisters," the oldest and most famous Eastern women's colleges, were not started until 1865. The men's colleges would not admit women, but in 1865 Matthew Vassar started Vassar College for Women. Vassar claimed that women had the same mental faculties as men and should have the same right to education, and the college he started could afford high standards and a good staff. Wellesley, Smith, and Bryn Mawr were

125

founded shortly afterward. Other colleges for women were formed as affiliates with the older Eastern men's schools, such as the Radcliffe-Harvard and Barnard-Columbia arrangements.

By the turn of the century, there were almost 120 women's colleges in the United States, and now there are around 150. There are few colleges in America that aren't co-ed, so despite some social pressures that discourage women from attending college, women have more chance to get a college degree in the United States than in any other country in the world. Despite what might be called a slow start, the United States has been a leader in education for women.

▲ (565 WORDS) ▲

PASSAGE 2-12

Circle the correct answer:

1. The main purpose of this passage is to
    a. trace the development of women's opportunities for higher education in the United States.
    b. compare men's and women's colleges in the United States.
    c. compare Eastern and Western colleges.
    d. discuss women's liberation.

2. Which of the following women's colleges was originally an affiliate of a men's college?
    a. Wellesley
    b. Radcliffe
    c. Smith
    d. Bryn Mawr

3. We can conclude from the passage that
    a. coeducational colleges developed as a response to the women's liberation movement.
    b. federal laws hindered the development of coeducational colleges.
    c. coeducational colleges developed with less difficulty in the East than in the West.
    d. coeducational colleges developed with less difficulty in the West than in the East.

4. The passage suggests that
    a. women were considered superior in intelligence to men.
    b. most women got at least a high school education.

c. college was considered immoral.
  d. women were considered "second-class" citizens.

5(a) As used in this passage, the word *era* means
  a. period
  b. position
  c. location
  d. kind

5(b) As used in this passage, the word *faculties* means
  a. abilities
  b. instructors
  c. advantages
  d. problems

5(c) As used in this passage, the word *affiliates* means
  a. gymnasiums
  b. antagonists
  c. partners
  d. religious schools

PASSAGE 2-13   SUBJECT:
The Tiny Island of Nauru
(nŏ oō′ roō)

The tiny island of Nauru is one of the richest countries in the world—not one of the seven thousand natives of Nauru works. There are no army, no war, no illiteracy; all health services are free, and there are no taxes to pay.

There's more—the climate is moderate, and the housing on Nauru is very modern; there are dozens of shops that specialize in luxury items. Naurans (nŏ oō′ rənz) are a racial mixture of Chinese, Polynesian, and European. For centuries, European visitors to the island have brought back stories of the beauty of the islanders and their good humor.

The island measures only eight square miles, and the islanders live on 15 percent of the land, along the coastline. The rest of the island holds the secret of Nauru's great wealth. The center of the island is covered with millions of tons of bird guano (gwŏ′ nō); centuries of bird droppings, collected on the coral mountains of the island, make the center of the island one huge phosphate mine.

The island was discovered in 1798 by U.S. whalers, who named it Pleasant Island. During the nineteenth century most of the Europeans who came to the island were sailors, convicts, or traders. Most who settled in Nauru were entranced by the climate, the natives, and the relaxed life-style.

But in 1900, the British found that the guano that made the center of the island useless was actually a high grade phosphate. The British and Germans began mining the guano for use as fertilizer.

Guano is the purest natural source for phosphate. As more and more fertilizer is needed in world farming, Naurans have found themselves growing richer; the per person income of $6,500 is one of the highest in the world, but there is really very little in Nauru left to spend this money on.

The guano industry brings in $10 million every year. The Naurans who own the guano deposits already own most of the consumer goods they could ever want—cars, stereos, jeeps, kitchen gadgets, boats, are all startlingly abundant on the island. A twelve-mile road encircles the island along its coastline, and the traffic on this one road is almost always bumper to bumper. The Naurans have no other place to drive the expensive jeeps, vans, cars, and trucks they have bought with their overflowing guano money.

The center of the island is now beginning to resemble a landscape from outer space. As the guano has been removed, tombstone-shaped pinnacles of coral are exposed. The sight has been described as "total and grotesque devastation . . . a vast cemetery." In fact, as each shipment of guano is removed for exportation, the island becomes smaller and less valuable; the coral plains in the center of the island, past the lush greenery along the coast, are becoming completely worthless.

The Naurans cannot agree on the future of the island. The guano will be all mined out in the next twenty years. The people of Nauru have resisted efforts to help them settle on other islands. Instead, they plan to import topsoil from New Zealand to make the island suitable for farming. No one knows if that will, in fact, work.

If importing topsoil turns out to be futile, the Naurans have one more scheme in mind: they've invested millions in hotels in Australia, and three-fourths of their money is being invested in trust funds to provide income when the guano is gone. If neither of these plans seems to be successful, there has been discussion about transforming Nauru into an international gambling center. Once again, outsiders may be lured into the island by its charms, whatever the Naurans decide these charms should be.

▲ (611 WORDS) ▲

PASSAGE 2-13

Circle the correct answer:

1. The main purpose of this passage is to
   a. describe phosphate mining.
   b. describe the unique economy of the island of Nauru.
   c. show how Western culture has corrupted the islanders of Nauru.
   d. trace the deterioration of the island of Nauru.

2. Which of the following statements is not true according to the passage?
   a. The islanders of Nauru are wealthy but ill-educated.
   b. The mountains of Nauru are made from coral.
   c. Nauru was first known as Pleasant Island.
   d. Guano is the purest natural source of phosphate.

3(a) We can conclude from the passage that
   a. the islanders of Nauru work hard in the phosphate mines to earn their riches.
   b. the islanders of Nauru have fought the temptation to embrace Western ways.
   c. the islanders of Nauru are increasing the price they charge for guano to try and force conservation.
   d. the islanders of Nauru are an industrious people who plan ahead.

3(b) Which of the following conclusions does the passage support?
   a. Phosphate fumes are destroying the coastal greenery of Nauru.
   b. Naurans prefer fuel-efficient cars because fuel is difficult to acquire.
   c. Guano is one of several exports that make the Naurans wealthy.
   d. The Naurans are quite optimistic about the future.

4. The passage suggests that
   a. the island of Nauru has benefited artistically from its involvement with the world.
   b. Naurans feel that importing soil is the most promising solution to their strip-mining problems.
   c. the coral in the mountains is almost as valuable as the guano that hides it.
   d. the island of Nauru may eventually be destroyed by tidal waves because of the erosion of the soil.

5(a) As used in this passage, the word *guano* means
   a. skeletons
   b. feathers
   c. eggs
   d. droppings

5(b) As used in this passage, the word *grade* means
   a. explosive
   b. text
   c. quality
   d. priced

5(c) As used in this passage, the word *pinnacles* means
   a. colors
   b. points
   c. depressions
   d. cemeteries

5(d) As used in this passage, the word *exportation* means
   a. sales outside the country
   b. sales within the country
   c. overuse
   d. fuel

5(e) As used in this passage, the word *import* means
   a. destroy
   b. steal
   c. to bring into the country
   d. plant

PASSAGE 2-14

SUBJECT:
Insomnia (ĭn sŏm′ nē ə)

When you were a youngster and couldn't sleep, your mother probably told you to drink a glass of warm milk; if she did, the folk remedy she prescribed had a scientific basis. The amino (ə mē′ nō) acids contained in milk have a sedative effect; various amino acids found in high protein foods promote heavy, relaxing sleep. So, if your mother really wanted to make sure you got plenty of sleep, the warm glass of milk should have been preceded or accompanied by a high protein dinner of meat and cheeses.

Other foods can, in fact, ensure sleeplessness, or insomnia. Caffeine is a stimulant; just as you take a cup of coffee to "wake up" in the morning, you should avoid coffee in the evening if you suffer from insomnia. Tea and cola should also be avoided, for they, too, contain caffeine, and in much larger proportions than people think. Two common stimulants an insomniac may overlook are tobacco and alcohol. One of the benefits of quitting smoking is better sleep. Other people may use alcohol to relax and get to sleep, but under some circumstances alcohol may be a stimulant itself. Besides, there is the added danger of just becoming addicted to the drug; some drinkers say their problems began with drinking to get to sleep.

The simplest cure for insomnia is to tire yourself out before going to bed at night. Exercise relaxes you enough for sleep, but only as long as the exercise is during the daytime. Exercise just before going to bed increases the heart and circulation rates and may actually leave you too stimulated to sleep well. Mental stimulation works precisely the same way. If you read or solve problems or perform other mental work during the day, you'll be left tired enough to sleep well; but if you excite your mental capacities just before going to bed, you may find it difficult to relax your mind for sleep.

Before attempting any cure for insomnia, you first should make sure you have insomnia. Many people worry about their sleeping habits because they don't get a full eight hours of sleep; these people don't realize that everyone doesn't require eight hours. Average amounts of sleep for perfectly healthy people may range from as little as five hours to as much as ten. There are instances of people throughout history, energetic artists and inventors, who needed as little as two hours sleep each night.

All of us sleep very lightly at several points during the night. One type of insomnia causes individuals to think they have not been asleep, when actually they have been sleeping very lightly. Also, most people find it difficult to judge time at night, so we may overestimate the amount of time we spend awake tossing and turning.

One kind of insomnia is called agrypniaphobia (ə grĭp′ nē ə phō′ bē ə), which is a fear of not being able to sleep. People with this phobia actually keep themselves awake, worrying about whether or not they sleep. These are the people who talk about insomnia constantly, making their sleeplessness the major problem in their lives.

Sometimes, of course, people are kept awake by very real problems in their lives. Money worries, family tensions, career problems may all literally keep you up at night. But when the problem is solved or disappears, the insomnia should disappear, too. Problems may <u>depress</u> you, or you may be suffering from a mental illness; waking up early each <u>morning</u> and being unable to go back to sleep may be a sign of depression. If you think your insomnia is the result of a mental problem, "sleep clinics" may be able to help you with relaxation techniques, hypnosis, or psychotherapy.

▲ (613 WORDS) ▲

PASSAGE 2-14

Circle the correct answer:

1. The purpose of this passage is to
   a. discuss the causes and cures of insomnia.
   b. discuss the causes of insomnia.
   c. discuss the cures of insomnia.
   d. discuss the effects of amino acids on insomnia.

2. According to the passage, which of the following statements is not true?
   a. The amino acids contained in milk have a sedative effect.
   b. Caffeine does not cause insomnia if it is consumed in foods other than coffee.
   c. Exercise can help cure insomnia.
   d. All people sleep lightly at several points during the night.

3. We can conclude from the passage that
   a. mothers are usually right about home remedies.
   b. alcohol seldom acts as a stimulant on alcoholics.
   c. both mental and physical stimulation immediately before going to bed can cause insomnia.
   d. hypnosis works better than psychotherapy in curing insomnia.

4. The passage suggests that
   a. anxiety can cause insomnia.
   b. people who do hard physical labor often have insomnia.
   c. mental activity during the day can cause insomnia.
   d. smoking helps relax people so they can sleep.

5(a) As used in this passage, the word *basis* means
   a. foundation
   b. fallacy

132

    c. training
    d. error

5(b) As used in this passage, the word *sedative* means
    a. negative
    b. interesting
    c. tensing
    d. calming

5(c) As used in this passage, the word *ensure* means
    a. guarantee
    b. help
    c. prevent
    d. restore

5(d) As used in this passage, the word *stimulant* means
    a. poison
    b. narcotic
    c. substance that excites
    d. addiction

5(e) As used in this passage, the word *depress* means
    a. hurt
    b. sadden
    c. improve
    d. excite

PASSAGE 2-15   SUBJECT:
Flexible Work Schedules

Flexible work days are transforming the character of the American worker's environment.

No longer do all office workers get out of bed before dawn. No longer do all factory workers show up at the plant gates while the sky is still dark. Now many workers are being given the opportunity to set their own schedules for each day, each week, or even each year.

For example, at one enormous New York insurance company, this new scheme, called "flextime," allows all office workers to adjust their schedules to suit their home schedules or personalities. During the "core hours" of 10 A.M. to 3 P.M., everyone must be at work, but each employee has the option of arriving at work anytime between 9 and 10 A.M. and leaving anytime between 3 P.M. and 6 P.M. At some companies, there are no core hours—employees can literally put in their forty hours per week any time they wish, even at night or on weekends.

As almost anyone could have predicted, the results have been very positive. In companies using flextime schedules, absence rates are lower and workers are happier. Working mothers can rise early, get their children off to school, and report for work without losing any time waiting around until nine o'clock for the office to open. After putting in a full day, a working mother can leave at three o'clock and pick up her children after school.

Flextime allows "night people" to adjust their schedules, too. Chronic sleepyheads don't have to feel exhausted all day or miss a day's work because they overslept, late sleepers can come to work at 10 A.M. and leave at 6 P.M., and workers with personal business to complete can schedule themselves lengthy lunch hours and return to finish regular workdays.

One great advantage of flexible work schedules is their effect on traffic. Either the late sleeper or the early riser can manage to avoid rush hour on the freeway or in the subway, and some European companies switched to flextime precisely because of this. At some German firms, for example, roads built before World War II just could not handle the traffic caused by twelve thousand workers reporting for work at a modern plant. Workers came in tired by the long traffic snarls outside the gates and angry at other drivers. Since the factory adopted flextime, the traffic flow is steady, but never overwhelming. Now traffic is spread out through a four-hour period.

Ironically, given Germany's reputation for precision and regimentation, it was here that flextime started. Many firms in Germany switched to flextime to help solve traffic and access problems at factories and office buildings. But the main reason behind massive shifts to flextime was a shortage of workers. Flextime was seen as a sensible, practical way to bring women and mothers into the labor force while disrupting family life as little as possible.

Acceptance of flextime was slow to come, however. There was no clock available that could keep track of each worker's hours and feed this information directly to payroll computers. By 1972, a million European workers had switched to flextime, once the benefits of the system were realized and the clock was being produced.

Thus, punching a time clock has become a way of letting workers set their own pace and schedule. Ironically, the symbol of job supervision, the time clock, is setting workers free from constant supervision and lessening the <u>alienation</u> many workers used to feel.

Flextime is speeding social change everywhere it's used; it is simpler to hire workers with children, and people are using flextime to schedule more time with their families. Soon workers may be able to schedule a vacation any time they wish, and retirement may be voluntary. Freedom on the job may prove to be the most important freedom of all.

▲ (636 WORDS) ▲

PASSAGE 2-15

Circle the correct answer:

1. This passage is mainly about
   a. the flextime schedule and its effect on the procrastinating employee.
   b. the benefit of flextime schedules as a traffic-controlling device.
   c. the beneficial effects of the flextime schedule on employees.
   d. the flextime schedule and the woman worker.

2. According to the passage, which of the following statements is not true?
   a. The flextime schedule is particularly beneficial to the woman worker who has school-age children.
   b. The flextime schedule helps control traffic on highways by spreading out the flow over a longer period of time.
   c. All flextime schedules involve some core hours when all employees are required to be at work.
   d. The main reason behind the massive shift to flextime was a shortage of workers.

3. We can conclude from the passage that
   a. workers are happier with the flextime schedule because they feel more in control of their lives.
   b. employers find it difficult to supervise their workers on a flextime schedule.

  c. many employees take advantage of the flextime schedule by lying about their reporting time.
  d. flextime scheduling need never rely on core hour scheduling.

4. The passage suggests that
  a. Daylight Saving Time greatly affected the development of flextime scheduling.
  b. the insurance industry must have some core hour scheduling.
  c. flextime scheduling has had more effect on blue-collar workers than on administration-level workers.
  d. flextime scheduling has had a positive influence on the family in most areas in which it's been implemented.

5(a) As used in this passage, the word *transforming* means
  a. destroying
  b. ruining
  c. changing
  d. negating

5(b) As used in this passage, the word *core* means
  a. useless
  b. central
  c. morning
  d. daily

5(c) As used in this passage, the word *option* means
  a. requirement
  b. choice
  c. obligation
  d. duty

5(d) As used in this passage, the word *alienation* means
  a. fatigue
  b. indifference
  c. hurry
  d. insecurity

PASSAGE 2-16

SUBJECT: Bullfighting

Bullfighting is a sport understood by very few people outside Spain and Latin American countries. Western tourists may spend hundreds of dollars on a tour of Spain that ends in a journey to the bullfighting arena and may take dozens of pictures to show that they've traveled to the arena. But most leave after taking their pictures, and most leave still with the notion that bullfighting is a cruel sport.

And—make no mistake about it—bullfighting is cruel. Ordinarily, the bull that is let into the arena must die. But the sport is equally cruel for the bullfighters themselves, many of whom are injured or killed each year. The matador (măt′ ə dôr), the bullfighter who actually makes the kill, is facing an animal specially bred to be mean, fast, and strong. The bull has almost as good a chance of winning as the matador, if not a better chance entirely.

As such, the sport of bullfighting compares favorably with sports such as boxing or automobile racing. In boxing, two well-trained fighters punch and stalk each other, looking for that one moment when a punch will knock the opponent unconscious. To win, a boxer must hurt his opponent; doctors are always present to ensure that no lasting damage occurs, but boxers have died from injuries received in the ring. And to be the victim of a simple, uncomplicated knockout punch is not without its dangers. Everyone is familiar with the stereotyped image of the punchy ex-fighter who simply got hit too many times.

Automobile racing is equally dangerous and may provide a better comparison for bullfighting. Probably very few people travel to an automobile race to witness a fiery crash. But a race driven at a slow, safe speed would be a bore; there would be no point in racing that way. The point of automobile racing is to drive as fast as possible, as close as possible to dangerous speeds, but always to be in control of the machine. And control is equally as important in bullfighting.

Actually, the English translation *bullfighting* is unfortunate. The Spanish means something more like "arranging" or "managing" the bull. The matador shows his own courage by working as close as possible to the bull's horns. He must also allow the bull to show his courage by allowing the bull chance after chance to kill the matador.

Rather than consider the elaborate ritual a sport, we might better consider bullfighting as a test of courage for the matador. Ancient athletes on the island of Crete (krēt) tested their courage by facing a charging bull and leaping over the deadly horns. The Portuguese (pôr′ chə gēz) are modern specialists in this art. For over two thousand years men have faced raging bulls to test their courage. During the long history of bullfighting, men have used lances, swords, axes, even specially trained bulldogs to fight bulls. In Spain, bullfighting was introduced by El Cid (ĕl cĭd), the nation's liberator, who lanced bulls from horseback.

In the eighteenth century, fighting the bull on foot became the accepted technique, and the cape became a means of moving the bull. The modern, rigid code of bullfighting, or toreo (tōr' ē ō), came into being about 150 years ago. The toreo is very carefully governed; any fakery, any showing-off is immediately noted by the very knowledgeable fans. The bull and the matador must face each other with nothing between them except the bull's fighting instinct and the matador's knowledge of bulls. Every matador works his way up through novice ranks painstakingly until he qualifies to work in big arenas in the large cities, sometimes earning $20,000 in an afternoon.

If the bull fights well, the matador may ask the arena president for a pardon of the bull's life. If granted, the pardon allows the bull to charge from the arena to a long, happy life on a breeding ranch, where bulls are bred and raised. Few realize that the bull has this possibility of winning, too. A fighting bull, in fact, has a much better chance of survival than a deer being stalked by a hunter. Now there is violence for you—and violence with no test of courage whatsoever.

▲ (690 WORDS) ▲

PASSAGE 2-16

Circle the correct answer:

1. The purpose of this passage is to
    a. compare automobile racing and bullfighting.
    b. discuss the training of matadors.
    c. show that bullfighting is not the cruel sport many people believe it to be.
    d. discuss the development of bullfighting in the eighteenth century.

2(a) Matadors must be
    a. brave
    b. knowledgeable
    c. well-trained
    d. all of the above

2(b) According to the passage, which of the following statements is not true?
    a. Bullfighting is equally cruel for bullfighter and bull.
    b. People in Spain and Latin America do not understand bullfighting.
    c. Automobile racing is just as dangerous as bullfighting.
    d. Fighting the bull on foot became the accepted technique in the 1700s.

3(a) We can conclude from the passage that
    a. boxing is as cruel a sport as is bullfighting.

    b. most boxers end up with brain damage.
    c. boxing is less cruel than bullfighting because no one ever dies.
    d. boxing and bullfighting aren't similar.

3(b) Which of the following conclusions does the passage support?
    a. Matadors are never hurt because of rigid safety precautions.
    b. Bulls never survive the arena.
    c. Bullfighting is very much a ritual in Spain and Latin America.
    d. Matadors are cheered for showing-off in the arena.

4. The passage suggests that
    a. bullfighting is banned in this country.
    b. bullfighting is not a very old art.
    c. many Americans refuse to see how cruel some of our favorite sports are.
    d. matadors never make very much money.

5(a) As used in this passage, the word *notion* means
    a. idea
    b. fear
    c. doubt
    d. reason

5(b) As used in this passage, the word *bred* means
    a. killed
    b. purchased
    c. feared
    d. developed

5(c) As used in this passage, the word *stereotyped* means
    a. actual
    b. strange
    c. uncommon
    d. typical

5(d) As used in this passage, the word *liberator* means
    a. person who set them free
    b. person who enslaved them
    c. dictator
    d. hunter

5(e) As used in this passage, the word *rigid* means
    a. benign
    b. inflexible
    c. inhuman
    d. flat

5(f) As used in this passage, the word *novice* means
    a. frightening
    b. religious

       c. expert
       d. beginner

5(g) As used in this passage, the word *stalked* means
       a. fed
       b. scared
       c. tracked
       d. surprised

PASSAGE 2-17

SUBJECT:
Fort Knox

The Pharaohs (fā′ rōz) of Egypt stored their gold in the pyramids, but the American taxpayers store their gold in an ugly little building on a military post in Kentucky. A few miles south of Louisville, on Gold Vault Road, lies the legendary Fort Knox. This unimposing structure, built in 1936 to help house the nation's wealth, holds more gold than any single ruler, including the Pharaohs, ever dreamed of.

Inside are huge stacks of gold bullion (bŏol′ yən) piled on shelves. The bars are of varying sizes and purity, but most are about 7 inches long, almost 4 inches wide, and 1¾ inches thick. Gold is twice as heavy as lead, so each gold bar weighs about 27 pounds. There are 147,342,320.272 ounces of gold at Fort Knox; at the price of gold in early 1980, that's $123 billion worth. As the price of gold rises and falls, it's not uncommon for the Fort Knox holdings to lose $14 billion in value in a single morning or to gain that much in an afternoon.

More amazingly, the Fort Knox gold is only a little more than half the gold the United States owns; the rest is scattered around the country in smaller, less famous vaults. The gold in Fort Knox was shipped there in 1937, in armored trucks and trains guarded by soldiers with machine guns and bayonets. Four years earlier, America abandoned the gold standard to back U.S. currency, and Americans turned in the gold coins then in circulation; the coins were melted down and formed into the bricks stacked on the Fort Knox shelves.

Besides all the gold stored in Fort Knox, there are several other kinds of items kept there. In case of shortages brought on by war or economic conditions, the government stores platinum (plăt′ i nŭm) and industrial diamonds. Many legal and necessary drugs can only be made from opium (ō′ pē əm) and morphine, so the government stores thousands of pounds of these two drugs in Fort Knox. If the Fort Knox drugs were sold "on the street," their value would be well over $25 billion.

During World War II, the original copies of the Constitution and the Declaration of Independence were kept in the vault, along with a copy of the Magna Carta and two of Lincoln's speeches. The crown jewels of Hungary were kept in Fort Knox until 1978; they had been taken out of Europe in 1945. All this time, the master dies for making U.S. coins and the master plates for printing paper money have been kept in the vault by the Bureau of Engraving and Printing.

All this wealth is in a two-story building made of stone, steel, and concrete, surrounded by an electrically charged steel fence. Television cameras on the roof rotate constantly, and the sentry boxes at each corner contain very serious military guards. In fact, the Depository Building is surrounded by a military post there to protect it. Visitors are stopped at the road before they even reach the fence.

The vault is in the middle of the building itself. No single person at Fort Knox knows the combination that would unlock the thirty-ton door, so getting inside the two-story vault requires the presence of several officials.

The walls of the vault are three-feet-thick layers of concrete poured over steel beams, steel plates, and steel cylinders. Inside the vault are almost thirty individual compartments, each with a key lock and a time lock. To ensure that no intruder has disturbed valuable materials, each compartment is sealed with steel bands and par-affin (păr' ə fin) seals. To each seal is attached a document signed by Fort Knox officials describing what they personally saw delivered into the compartment. The gold compartments are about the size of a small room in a modern house; each one holds 36,000 gold bars, so each compartment contains gold bars worth about $10 billion.

Any people going into the Depository Building or into the vault must empty their pockets going in and coming out, as well as walk through a metal detector. Usually, no one not directly employed by the Depository can gain entry to the vault. Franklin Roosevelt once inspected the vaults, and in 1974 a group of congressmen were allowed inside. This list of visitors also emphasizes the fact that all this security has worked. Not only has Fort Knox never been robbed—despite the novels and films that describe some archvillain's plot to do so—no one has ever even made an attempt.

▲ (743 WORDS) ▲

PASSAGE 2-17

Circle the correct answer:

1. The purpose of this passage is to
   a. describe America's gold reserves.
   b. discuss military security measures.
   c. discuss gold and silver.
   d. describe Fort Knox.

2. According to the passage, which of the following statements is not true?
   a. There is more gold in Fort Knox than was held by any of the Pharaohs.
   b. The gold in Fort Knox has been placed there primarily since the beginning of the rises in oil prices.
   c. Large quantities of certain drugs are stored at Fort Knox.
   d. All visitors to Fort Knox are stopped at the gate.

3. We can conclude from the passage that
   a. America stores drugs because they are more valuable than gold.
   b. opium and morphine are stored at Fort Knox because of the incredible security there.

c. industrial diamonds are worth more than gold on the open market.
   d. platinum is used in processing opium and morphine into legal drugs.

4(a) The passage suggests that
   a. The Constitution and the Declaration of Independence were placed in Fort Knox because they were beginning to deteriorate.
   b. The Constitution and the Declaration of Independence were stored in Fort Knox during World War II because of the political unrest they caused in this country.
   c. The Constitution and the Declaration of Independence were stored in Fort Knox to keep them from being sold.
   d. The Constitution and the Declaration of Independence were stored in Fort Knox during World War II to protect them in case of attack.

4(b) How does the author seem to feel about the security at Fort Knox?
   a. offended
   b. negative
   c. impressed
   d. skeptical

5(a) As used in this passage, the word *legendary* means
   a. famous
   b. useless
   c. deteriorating
   d. unsafe

5(b) As used in this passage, the word *unimposing* means
   a. curious
   b. bizarre
   c. impressive
   d. unimpressive

5(c) As used in this passage, the word *circulation* means
   a. need
   b. paper money
   c. use
   d. movement

5(d) As used in this passage, the word *paraffin* means
   a. broken
   b. wax
   c. open
   d. useless

PASSAGE 2-18   SUBJECT:
Common Foot and Leg Injuries to Exercisers

In an effort to increase their physical fitness, millions of people are exercising. Many people who never exercised in any regular, routine way are jogging, swimming, riding bicycles, playing tennis or other sports for the first time in their lives. The magazine *Runner's World* once took a poll of its readers, all long-time joggers and exercisers. Nearly two-thirds of all their readers had injured themselves badly enough to be forced to stop exercising. The magazine's staff also discovered that most of their readers had been injured at least twice during their first year of exercise.

Now that's not an argument against the very obvious benefits of exercise. But many people who are now exercising have little experience with common athletic injuries, much less training in their treatment.

The most common injuries are to the feet and legs; among these, the single most common complaint is shin splints, sharp pains just to the inside of the shinbone. Shin splints are common because there are so many possible causes, ranging from simple overexertion to too much running uphill. Another common cause of shin splints is inadequate heel support in athletic shoes. The only treatment is rest, and shin splints are so painful that no one will have to tell you to rest. The pain is caused by muscle cramps in the thin muscles in the shin area; anything to help speed up circulation in the feet and legs will help drive away the stiffness. Some doctors prescribe vitamin E for this purpose.

Another painful injury to the area is inflammation or breaking of the Achilles (ə kil′ ēz) tendon; this tendon is the long thin tendon at the back of the ankle that connects the heel with the calf muscles above it. According to Green legend, the warrior Achilles was made invulnerable to harm when his mother dipped him into the river Styx (stĭx). But she held him by the heel, and this was left the one spot where he could be injured; the legend ends when the famous warrior was killed by an arrow in the heel. The phrase "Achilles' heel" has come to mean a weak spot, and for many athletes, it's an apt name for this tendon. The tendon tightens with age and loses its flexibility, so that a sudden flexing of the foot may cause soreness. Worse, the tendon can snap in half; several athletes have had their professional careers end this way. Careful warm-up exercises, along with a stretching and flexing routine, are necessary if your Achilles tendon is too tight to allow full movement.

There are several abnormal conditions of the foot that may need medical treatment before vigorous exercise is possible. A sharp pain in the arch of the foot, called plantar fasciitis, can make running or a fast game of tennis impossible. If you have this problem, a doctor can prescribe medicines to reduce the inflammation causing the pain. Another, more common problem is Morton's toe, a condition named after the doctor who first described this condition. People with short first toes may develop a very painful, almost arthritislike condition in which the bones behind the first toe actually move forward to compensate for the toe's short length. If you have burning pain between the first and second toes or if you cannot move your first toe, you may have Morton's toe. A podiatrist (pə dī′ ə trĭst) can construct polyurethene (pŏl ē yoŏr′ a thān) pads for the arch or front of the foot that will relieve pressure on the toe by distributing your weight more regularly over the entire foot. Pads are also the correct treatment for heel spurs; a polyurethene pad should be constructed in the heel of athletic shoes to pad the area where the pain is occurring. Be sure that the pad isn't too thick, or it will cause your heel to wobble in the shoe without support. You also must be sure to pad the other shoe to precisely the same thickness, or you'll be running off balance and cause even more problems.

Other problems, like neck or back pain, can be avoided by careful warm-up and stretching exercises before beginning any strenuous exertion. If you're out of shape, don't try to get into perfect condition in two days by driving yourself to the point of serious injury. And buy good equipment; cheap running shoes or tennis shoes are no bargain. They can literally cause injury. Get expert advice, and make sure that equipment, like a bicycle or rowing machine, is correctly adjusted before you use it.

These four rules can help keep you exercising without interruption and can keep you out of the doctor's office. But the fifth rule is this: if you do injure yourself or if you have severe pain or rest doesn't help, admit it and see a doctor.

▲ (793 WORDS) ▲

PASSAGE 2-18

Circle the correct answer:

1(a) The main idea of this passage is that
    a. many painful injuries can result from not taking the correct approach to exercising.
    b. exercising is dangerous for older adults.
    c. exercising is a beneficial, but dangerous activity.
    d. most people don't really need much exercise.

1(b) A good title for this passage might be
    a. Exercising
    b. Injuries and Their Cures
    c. Injuries That Can Result from Exercising
    d. How to Train

2. According to the passage, which of the following statements is not true?
   a. The most common injury to the leg is heel spur.
   b. Achilles tendons can actually snap under stress.
   c. Inadequate heel support can cause shin splints.
   d. People with short first toes may develop Morton's toe.

3. We can conclude from the passage that
   a. injuries to the Achilles tendon are the most common injuries among joggers.
   b. only joggers have problems with their legs and feet.
   c. buying the right equipment can prevent injuries.
   d. bicyclists are more likely to injure their legs than are joggers.

4(a) The passage suggests that
   a. people often begin exercising without realizing some of the problems they can encounter.
   b. no one but doctors should jog.
   c. having a checkup by your doctor periodically can prevent all injuries.
   d. people who are not in good shape should exercise vigorously at first to warm up.

4(b) The author probably believes that
   a. exercising is too dangerous for most people.
   b. exercising is not dangerous if approached correctly.
   c. exercising is of little benefit because it causes so many injuries.
   d. many aches and pains of exercising are just psychological.

5(a) As used in this passage, the word *complaint* means
   a. benefit
   d. disease
   c. advantage
   d. ailment

5(b) As used in this passage, the word *overexertion* means
   a. deformities
   b. overexercising
   c. accidents
   d. falls

5(c) As used in this passage, the word *flexibility* means
   a. contracting ability
   b. shape
   c. tone
   d. stretching ability

5(d) As used in this passage, the word *inflammation* means
   a. exercise
   b. activity

    c. irritation
    d. disease

5(e) As used in this passage, the word *podiatrist* means
    a. a doctor who specializes in skeletal surgery
    b. coach
    c. a doctor who specializes in foot care
    d. trainer

5(f) As used in this passage, the word *strenuous* means
    a. vigorous
    b. easy
    c. fatal
    d. temporary

PASSAGE 2-19

SUBJECT: Chinese Bronzes

Bronze is an alloy, a mixture of two metals, usually copper and tin. The result is a very durable metal, which can withstand constant use and even neglect. Some of the most famous bronze artifacts ever discovered were buried in the wet soil of the Yellow River basin in China for almost two thousand years without damage.

Because these bronzes were in such good condition and because Western artists could not match the craftsmanship of the pots and dishes, some experts claimed it was impossible that they had been products of the Shang (Shŏng) dynasty. This dynasty, which ruled China from 1765 to 1122 B.C., and the succeeding Chou (jō) dynasty first discovered and used bronze for everyday tools and utensils in preparing food and wine. Later, bronze began to be used to make ceremonial vessels, bells, and weapons. Bells and urns were often cast to commemorate a ceremonial occasion.

Two methods of casting were apparently used by the Shang bronze workers: The first method used a highly detailed wax model; the artist used this to shape a clay mold. The hot bronze was poured into the clay mold actually to make the bronze object. The second method was probably much more difficult to use, requiring the creation of several different pottery molds, one for each section of a large object. After the molten bronze had been poured and cooled, the bronze sections were carefully fitted together and welded to create the finished object.

Metals other than tin were often mixed with the copper to create variously colored bronzes. Early Chinese bronzes range from a deep red, which is created with a high proportion of copper, to a very lustrous silver for mirrors, which are half tin and half copper. Other metals used to color the bronze include lead, antimony (ăn' tə mō nē), zinc, iron, and silver.

There are many collectors who specialize in Chinese bronzes. Many museums have large collections of these artifacts, but many are owned by private collectors who bought them from the Chinese farmers who found the bronzes. The most common of the food and wine containers are generally one of seven types of vessel:

Tǐng were bowls used at formal banquets; their diameter ranged from two inches to twenty-four inches across. All have indentations or projections that aided pouring, and most rest on three or four solid legs. *Hsien* are two-piece bowls with a bronze screen used to steam vegetables.

The other five common utensils were designed for storing, serving, or transporting sacrificial wine. A *yü* is a bucketlike vessel with a swinging handle for carrying sacrificial wine, as was the *lei* (lā' ē) and the *hui* (hü ē), both round pots with ring handles at each side; the *kü,* a beaker used to drink wine both in ceremonies and at meals, is probably the most common of all the Chinese bronzes. A *kü* is generally shaped like a tall, graceful glass, but is heavily decorated.

The most prized of the common utensils is the *chueh* (jü ə), a ceremonial wine dish used to pour offerings to the gods. It has a pouring lip and rests on a tripod base, so most collectors assume the *chueh* held wine for warming as well. Early examples look like helmets turned upside down and resting on three legs; *chueh* from the later Chou dynasty were decorated very elaborately, often cast in the shapes of various animals, such as tigers or birds. In fact, one old legend says that *chueh* look like birds, so they are called by a name that resembles the chirping call of a bird.

The majority of these pieces come from the Shang dynasty, the oldest rulers about whom written records exist. (And many of these records are inscribed on the surface of bronze ceremonial vessels.) The later Chou dynasty is responsible for many beautiful pieces, though. In the later period, bronze casting techniques were improved. Gold and silver were often inlaid on the bronze vessels, along with other changes in the casters' art.

In 1974 the greatest single collection of bronzes in China was found by farmers digging wells along the Yellow River. They found a burial vault of the Emperor Quin (kwĕn), the tyrant who built the Great Wall of China at the cost of a million lives. He was a ruler of the late Chou dynasty, when iron had replaced bronze for daily use; bronze was reserved for ceremonial vessels and weapons, thousands of which were buried with the emperor for his use in the afterlife. An entire army of 7,500 life-size clay soldiers carrying bronze weapons was also buried with the emperor in the belief that they, too, could aid him in the afterlife. Most of the bronze weapons were looted from the burial vaults centuries ago, but no one knows where they are today. These treasures may have been melted down to make other bronze objects for some other ruler.

▲ (809 WORDS) ▲

PASSAGE 2-19

Circle the correct answer:

1. The purpose of this passage is to
    a. discuss the making of bronze.
    b. discuss bronze artifacts of the Shang and Chou dynasties.
    c. describe methods of casting bronze.
    d. discuss ancient Chinese culture.

2. a *yü* is used for
    a. drinking wine.
    b. pouring offerings to the gods.
    c. steaming vegetables.
    d. carrying sacrificial wine.

3(a) We can conclude from the passage that
    a. large objects were more difficult to cast than small objects.
    b. small objects were more difficult to cast than large objects.
    c. only small objects could be decorated during the casting.
    d. large objects were less durable casts than were small objects.

3(b) Which of the following conclusions does the passage support?
    a. The bronzes made by the Shang dynasty were more advanced than those made by the Chou dynasty.
    b. The bronzes found in the Yellow River basin were later found to have been misdated by the archaeologists.
    c. Experts did not believe the Shang dynasty's metal-working skills could have been as advanced as those of modern metal workers.
    d. The bronze workers of the Shang dynasty apparently used three different methods of casting.

4(a) The passage suggests that
    a. the ancient Chinese believed in only one god.
    b. the ancient Chinese believed the afterlife to be much like life on earth.
    c. the ancient Chinese killed soldiers and buried them with the dead emperors.
    d. the ancient Chinese were terrified of the dead.

4(b) The author's tone is
    a. admiring
    b. subjective
    c. negative
    d. skeptical

5(a) As used in this passage, the word *artifacts* means
    a. weapons
    b. alloys
    c. objects from another culture
    d. fakes

5(b) As used in this passage, the word *succeeding* means
    a. more successful
    b. following
    c. gaining
    d. cruel

5(c) As used in this passage, the word *commemorate* means
    a. dishonor
    b. ridicule
    c. create
    d. honor

5(d) As used in this passage, the word *casting* means
    a. building
    b. molding

c. assembly
   d. melting

5(e) As used in this passage, the word *tyrant* means
   a. architect
   b. absolute ruler
   c. laborer
   d. queen

PASSAGE 2-20

SUBJECT: First Aid

The major causes of death in America today are heart attack and sudden injury. Most people have been, or will be, present as a victim of one of these sudden attacks waits for an ambulance. If the victim loses pulse and breathing, the chances for survival decrease tremendously. Only 18 percent survive if no one present can assist the victim to maintain pulse and breathing until an ambulance arrives.

If, however, the victim receives vital aid within the first minute, there is a 98 percent chance for survival. As aid arrives later and later, these chances decrease. In fact, after four minutes without a pulse, the brain begins to deteriorate. If help is delayed for six minutes, the victim's chances decrease to 11 percent. It is vitally important that all of us understand the measures to take when someone's pulse or respiration stops suddenly.

Of all deaths, 50 percent are at least partially caused by choking. If a victim struggles to force air into his or her lungs, immediately check for blockage in the mouth or throat. Sometimes, a wheezing noise indicates that the airway is partially blocked. An absence of noise is even more serious, indicating a completely blocked airway.

Many people believe that people who are unconscious can "swallow their tongues." What actually happens is that the completely relaxed tongue falls against the opening of the throat, but the resulting choking is the same as if the victim had "swallowed" the tongue. If the victim is lying on his or her back, elevate the chin and point the top of the head toward the floor; this should allow the tongue to permit unrestricted breathing once again.

Other victims may have foreign objects in the airway—food particles, false teeth, or other objects that the victim may have had in the mouth can block or close off the vocal cords. Sometimes small foreign objects may cause a spasm in the vocal cords themselves, closing off the throat. If a patient cannot remove the object by coughing, you should hold the person in a "bear hug" position. Place both fists in the lower chest or upper abdominal area and squeeze suddenly, violently, and repeatedly. This may expel the foreign object or at least move it to the upper throat, where it can be removed with the fingers.

Some parts of the throat and bronchial tubes are narrow; others much wider, so foreign objects are of immediate concern only if they are blocking the airway, causing the victim to suffocate. If the object can be expelled or blown into a wider area of the airway where it does not cause blockage, then the immediate problem has been solved. Later, doctors can use a long, thin, hollow tube to direct forceps into the throat, even into the lungs if need be, to remove the object. This is a simple, almost painless procedure, so it is obviously better to blow the object further downward than to allow the victim to continue choking.

If the victim is no longer choking or if you have tried the other methods to remove the object, you may use mouth-to-mouth resuscitation. This is an artificial method of inflating the lungs, and it may dislodge foreign objects by blowing them downward into the lungs. With the victim lying or his or her back, once again tilt the top of the head toward the floor. Close off the victim's nostrils with one hand, and exhale forcefully into that person's mouth; the victim's chest should expand as oxygen rushes into the lungs. When you lift your head to inhale oxygen yourself, the victim's lungs should relax and exhale the air; this routine is performed fairly rapidly, but not so rapidly that you grow faint. Mouth-to-mouth resuscitation restarts respiration for the victim.

To restart circulation, you should begin external heart massage. At one time, it was thought necessary to open the chest surgically to massage the heart between the hands. Now, however, a method has been developed to massage the heart between the hard breastbone and the spinal column. Put the heel of one hand on the lower breastbone, and use the other hand to press down firmly on that hand; squeezing the heart between the breastbone and the spinal column compresses it and pumps blood from the heart into the arteries. When this pressure relaxes, the heart automatically refills with blood, so give the heart enough time to fill with blood, but try to strike an even rhythm of about sixty beats per minute.

If two people are attempting resuscitation, one should give mouth-to-mouth resuscitation while the other massages the heart externally. If you are working alone, use your strength in external heart massage. But stop the massage after fifteen beats to force two breaths into the victim, ensuring that the victim's blood maintains its oxygen level. If the heart massage is being done well, the veins in the neck should move as pressure is applied.

This artificial respiration and circulation should continue until help arrives, if necessary. Most ambulances have all the machines needed to stimulate the heart, as well as oxygen supply equipment. If the ambulance does not have these machines, you should keep "breathing" for the victim until the latter begins to breathe without help or is delivered to a hospital that has the equipment.

Organizations such as the Red Cross and the Heart Association regularly offer classes to train people to use these techniques. The techniques should be practiced, not merely read, and there is more to learn than the mere outline provided here. Everyone should become familiar with these methods, for the chance to save a life may come only once.

▲ (944 WORDS) ▲

PASSAGE 2-20

Circle the correct answer:

1(a) This passage is mainly about
    a. the causes of heart attack and sudden injury.
    b. first aid steps to take to restore breathing.

      c. first aid steps to take to aid choking victims.
      d. first aid steps to take to restore pulse and breathing.

1(b) A good title for this passage might be
      a. How to Save a Life by Restoring Pulse and Breathing
      b. How to Aid Choking Victims
      c. How to Restore Breathing
      d. What Causes Heart Attack?

2(a) According to the passage, which of the following statements is not true?
      a. Heart attack causes more deaths in America than does sudden injury.
      b. Of all deaths, 50 percent are at least partially caused by choking.
      c. Unconscious people do not actually "swallow" their tongues.
      d. Some parts of the throat and bronchial tubes are narrower than other parts.

2(b) To perform mouth-to-mouth resuscitation
      a. have the victim lying on his or her back.
      b. close off the victim's nostrils with one hand.
      c. exhale forcefully into his or her mouth.
      d. all of the above.

3. We can conclude from the passage that
      a. only 11 percent of victims of sudden injury survive.
      b. choking has little to do with most deaths.
      c. only about 10 percent of victims who receive first aid within the first minute do not survive.
      d. the possibility of swallowing the tongue is the most dangerous threat to an unconscious person.

4(a) The passage suggests that
      a. foreign objects in the throat cause most heart attacks.
      b. external heart massage bruises the heart.
      c. everyone has an obligation to learn basic resuscitation and heart massage techniques.
      d. mouth-to-mouth resuscitation is of little use if a person is unconscious.

4(b) The author's tone is
      a. objective
      b. negative
      c. subjective
      d. sarcastic

5(a) As used in this passage, the word *deteriorate* means
      a. bleed
      b. decay
      c. forget
      d. function

5(b) As used in this passage, the word *partially* means
- a. in part
- b. totally
- c. believed
- d. eventually

5(c) As used in this passage, the word *elevate* means
- a. raise
- b. lower
- c. stretch
- d. level

5(d) As used in this passage, the word *foreign* means
- a. normal
- b. poison
- c. external
- d. imported

5(e) As used in this passage, the word *spasm* means
- a. hemorrhage
- b. deterioration
- c. contraction
- d. opening

5(f) As used in this passage, the word *expel* means
- a. enlarge
- b. remove
- c. crush
- d. melt

5(g) As used in this passage, the word *suffocate* means
- a. vomit
- b. turn blue
- c. scream
- d. smother

5(h) As used in this passage, the word *resuscitation* means
- a. revival
- b. suction
- c. massage
- d. degrees

5(i) As used in this passage, the word *exhale* means
- a. take in air
- b. blow out air
- c. scream
- d. push

5(j) As used in this passage, the word *compresses* means
   a. enlarges
   b. bruises
   c. squeezes
   d. damages

5(k) As used in this passage, the word *rhythm* means
   a. relaxation
   b. tension
   c. compression
   d. pattern

5(l) As used in this passage, the word *ensuring* means
   a. guaranteeing
   b. hoping
   c. doubting
   d. relaying

SECTION 3 | READING PASSAGES

DIRECTIONS: Read all of the passages that your instructor has assigned in this section. Answer the comprehension items that have been assigned on your Student Score Sheet. Be sure to read each passage carefully and to refer to the passage to check your answers to the comprehension questions.

PASSAGE 3-1

SUBJECT:
Operation Red Flag

Picture American pilots using enemy tactics, flying F-5E Tigers painted to look like MiGs, and lining other American planes up in the cross hairs of their weapons. Are these men traitors?

Operation Red Flag is a training program operated by the U.S. Air Force at Nellis Air Force Base in Nevada, where pilots from all over the United States come to complete their training or to take "refresher courses," as, each day, mock battles are staged high over the Nevada desert. Trainees in American planes try desperately to fend off the planes from the Operation Red Flag squadron.

Only the best pilots fly the Red Flag planes. The F-5E was chosen because it looks and performs like a Russian fighter, the MiG. The pilots in these planes have gone through extensive training to enable them to impersonate Russian pilots: they read Russian newspapers; their briefing room has Russian posters on the walls; the pilots learn how Russian pilots grow up, how they are trained, how they think; and in their planes, flying over wooden models of Russian tanks and trucks, they fly like Russian pilots. After each day's battle is over, they lecture the new pilots about the day's failures or successes and about Russian tactics.

Until Operation Red Flag began, American pilots finished their training by staging battles against other American pilots. But enemy pilots use different tactics, relying on radar rather than sight to spot the enemy, for example. Operation Red Flag ended all that. Now the training of American pilots is much more realistic. Computers and gun cameras record the battles for later analysis. Now a pilot can fly against an "enemy" and have a chance to learn from his mistakes—before the mistakes have become fatal.

▲ (290 WORDS) ▲

PASSAGE 3-1

Circle the correct answer:

1. The main idea of this passage is that
    a. learning to fly Russian MiGs is essential for American pilots.
    b. Operation Red Flag offers American pilots training under the same conditions they might encounter in a real battle.

c. the Air Force trains its pilots well.
   d. Russian pilots fly differently from American pilots.

2. According to the passage, which of the following statements is not true?
   a. Actual Russian MiGs are used in Operation Red Flag.
   b. Operation Red Flag is a training program for American pilots.
   c. Russian pilots rely heavily on radar to sight enemy planes.
   d. Operation Red Flag is carried out over the Nevada desert.

3. We can conclude from the passage that
   a. several pilots in Operation Red Flag have been killed because they made mistakes.
   b. most of the time allotted for Operation Red Flag is spent in lectures.
   c. Russia provides a similar program to train Russian pilots in American tactics.
   d. Operation Red Flag tries to make the program as realistic as possible.

4. The passage suggests that
   a. funds for Operation Red Flag have been cut back since the end of the cold war.
   b. the Air Force recruits only ex-Russian pilots for Operation Red Flag.
   c. classroom training and basic flying lessons are not enough to prepare a pilot for combat.
   d. Russian pilots are better fighters than American pilots.

5(a) As used in this passage, the word *tactics* means
   a. pilots
   b. maneuvers
   c. weapons
   d. planes

5(b) As used in this passage, the word *mock* means
   a. ridiculous
   b. scornful
   c. surreal
   d. simulated

5(c) As used in this passage, the word *fend* means
   a. invite
   b. survive
   c. pretend
   d. fight

5(d) As used in this passage, the word *impersonate* means
   a. domineer
   b. specify
   c. imitate
   d. trick

PASSAGE 3-2

SUBJECT: McDonald's

In 1939 two brothers, Mac and Dick McDonald, started a drive-in restaurant in San Bernadino, California. They carefully chose a busy corner for their location. They had run their own businesses for years, first a theater, then a barbecue restaurant, then another drive-in. But in their new operation, they offered a new, shortened menu: french fries, hamburgers, and sodas. To this minimal selection they added one new concept: quick service, no waiters or waitresses, and no tips.

Their hamburgers sold for fifteen cents. Cheese was another four cents. Their french fries and hamburgers had a remarkable uniformity, for the brothers had developed a strict routine for the preparation of their food, and they insisted on their cooks' sticking to their routine. Their new drive-in became incredibly popular, particularly for lunch. People drove up by the hundreds during the busy noontime. The self-service restaurant was so popular that the brothers had allowed ten copies of their restaurant to be opened. They were content with this modest success until they met Ray Kroc (krŏk).

Kroc was a salesman who met the McDonald brothers in 1954, when he was selling milkshake-mixing machines. He quickly saw the unique appeal of the brothers' fast-food restaurants and bought the right to franchise other copies of their restaurants. The agreement struck included the right to duplicate the menu, the equipment, even their red and white buildings with the golden arches.

Today McDonald's is literally a household name. Its names for its sandwiches have come to mean hamburger in the decades since the day Ray Kroc watched people rush up to order fifteen-cent hamburgers. In 1976, McDonald's had over $1 billion in total sales. Its first twenty-two years is one of the most incredible success stories in modern American business history.

▲ (292 WORDS) ▲

PASSAGE 3-2

Circle the correct answer:

1. This passage is mainly about
   a. the business careers of Mac and Dick McDonald.

b. how McDonald's became a billion-dollar business.
   c. Ray Kroc's business abilities.
   d. the development of fast-food services.

2. Mac and Dick McDonald had experience in managing all of the following businesses except
   a. a barbecue restaurant.
   b. a drive-in.
   c. an ice-cream parlor.
   d. a theater.

3. We can conclude from this passage that
   a. Mac and Dick McDonald never became wealthy because they sold their idea to Kroc.
   b. Ray Kroc was a good businessman.
   c. the location the McDonalds chose was the only source of the great popularity of their drive-in.
   d. forty years ago there were numerous fast-food restaurants.

4. The passage suggests that
   a. creativity is an important element of success.
   b. Ray Kroc spent long hours working in the first McDonald's.
   c. the McDonalds sold only fresh homegrown vegetables.
   d. California is the best place to go into business.

5(a) As used in this passage, the word *minimal* means
   a. attractive
   b. menial
   c. basic
   d. novel

5(b) As used in this passage, the word *uniformity* means
   a. flavor
   b. success
   c. consistency
   d. appeal

5(c) As used in this passage, the word *unique* means
   a. aesthetic
   b. financial
   c. ethnic
   d. unparalleled

5(d) As used in this passage, the word *franchise* means
   a. a privilege
   b. authorization granted by a distributor
   c. a statutory right
   d. a constitutional right

PASSAGE 3-3 SUBJECT: The Madrid (mə drĭd′) Fault

Everyone has heard of the San Andreas (săn ăn drā′ ɔs) fault, which constantly threatens California and the West Coast with earthquakes. But how many people know about the equally serious New Madrid fault in Missouri?

Between December of 1811 and February of 1812, three major earthquakes occurred, all centered around the town of New Madrid, Missouri, on the Mississippi River. Property damage was severe. Buildings in the area were almost all destroyed. Whole forests fell at once, and huge cracks opened in the ground, allowing the odor of sulfur to filter upward.

The Mississippi River itself completely changed character, developing sudden rapids and whirlpools. Several times it changed its course, and once, according to some observers, it actually appeared to run backwards. Few people were killed in the New Madrid earthquakes, probably simply because few people lived in the area in 1811; but the severity of the earthquakes are shown by the fact that the shock waves rang bells in church towers in Charleston, South Carolina, on the coast. Buildings shook in New York City, and clocks were stopped in Washington, D.C.

Scientists now know that America's two major faults are essentially different. The San Andreas fault is a horizontal boundary between two major land masses that are slowly moving in opposite directions. California earthquakes result when the movement of these two masses suddenly lurches forward.

The New Madrid fault, on the other hand, is a vertical fault; at some point, possibly hundreds of millions of years ago, rock was pushed up toward the surface, probably by volcanoes under the surface. Suddenly, the volcanoes cooled and the rock collapsed, leaving huge cracks. Even now, the rock continues to settle downwards, and sudden sinking motions trigger earthquakes in the region. The fault itself, a large crack in this layer of rock, with dozens of other cracks that split off from it, extends from northeast Arkansas through Missouri and into southern Illinois.

Scientists who have studied the New Madrid fault say there have been numerous smaller quakes in the area since 1811; these smaller quakes indicate that larger ones are probably coming, but the scientists say they have no method of predicting when a large earthquake will occur.

▲ (364 WORDS) ▲

PASSAGE 3-3

Circle the correct answer:

1. This passage is *mainly* about
    a. the San Andreas and the New Madrid faults.
    b. the New Madrid fault in Missouri.
    c. the causes of faults.
    d. current scientific knowledge about faults.

2. The New Madrid fault is
    a. responsible for forming the Mississippi River.
    b. a horizontal fault.
    c. a worse fault than the San Andreas fault.
    d. a vertical fault.

3. We can conclude from the passage that
    a. it is probably as dangerous to live in Missouri as in California.
    b. the New Madrid fault will eventually develop a mountain range in Missouri.
    c. in the future California will become an island.
    d. California will be broken into small pieces by an eventual earthquake.

4. The passage suggests that
    a. earthquakes occur only around fault areas.
    b. horizontal faults are more dangerous than vertical faults.
    c. vertical faults are more dangerous than horizontal faults.
    d. faults are cracks in the earth's surface caused by past movement of the earth's land masses.

5. As used in this passage, the word *essentially* means
    a. basically
    b. dangerously
    c. slightly
    d. frighteningly

PASSAGE 3-4

SUBJECT:
Opinion Polls

One presidential candidate has just taken a poll of public opinion, and he says he has a 6 percent lead over his opponent; the other candidate, though, has <u>commissioned</u> his own survey, and he publicizes results that show him with a four-point lead over the other candidates if the election were taken tomorrow. Whom do you believe? Should you, in fact, believe the results of either poll?

Standards for interpretation of opinion polls are difficult to come by because, so far, the polling industry regulates itself. There are two organizations that try to assure that only reliable polls are used to survey opinion. The first, the <u>American Association for Public Opinion Research</u> (AAPOR), now has over one thousand members. The AAPOR asks its members to pledge that they will not report misleading facts or run polls just to prove some client's point. The second group, the <u>National Council on Public Polls</u> (NCPP), was founded in 1969 to stop abuses of the polling process. The NCPP hopes to teach the public how to use its polls. The members of NCPP swear always to disclose data that are needed for current understanding of the results. Polls conducted by NCPP members are always accompanied by copies of the questions asked as the poll was taken and also the names of the people who asked that the survey be taken. Moreover, these polls report the number of people who answered the questions and the date on which they answered them and the method by which each person was contacted.

A well-informed public should be <u>reluctant</u> to interpret results of these surveys; always ask yourself, "Who is reporting this poll?" If the results are positive, who is benefiting from the publicity? And, more importantly, look for the date on which the poll was taken. Only recent information is valuable; an ex-manager of ABC news claims that the public can completely change its opinions on an issue in less than a day.

▲ (377 WORDS) ▲

PASSAGE 3-4

Circle the correct answer:

1. The main idea of this passage is that
   a. the AAPOR attempts to control the taking of polls so that the public can rely on the results.

b. political figures seldom misuse the data provided them by surveys.
   c. the results of a survey or poll are worthless unless the reader knows something of the conditions and methods used in the poll.
   d. the NCPP attempts to ensure honest reporting of opinion poll results.

2. According to the passage, which of the following statements is not true?
   a. Standards for the interpretation of opinion polls are difficult to obtain.
   b. The NCPP is more successful at controlling the polls taken by its members than is the AAPOR.
   c. The public should always be wary of poll results until they have studied them very carefully.
   d. The NCPP was founded in 1969.

3. We can conclude from the passage that
   a. most presidential polls are reliable.
   b. the AAPOR and the NCPP have eliminated the reporting of misleading statistics.
   c. presidential polls are less reliable than other polls.
   d. polls must be closely controlled if they are to be of use to the public.

4. The passage suggests that
   a. people will use polls to mislead the public.
   b. political candidates cannot be trusted.
   c. all polls are unreliable because the survey of a poll is biased to prove the point of the poll's clients.
   d. older surveys are more reliable than the more recent ones.

5(a) As used in this passage, the word *commissioned* means
   a. invented
   b. doubted
   c. authorized
   d. sold

5(b) As used in this passage, the word *data* means
   a. finances
   b. persons
   c. confusion
   d. information

5(c) As used in this passage, the word *reluctant* means
   a. eager
   b. impossible
   c. unable
   d. hesitant

PASSAGE 3-5   SUBJECT:
Cheating on Job Applications

You're busy filling out the application form for a position you really need; let's assume you once actually completed a couple of years of college work or even that you completed your degree. Isn't it tempting to lie just a little, to claim on the form that your diploma represents a Harvard degree? Or that you finished an extra couple of years back at State University?

More and more people are resorting to outright deception like this to land their first job or to move ahead in their careers, for personnel officers, like most Americans, value degrees from prestige schools. A job applicant may have a good education anyway, but he or she assumes that chances of being hired are better with a diploma from a well-known university. Registrars at most well-known colleges say they deal with fraudulent claims like these at the rate of about one per week.

Personnel officers do check up on degrees listed on application forms, then. If it turns out that an applicant is lying, most colleges are reluctant to accuse the applicant directly. One Ivy League school calls them "impostors"; another refers to them as "special cases." One well-known West Coast school, in perhaps the most delicate phrase of all, says that these claims are made by "no such people."

To avoid outright lies, some job-seekers claim that they "attended" or "were associated with" a college or university. After carefully checking, a personnel officer may discover that "attending" means flunking out after one semester. It may be that "being associated with" a college means that the job-seeker visited his younger brother for a football weekend. One school that keeps records of false claims says that the practice dates back at least to the turn of the century—that's when they began keeping records, anyhow.

If you don't want to lie or even stretch the truth, there are companies that will sell you a phony diploma. One company, with offices in New York and on the West Coast, will put your name on a diploma from any number of nonexistent colleges. The price begins at around twenty dollars for a diploma from "Smoot State University." The prices increase rapidly for a degree from the "University of Purdue." As there is no Smoot State and the real school in Indiana is properly called Purdue University, the prices seem rather high for one sheet of paper.

▲ (399 WORDS) ▲

PASSAGE 3-5

Circle the correct answer:

1. The main idea of this passage is that
   a. employers are checking more closely on applicants now.
   b. lying about college credentials has become a widespread problem.
   c. bogus college degrees can now be purchased through the mail.
   d. employers are no longer impressed by college degrees because they can't be sure they're authentic.

2. According to the passage, "special cases" refers to
   a. students who attended a school only part-time.
   b. students who never attended a school they listed on their application.
   c. students who attended a prestigious school as transient students.
   d. students who purchase phony degrees from commercial firms.

3. We can conclude from the passage that
   a. performance is a better judge of ability than is a college degree.
   b. experience is the best teacher.
   c. a degree from a prestigious school gives an applicant the "edge" in job competition.
   d. past work histories influence personnel officers more than degrees do.

4. The passage suggests that
   a. buying a bogus degree is immoral.
   b. personnel officers only consider applicants from prestigious schools.
   c. most people lie on applications because they failed out of college.
   d. society is largely responsible for the practice of lying on applications.

5(a) As used in this passage, the word *fraudulent* means
   a. actual
   b. amorphous
   c. deceptive
   d. diabolical

5(b) As used in this passage, the word *delicate* means
   a. careless
   b. subtle
   c. indecisive
   d. ridiculous

PASSAGE 3-6

SUBJECT: Vitamin C

Vitamin C, or ascorbic (ə skôr′ bǐk) acid, is found in fruits, in salad greens, and in many vegetables such as tomatoes and cabbage. Some foods, such as eggs, cheese, or cereals, contain no vitamin C. For animals, eating these foods would cause no problems because most animals can produce ascorbic acid from their own bodies. But humans must obtain this vitamin from their diets—and they cannot store ascorbic acid.

This extremely important vitamin is used in maintaining blood vessels, bones, and teeth. If a human cannot obtain enough vitamin C, the deficiency causes scurvy (skûr′ vē), a general weakening of the body that can result in hemorrhages (hĕm′ ə rĭj ĕz) and eventual death. But this disease was understood long ago and is extremely rare in the United States.

Vitamin C may play a role in the prevention of colds, though there is very little agreement on this. Linus Pauling, a Nobel Prize-winning Ph.D., published a very popular book on the subject, *Vitamin C and the Common Cold,* which claimed that proper dosages of vitamin C both prevented and reduced the severity of cold symptoms. But most dietitians and doctors do not agree with Pauling. Studies that have been made have been inconclusive. Dr. Pauling has been proven neither right nor wrong by studies using groups taking vitamin C and groups taking inactive substances. The vitamin C groups appear to have fewer colds and colds that last for fewer days. For example, Navaho (Nă′ və hō) schoolchildren who took vitamin C supplements had 26 percent fewer days of illness than children who did not take the supplement, but the effect of the vitamin C seems to be less significant with older children.

Researchers are not anxious to claim that everyone should start taking vitamin C because very little is known about the effects of taking in too much ascorbic acid. One researcher claims that too much vitamin C causes scurvy, just like the scurvy caused by a vitamin C deficiency. Other possible side effects may be the formation of kidney stones or liver disease. In addition, high levels of vitamin C may make the diagnosis of diabetes or liver disease impossible. Until more is known about vitamin C, the best thing for the average person to do is to wait for expert opinion to settle on one side of the issue or the other. And—though it's dull and familiar-sounding advice—the least risky source of most vitamins is a balanced diet.

▲ (401 WORDS) ▲

PASSAGE 3-6

Circle the correct answer:

1. The main idea of this passage is that
   a. Navaho children benefit from vitamin C supplements.
   b. vitamin C can act as a deterrent to the common cold.
   c. vitamin C is harmful and should be avoided in supplement form.
   d. there is no consensus on the benefits of high-level doses of vitamin C.

2. Vitamin C is found in all of the following foods except
   a. salad greens
   b. cereal
   c. tomatoes
   d. cabbage

3. Which of the following conclusions does the passage support?
   a. Vitamin C taken in through a balanced diet is the only prevention of scurvy.
   b. Animals need more vitamin C than humans.
   c. The known disadvantages outweigh the known advantages of vitamin C supplements.
   d. Navaho Indian children suffer from vitamin C deficiencies.

4. The passage suggests that
   a. Dr. Pauling used biased data in his study.
   b. vitamin C can be used to control colds.
   c. people don't fully understand the human body's reaction to vitamin C.
   d. vitamin C's effect on the common cold is mostly psychological.

5(a) As used in this passage, the word *deficiency* means
   a. incompleteness
   b. insufficiency
   c. desert
   d. disease

5(b) As used in this passage, the word *inconclusive* means
   a. indecisive
   b. inaccurate
   c. successful
   d. encouraging

PASSAGE 3-7   SUBJECT:
Matinicus (mă tĭn′ ĭ cŭs) Island

The rocky, tiny islands off the coast of Maine attract a particular kind of people. The population of these islands triples or quadruples in the summer, but in the winter, only the very independent, self-reliant types remain.

Matinicus is an island one mile wide and two and a half miles long. There are only forty-five winter residents. After the tourists have gone, many of the year-round residents gather for conversation at the island's post office and store—located at the only traffic light on the island, at the intersection of two gravel roads. People on Matinicus don't stay home to watch television—though reception on the island is excellent. There are no central electric utility lines, so each home uses a diesel generator as a power supply. Diesel fuel is expensive, so the residents are very careful about their use of electricity.

Most of the winter people are fishermen, lobstermen, storeowners, and their families. They still enjoy a way of life largely the same as life in the early twentieth century. Women knit and get together to visit and talk while sewing clothes; children read or play games together because their television viewing is limited. There are only six children on the island in the winter, so they all attend a one-room schoolhouse, where grades one through eight are taught by one teacher.

The most common method of transportation is the mail ferry; it comes to the island every day in the summer, but in the winter it only stops at Matinicus twice a week. Because everything must be shipped to Matinicus by ferry, many goods, such as school supplies, are quite scarce; and the goods that are in good supply are more expensive than on the mainland, for the expense of ferrying them is added by the storekeepers. All fuel averages ten cents a gallon more on Matinicus, so most of the islanders use wood to heat their houses. The spruce on the island doesn't burn well, though, so the winter people pay from $90 to $150 for a load of wood to be delivered.

The one form of transportation faster than the ferry is the Coast Guard helicopter. In an emergency such as an accident or sudden illness, the helicopter can reach the island in a little less than half an hour. Other islands are more <u>accessible</u>, of course; Vinalhaven (vĭ′ nŭl hā vĕn) and Peaks are very short ferry rides away from the mainland, and Peaks is even within the city limits of Portland. But most of the tiny islands are like Matinicus and its sister island Monhegan (mŏn hē′ găn), miles away from the mainland. They offer a <u>secluded</u>, hardy life that the winter people love—few ever leave these islands.

▲ (448 WORDS) ▲

PASSAGE 3-7

Circle the correct answer:

1. This passage is mainly about
    a. the economy of Matinicus Island.
    b. life-style on Matinicus Island.
    c. tourism on Matinicus Island.
    d. life-styles in New England.

2. Many of the winter people are
    a. storekeepers
    b. tourists
    c. retired
    d. teachers

3. We can conclude from this passage that
    a. children dislike living on the island.
    b. tourism is destroying the charm of Matinicus Island.
    c. the people of Matinicus Island prefer a quiet rural life.
    d. the children don't get a very good education.

4. The passage suggests that
    a. there are no cars on the island.
    b. there is no paved road leading to the island.
    c. television reception is poor on the island.
    d. the residents gather their firewood on the island.

5(a) As used in this passage, the word *accessible* means
    a. distant
    b. populated
    c. easily approached
    d. entertaining

5(b) As used in this passage, the word *secluded* means
    a. crowded
    b. carefree
    c. isolated
    d. dull

PASSAGE 3-8

SUBJECT:
Henry Kissinger

Henry Kissinger may be the most successful, certainly the most flamboyant, secretary of state to hold that office in modern times. When he was appointed in the late 1960s, there were no American ties with Communist China, Vietnam and Berlin seemed ready to draw the United States into a third world war, and Russia was seen as "the enemy."

But all this has changed, and Henry Kissinger caused much of that change; in 1971, he made his first trip to China, a trip that was the beginning of the current ties between the United States and China. He brought the United States and Russia closer together on major issues by the policy he called "détente," literally meaning a relaxation. His philosophy was always to talk and to bring together. With these two policies, Kissinger did much to draw attention away from any possible Russian-American friction.

In 1973 he made his first visit to Egypt. Here he was able to begin U.S. relations with Egypt. He used this contact later to begin the sort of talks that the American press called "shuttle diplomacy." For ninety-nine days, he "shuttled" back and forth on flights between Cairo and Jerusalem to work out a step-by-step withdrawal of Israeli troops from the Sinai desert. His wit, his careful approach to detail, and his presence made "shuttle diplomacy" work. It was the only successful approach to Mideast peace in the thirty years since the state of Israel was founded.

Another major work was the Strategic Arms Limitation Talk. Though his term in office passed with the treaty unsigned, Kissinger left a draft of the treaty to which the Russians had already agreed. The SALT treaty spelled out a one-tenth reduction in nuclear arms, a major accomplishment by any standard, even if one does not consider all the other conditions and limitations included in the treaty.

Even though he successfully helped bring an end to the Vietnam War, Kissinger's final days in office were affected, as was the entire executive branch in one way or another, by the scandals of the Nixon White House. Kissinger's critics point to his role in placing wiretaps on the phones of reporters and officials and to what they consider his "high-handed" approach to setting foreign policy. But Kissinger, during the last few months of the Nixon presidency, limited the effects of American domestic problems on our foreign policy. He continued talks in the Middle East. He continued close contact with the Soviet Union.

History will decide in the final view, as Kissinger—and many presidents—often said, on the value of his service. Whatever they decide, whether his actions are finally to be considered wise or foolish, he had a personal vision that will be difficult to match.

▲ (459 WORDS) ▲

PASSAGE 3-8

Circle the correct answer:

1. The main idea of this passage is that
   a. Kissinger helped smooth out the trying times of Watergate.
   b. Kissinger was very influential in American foreign policy.
   c. peace in the Middle East would have been impossible without Kissinger.
   d. Kissinger helped end the cold war with Russia.

2. Kissinger's version of the SALT treaty was most important because
   a. it spelled out a one-tenth reduction in nuclear arms.
   b. the Russians had already agreed to it.
   c. it set a standard for nuclear missile development.
   d. it effectively halted the proliferation of nuclear weapons in nonaligned countries.

3. We can conclude from the passage that
   a. "shuttle diplomacy" greatly affected the SALT treaty.
   b. Watergate made Kissinger ineffective.
   c. some of the things that Kissinger began are still being worked out.
   d. Kissinger was not a humanitarian.

4(a) The passage suggests that
   a. Kissinger was driven by ego.
   b. Kissinger was unsuccessful in bringing about peace in the Middle East.
   c. Kissinger significantly altered the direction of international relationships.
   d. Kissinger was more important than the president during the Nixon administration.

4(b) Which of the following words best describes the author's tone in this passage?
   a. objectivity
   b. indifference
   c. contempt
   d. admiration

5(a) As used in this passage, the word *flamboyant* means
   a. showy

    b. intelligent
    c. famous
    d. revered

5(b) As used in this passage, the word *detail* means
    a. the individual parts of the whole
    b. the outline
    c. protocol
    d. emotions

PASSAGE 3-9

SUBJECT: Women Pilots

Don't be surprised if your next airline flight is piloted by a woman. In this traditionally male occupation, women are beginning to be regularly accepted.

In the years since World War II, more women than ever before have entered the labor force. Experts say social trends such as later marriage, high divorce rates, and better schooling for women may be responsible. Other people claim more practical reasons such as inflation, higher housing costs, and other economic reasons. But, of course, one very important reason women are working in greater numbers may be a search for self-fulfillment.

Flying for a commercial airline offers this self-fulfillment to women. Airline pilots are highly trained, highly paid professionals whose jobs offer a great deal of pride. There are 34,000 male pilots for U.S. airlines, and by 1978 there were only about 80 women pilots. But the number of women pilots is doubling every year. Many major airlines are aware of their need to hire women and minority pilots and are actively recruiting women for their training programs.

Most male pilots received their training during military service. Many female pilots, on the other hand, learned to fly in school or college. Some originally trained to serve as hostesses, but other female pilots come from more varied backgrounds. Claudia Jones, a pilot for Continental, learned to fly to take her musical group to club dates. One female pilot's first job after college was transporting corpses for a mortician.

Though airlines are searching for women pilots, they are very selective when choosing. Women pilots are every bit as qualified to fly as any male, and many passengers seem to prefer women pilots at the controls. Male pilots are generally in favor of women's breaking into the field. One's skills are the most important characteristic that other pilots are interested in.

Emily Warner, who flies with Frontier, was the first female to assume full command of a commercial airline in 1973. The ladder to command of a plane is a long one. Male and female pilots generally are assigned to a plane as second officers when first hired; a second officer is allowed to fly the plane, but generally doesn't, and must wait one to several years before becoming a first officer, or copilot. Warner sidestepped this problem by choosing Frontier, which flies smaller planes that require only two people in the cockpit.

So, though most women in the labor market—like most men—enter the job market for low-paying jobs, women are being accepted in one of the most glamorous jobs available. Between 1960 and 1977, the percentage of accountants who are female rose from 17 to 28 percent. The percentage of medical doctors who are women increased from 7 to 11 percent, and the number of female lawyers and judges rose from 4 to 10 percent. The airlines may be lagging behind in their hiring of women pilots, but there are many more women being trained now or working their way up through the ranks to take the controls of airliners.

▲ (506 WORDS) ▲

PASSAGE 3-9

Circle the correct answer:

1. The main idea of this passage is that
   a. women are not as qualified to be pilots as men are.
   b. women are now entering the airline pilot field in increasing numbers.
   c. women are now seeking employment in high-paying professions.
   d. women have more chance for promotion with smaller airlines.

2. Which of the following statements is true?
   a. There are 34,000 female pilots for U.S. airlines.
   b. Emily Warner was the first female to assume full command of a commercial airliner.
   c. In 1960, 28 percent of all accountants were female.
   d. In 1977, 7 percent of all medical doctors were female.

3. We can conclude from the passage that
   a. it is easier to become a first officer with a smaller airline than with a larger one.
   b. women are restricted from becoming first officers by most large airlines.
   c. most women are hired as assistant second officers.
   d. women are better pilots than men are.

4. The passage suggests that
   a. the percentage of women holding jobs in the higher-paying professions is on the decline.
   b. the percentage of women holding jobs in the higher-paying professions is remaining stable.
   c. some high-paying professions are now dominated by women.
   d. the percentage of women holding jobs in the higher-paying professions is on the increase.

5. As used in this passage, the word *lagging* means
   a. falling
   b. proudly
   c. purposely delaying
   d. not keeping pace

PASSAGE 3-10   SUBJECT:
Quarter Horses

The quarter horse is the world's most popular horse. Each year there are over 2,000 quarter horse shows held in the United States. In fact, over 400,000 Americans own quarter horses.

    The quarter horse is an extremely versatile horse. Apparently bred from English horses brought to America in colonial days, the quarter horse is considered a "light horse." The American Quarter Horse Association sponsors competitions for these horses in three areas. They are raced, they are shown, and they take part in cutting competitions.

    The cutting competition is most similar to a horse's daily work on a ranch. A horse separates a cow out of a herd and then prevents the cow from returning to the herd for a specified period of time. To perform well, the horse must continually block the cow, wheel around quickly and head the cow off, and herd the cow from side to side. One reason this event is popular with spectators is that the horse does this without any human direction; the rider is doing only that—riding. Judges penalize riders who signal their horses or who control the reins, so the animal must be intelligent and surefooted.

    When away from competition, champion cutting horses can earn their keep on the ranch because herds of cattle are constantly being driven from one place to another. One cow or another is constantly being cut from a herd for taking to market, branding, or "doctoring." The quarter horse is uniquely suited to this sort of quick, athletic work, yet still can stand the daily routine of hard labor. For generations, cowboys have used the quarter horse for cutting, roping, and for traveling the vast distances required for roundups on the giant ranches of cattle country. Quarter horses are light, compact, but tremendously strong; they are quick, intelligent, and fantastically well balanced; quarter horses stand with their legs gathered beneath them, ready to spring in any direction.

    By 1940 the quarter horse became an official breed when the AQHA was founded to keep track of the pedigrees. The first secretary of the association kept all the horses' records in a filing cabinet in his bedroom; six years later the records filled a half-ton truck when the association moved its headquarters to Amarillo, Texas. Now the association has 240 full-time workers helping to manage the records and activities. Their next project is a Hall of Fame and library adjoining the AQHA main offices.

    Quarter horses may be shown or raced, but it is as cutting horses that they are actually most popular. Watching a cutting horse as it anticipates the moves of a cow or a herd shows the spectator a bit of what work on the ranch was actually like. The horse actually develops this ability from experience on the range, working daily with cattle. As the horse stops and turns and starts again, one can actually see the horse making judgments from its experience. This judgment and the horse's performance in the arena and on the ranch are the guides to the value of a cutting horse.

▲ (511 WORDS) ▲

PASSAGE 3-10

Circle the correct answer:

1. The main purpose of this passage is to
    a. discuss quarter horses.
    b. discuss the origin of the cutting horse.
    c. describe cutting horse competitions.
    d. discuss the uses of quarter horses on a ranch.

2. The quarter horse was bred
    a. in England.
    b. by the AQHA.
    c. for show competition.
    d. in America, from English stock.

3. We can conclude from the passage that
    a. in 1930 the quarter horse was not an official breed.
    b. quarter horses respond well to verbal directions.
    c. quarter horses are too slow for racing.
    d. quarter horses can't stand hard labor.

4. The passage suggests that
    a. quarter horses are temperamental.
    b. quarter horses memorize their routines for competition.
    c. quarter horses apply experience to new situations.
    d. a quarter horse can only do what its rider directs it to do.

5(a) As used in this passage, the word *versatile* means
    a. virile
    b. adaptable
    c. beautiful
    d. temperamental

5(b) As used in this passage, the word *pedigrees* means
    a. training
    b. owners
    c. lineage
    d. competitions

PASSAGE 3-11

SUBJECT: Robert E. Lee

During the Civil War itself, from 1861 to 1865, Robert E. Lee was not the idol of the Southern people at all. Stonewall Jackson, partly because of his courageous exploits and partly because of the image summoned up by his name, was far more popular with the Confederate masses. Lee's first few biographers, who wrote between 1865 and 1870, emphasized his military errors. In fact, they blamed Lee for his own defeat at Gettysburg, which most of them claimed cost the South the war.

Lee was far from a hero. He was born into a debt-ridden family. For all his fabled love for Virginia, he never owned a single ounce of her soil. His early educational career was hindered by his duty to care for his family, but he attended West Point and graduated in 1829 with distinction. In 1831 he married well, but his marriage often brought him sadness and depression. His wife became chronically ill, essentially an invalid, and his jobs in the army often caused long separations.

Except for one short tour of service as a reconnaissance officer in the war with Mexico, Lee's career was dull, and he was slow to be promoted. As an officer in the engineer corps, he served at Savannah, Georgia; at St. Louis; at Washington; at Long Island; and finally at San Antonio. Even after he became a colonel, Lee's pay was only $4,000 a year. He despised the system of political favoritism, which brought quicker promotions, so he watched many capable officers leave the service. W. T. Sherman left to become a banker; U. S. Grant left the army to farm in Missouri; George McClellan became a bank executive. Lee served thirty years in the regular army before the outbreak of the Civil War, but he was unknown outside a small circle of professional soldiers. In fact, he was not highly thought of even in Virginia.

But the war changed all that. As happens with many defeated leaders, his image actually improved after losing a great war. He came to represent the perfect Southern gentleman, much more so than the Confederacy's political leader, Jefferson Davis. By 1885, Lee had become an idol. By the turn of the century Lee's birthday had become a Southern regional holiday, a day of commemoration for both Lee and the fallen South. President Roosevelt and President Wilson praised Lee for his intelligence and his conduct in defeat after the war. President Coolidge even struck a new coin to help construct a massive monument to Lee in Atlanta.

Legends grew up about Lee in the years before his death. He was supposed to have rescued a fledgling bird under enemy fire in a Civil War battle. He became an invincible military commander, a great thinker, a perfect man of absolute integrity. His popularity threatened at one point to be greater than Washington's, and some Lee admirers even dared compare his behavior to that of Christ.

Lee was, in fact, a man of irreproachable character, and he was a magnificent military thinker. Some of his campaigns were incredibly successful, but his mistakes have been explained away. The legend has it that he could have won the war for the South if a jealous Davis had not hampered him; possibly he could have. One thing, though, is certain: Robert E. Lee, whatever would have happened to him in victory, became the noble image of the destroyed, aristocratic, even mythic South in defeat.

▲ (575 WORDS) ▲

PASSAGE 3-11

Circle the correct answer:

1(a) A good title for this passage might be
    a. Robert E. Lee: Myth and Fact
    b. The Civil War
    c. The Fallen South
    d. Robert E. Lee's Military Strategy

1(b) The main idea of this passage is that
    a. in reality Robert E. Lee was ill-fitted for his job as Southern commander during the Civil War.
    b. Robert E. Lee's military career was destroyed by his alliance with the South during the Civil War.
    c. Stonewall Jackson was a better military strategist than Lee.
    d. a lot of the current feelings about Robert E. Lee are based on myths that developed about Lee after the Civil War.

2. Which of the following leaders did not leave the military because of the system of political favoritism?
    a. W. T. Sherman
    b. U. S. Grant
    c. Jefferson Davis
    d. all of the above

3. We can conclude from the passage that
    a. had Jackson been the commander of the Southern forces, the South might have won the Civil War.
    b. without his involvement in the Civil War, Lee's military career might have continued to be uneventful.
    c. the South lost the Civil War because Davis always approved Lee's strategies for battles.
    d. Robert E. Lee stayed in the army while his colleagues were leaving for civilian jobs because of his fear of failure.

4(a) Which of the following statements would the author most likely support?
   a. Robert E. Lee was a man of mediocre ability who rose to fame because of the circumstances surrounding him.
   b. Robert E. Lee should have replaced Jefferson Davis as president of the Confederacy.
   c. Robert E. Lee was too gentle a personality for the tasks thrust on him by the Civil War.
   d. Robert E. Lee was inept at military strategy and didn't deserve all the fame he achieved.

4(b) The author's tone is
   a. negative
   b. objective
   c. humorous
   d. sarcastic

5(a) As used in this passage, the word *chronically* means
   a. timely
   b. sporadically
   c. emotionally
   d. continually

5(b) As used in this passage, the word *commemoration* means
   a. shame
   b. remembrance
   c. sympathy
   d. exultation

PASSAGE 3-12

SUBJECT:
Brass Rubbing

In England and in Europe during the early medieval period, most aristocrats and nobles were buried inside their church. The size of aristocrats' graves and the decoration of their surfaces became symbols of status, but for 500 years the most popular status symbol was to commission an image of oneself carved to cover one's grave. Flat sheets of brass, about a half-inch thick, covered the graves, which might be six feet long or shorter; and on these covers of brass were carved representations of the dead, or of the dead and their families.

One of the most popular amateur art forms in Europe and America are rubbings of these brass gravestones. A rubbing is created by the same process children use to rub coins, by placing a sheet of paper over a coin and then rubbing the paper with a pencil to create the image of Washington or Jefferson. A brass rubber uses black, white, or blue paper; the "heel ball" or crayon used instead of a pencil is a wax and may contain lampblack or metallic dye to color the paper. The results are beautiful and inexpensive; many collectors take vacations in Europe and England to add to their collections of brass rubbings.

So popular is the hobby that many of the more popular brass gravestones in England are in danger of being worn smooth. Many stones have been restricted, so that only professional members of brass societies may rub them. Many of the brass stones have been copied, so that amateurs can use the duplicates to take rubbings. Although the duplicates are very detailed and provide quite beautiful rubbings, these second generation rubbings are not really collector's items.

Because there is such a huge demand for rubbings, even the duplicates are now constantly copied. In Westminster Abbey in London, hundreds of people make reservations to copy the brasses every day. For some of the more popular stones, people waited for hours to get the chance to take a rubbing. Even with several duplicates available, crowds are enormous.

A rubbing taken from an original stone has a certificate, often a handwritten statement on the back; this certificate identifies the subject and the church in which the rubbing was taken.

Parliament has long considered the rubbing of original stones to be a threat to national treasures and monuments and has long considered a law restricting all brass rubbings to professionals. Some suggest that all brass rubbing of original stones should be made illegal. The people would have to content themselves with rubbings from the duplicates.

In the meantime, one of the most popular brasses that can still be rubbed covers the grave of Sir Thomas Bullen (bŏŏl′lĕn). Bullen was the grandfather of Queen Elizabeth and the father of Anne Boleyn (bō' lĭn), the second wife of Henry the Eighth; his gravestone, an enormous one, represents Sir Thomas dressed in full armor and cloak. His effigy wears the medal and the Order of the Garter; at its feet are an eagle and griffin, symbols of his family. A rubbing of Sir Thomas Bullen's gravestone is nearly six feet long when it is framed.

If access to brasses like the Bullen gravestone is restricted by Parliament, the rubbings that have already been taken would suddenly increase in value. But it is difficult to believe that collectors look on their rubbings as investments. Taking a rubbing is much like creating your own work of art, but more important, probably, is the sense of touching history enjoyed by each brass rubber.

▲ (588 WORDS) ▲

PASSAGE 3-12

Circle the correct answer:

1. The main purpose of this passage is to
   a. describe the art of brass rubbing.
   b. discuss the financial advantages of collecting brass rubbings.
   c. discuss the burial customs during the medieval period.
   d. discuss the need for legislation restricting brass rubbing.

2(a) Which of the following statements is not true?
   a. Grave decorations were status symbols in the medieval period.
   b. Brass rubbing is a popular amateur art form.
   c. Second generation rubbings are collector's items.
   d. Sir Thomas Bullen was the grandfather of Queen Elizabeth.

2(b) Which of the following items is not a tool used in brass rubbing?
   a. a "heel ball"
   b. black, white, and blue paper
   c. flat sheets of brass
   d. crayon

3. We can conclude from the passage that
   a. the English government wants to charge people for brass rubbings.
   b. brass rubbing can eventually deface the original brass stones.
   c. the English fear tourism will drop because of an overabundance of brass rubbings.
   d. only professionals do brass rubbings.

4. The passage suggests that
   a. amateurs are defacing the brass stones with sharp instruments.

b. brass rubbing is the most popular hobby in England.
   c. rubbings made from duplicates are as desirable as those made from the original brass stones.
   d. the prices of brass rubbings are affected by supply and demand.

5(a) As used in this passage, the word *status* means
   a. social position
   b. solidity
   c. strength
   d. tradition

5(b) As used in this passage, the word *effigy* means
   a. armor
   b. rubbing
   c. casket
   d. image

PASSAGE 3-13

SUBJECT:
Salmon

Fishermen enjoy catching an Atlantic salmon, a silvery, fork-tailed fish that looks rather like an overgrown trout. Salmon, when hooked, put on a brilliant struggle; they run rapidly with line and tumble upward out of the water, flipping to disengage the hook. It may take half an hour of expert handling of a rod and reel to overcome a fully matured salmon, and very frequently the fish will escape. Because of the thrill of landing a salmon and because really big salmon are rare, many a fisherman's top-of-the-evening fish story revolves around the time he landed—or missed—an Atlantic salmon. The fine taste of the salmon no doubt adds to their value; because their clean, pink salmon steaks have such a rich, distinct flavor, fresh salmon sells for outrageous prices.

Biologists are as fascinated by the salmon as fishermen are. After decades of studying the salmon's life cycle, biologists recognize that they know plenty about the fish, but many details are yet to be discovered. And, as with many life cycles, the salmon's life is too complex for man to be very successful at artificially increasing the salmon's numbers.

Atlantic salmon are hatched in freshwater rivers that flow into the Atlantic Ocean. The salmon remain in freshwater rivers precisely two years, feeding constantly until they are about nine inches long; when they attain this size, they begin swimming downriver. The trip downriver is a rugged journey, taking a heavy toll on the immature salmon; many are caught by predators including men and bears, before reaching the ocean. Those that survive the journey and make it to the Atlantic swim far out to the shallow banks around the island of Greenland, where they feed for two or three years, growing sometimes to weights of twenty pounds or more.

At the age of four or five, the salmon return to their original hatching grounds to spawn. Scientists cannot explain why they return, nor can they explain why all salmon return at once—in fact, no one knows how the salmon locate the mouth of freshwater rivers to swim back upstream to hatching areas, but they do. Unless the salmon are caught by fishermen or other predators, unless they come to an obstruction impossible to leap over (most salmon can leap about five feet), the salmon swim to the headwaters, spawn, and return to the ocean again.

Despite the unrelenting urge that drives the salmon and despite the salmon's "courage," this cycle is a fragile one. In the early nineteenth century, for instance, the Connecticut River was full of these fish, but the last one was caught in 1874. The modern world humans created had wrecked the salmon's environment. Power dams were built that kept the fish from swimming upstream to their spawning grounds. The flow of the river became uneven—possibly confusing the fish—and industries dumped pollution into the Connecticut, along with hot waste water that made the river impossible for the fish. The Atlantic salmon disappeared from the Connecticut River, and they disappeared from almost all the New England waterways.

Officials for four states banded together to return the salmon to the Connecticut River. In 1967, they began building ladders alongside the power dams to allow the fish to jump over the dams a few feet at a time. Industries along the river were pressured by various agencies to control both the temperature and the waste being dumped into the river. The dams were more carefully regulated to maintain even flow and level in the river. Hatchery salmon were dumped into the headwaters of the river each year while everyone waited to see if the fish would return. Finally, in 1977, a schoolboy caught an eight-pound salmon in the Connecticut River. Humans had been able to restore the Atlantic salmon to its natural habitat.

▲ (637 WORDS) ▲

PASSAGE 3-13

Circle the correct answer:

1(a) The purpose of this passage is to
   a. discuss the life cycle of the salmon.
   b. discuss the Atlantic salmon.
   c. discuss the spawning habits of the salmon.
   d. discuss the restocking of salmon into freshwater rivers.

1(b) A good title for this passage might be
   a. The Spawning Habits of Salmon
   b. Save the Salmon!
   c. Common Myths About Salmon
   d. The Atlantic Salmon

2. According to the passage, which of the following statements is not true?
   a. The salmon return to their birthplace to spawn.
   b. Salmon are tremendous game fish.
   c. The salmon's life cycle is not very complex.
   d. Salmon are capable of swimming upstream.

3. We can conclude from the passage that
   a. salmon use sonar to find the mouth of freshwater rivers.
   b. scientists now fully understand the salmon's life cycle.
   c. the salmon is more difficult to restock in rivers than are some fish.
   d. the normal life expectancy of salmon is three years.

4. The passage suggests that
   a. environmental changes could easily make the Atlantic salmon extinct.
   b. salmon are not valued as a food source.
   c. very few of the young salmon are killed on the trip from the freshwater rivers to the ocean.
   d. salmon can live in freshwater for only a short time.

5(a) As used in this passage, the word *disengage* means
   a. surprise
   b. distract
   c. secure
   d. dislodge

5(b) As used in this passage, the word *complex* means
   a. short
   b. simple
   c. complicated
   d. confused

5(c) As used in this passage, the word *attain* means
   a. surpass
   b. reach
   c. lose
   d. double

5(d) As used in this passage, the word *spawn* means
   a. reproduce
   b. die
   c. be reborn
   d. feed

5(e) As used in this passage, the word *unrelenting* means
   a. vague
   b. slight
   c. horrible
   d. constant

5(f) As used in this passage, the word *fragile* means
   a. hopeless
   b. secure
   c. strong
   d. delicate

5(g) As used in this passage, the word *habitat* means
   a. environment
   b. pollution
   c. dominance
   d. courage

PASSAGE 3-14

SUBJECT: Rock Concerts

You've paid your ten or twelve dollars, handed your ticket to the guard, and you walk into the auditorium, ready to see your favorite musical group. Thousands of people are already in their seats, and taped music is playing through a mammoth sound system, soothing the crowd's expectations. Far below, at one end of the auditorium, the stage is bathed in light, the amplifier, drums, and instruments glistening like jewels. As excitement mounts, as warm-up acts run through their paces, few people in the audience stop to think just how much sheer physical labor goes into creating a concert.

In the fifties and sixties, artists could tour in just a bus or a van; all they needed to play a date was their instruments. But as the volume of the music increased, artists found that they could not rely on the microphones and public address systems at the auditoriums they played. As stage shows became more and more elaborate—whirling pianos, light shows, stage props—rock-and-roll artists found that they needed tractor-trailer trucks to carry their equipment. Touring has become a giant business enterprise; over one hundred people may be involved in the production of a rock and roll concert.

The tour itself is planned with the accuracy of a military campaign. A tour will usually open in a smaller city, so that any problems with the performance or with the equipment can be ironed out before the tour gets to a major market like Los Angeles or Dallas. Performances are scheduled one or two days apart because the performers must play in enough cities to make money, but the cities must be close enough to allow the band's equipment to arrive at the next city on time.

Early on the morning of a concert, the performers' equipment will arrive at the back door of the auditorium. If the act is an act that requires little lighting or sound other than that already at the auditorium, there will be only one or two truckloads. But most rock shows carry much more equipment with them; ZZ Top, for example, carries five truckoads of equipment with them on concert tour, as does Heart, another band now touring. But the performers will be sleeping on the buses or in a hotel room, waiting to fly to the location of the performance. They must rest after performances, so the only people working now are the truck drivers, the roadies—equipment handlers for the performers—and up to twenty-five or so stagehands who actually unload the equipment.

Lighting trucks are unloaded first, and the lighting that you see suspended overhead at the concert is assembled on the stage. Earlier in the morning, riggers will have climbed into the rafters and attached chains and motors to lift the lights up once they are assembled. Almost all touring performers carry their own lighting systems because they never know what type of lighting will be available at the auditoriums where they play.

Once the lighting is assembled and the rigging suspended, the stagehands unload the sound trucks; those giant stacks of speakers that concertgoers see at the corners of the stage are all unpacked, stacked, and rewired for each show. Each year, touring bands find themselves forced to carry more speakers; ZZ Top, for example, now tours with almost 40,000 pounds of speakers. As most stages won't hold such weight, they hoist the speakers into the air and suspend them as they do their lighting.

All this equipment is expensive, to say the least, so most performers rent from lighting and sound companies that also provide touring light and sound engineers for the performers, but wealthy bands own their trucks and equipment. The work is exhausting physical labor for stagehands, roadies, and performers alike. Producing a tour is complicated and expensive; it's no wonder that most bands prefer to live from the proceeds of their recording and stop touring as soon as possible.

▲ (654 WORDS) ▲

PASSAGE 3-14

Circle the correct answer:

1. The purpose of this passage is to
   a. discuss two rock bands who are currently on tour.
   b. discuss how lighting is provided for rock concerts.
   c. discuss the work that goes into preparing for a rock concert.
   d. discuss how rock concerts are financed.

2. According to the passage, which of the following statements is not true?
   a. Some rock and roll bands have elaborate light shows and stage props.
   b. In setting up a concert, the lighting truck is unloaded first.
   c. In the fifties and sixties rock and roll bands needed only a van or bus to tour.
   d. Most touring rock bands use only the lighting provided by the auditorium in which they appear.

3. We can conclude from the passage that
   a. rock performers don't appreciate their roadies.
   b. most rock and roll bands find touring too demanding.
   c. most concert tours are planned on the road.
   d. fans in Los Angeles are harder to please than other fans.

4. The passage suggests that
   a. most bands only use one tractor-trailer truck when they tour.
   b. the stages in most auditoriums are poorly constructed.

c. most of the work on a rock concert is done before the actual performance.
   d. stagehands don't get paid very well.

5(a) As used in this passage, the word *mammoth* means
   a. gigantic
   b. small
   c. poor
   d. quiet

5(b) As used in this passage, the word *paces* means
   a. practices
   b. performances
   c. warm-ups
   d. trials

5(c) As used in this passage, the word *sheer* means
   a. impossible
   b. barely
   c. thin
   d. purely

5(d) As used in this passage, the word *volume* means
   a. quality
   b. loudness
   c. ability
   d. need

5(e) As used in this passage, the word *elaborate* means
   a. complex
   b. average
   c. normal
   d. heavy

5(f) As used in this passage, the word *suspended* means
   a. flashing
   b. hung
   c. balanced
   d. handled

5(g) As used in this passage, the word *proceeds* means
   a. hopes
   b. fans
   c. financial gains
   d. debts

PASSAGE 3-15

SUBJECT: Dinosaurs (dī′ nə sôrz)

Late in the 1700s, the first fossilized dinosaur bones were discovered. The word *dinosaur* was created in 1842 by Richard Owen. Owen was a foe of the theory of evolution, so he used a word meaning "terrible lizard." But his word had the opposite effect; it caught on and people everywhere began talking about the huge beasts. It was in the later half of the nineteenth century that most of the bones and fossils in museums now were found. Americans and Europeans worked diligently to uncover the most, and the biggest, bones for their museums, so that today the sight of a huge dinosaur skeleton suspended in a museum is a common sight.

Popular literature portrays the dinosaur as a huge lizard, stupid, scaly, and cold-blooded like a lizard or a snake. But since the nineteenth century, the methods of digging for fossils and the methods of interpreting the discoveries have changed many of our ideas about these ancient animals. Some dinosaurs may have been small, almost like birds, and some may even have been warm-blooded animals. And many more dinosaurs ate meat than was previously thought.

A cold-blooded animal may not really have cold blood. What a cold-blooded animal lacks is a way to keep its body temperature constant. These animals simply take on the temperatures of their surroundings. In cold water, they are as cold as the water; to warm themselves, cold-blooded animals must expose themselves to a source of warmth such as direct sunlight. Hence, the common sight of lizards, snakes, or crocodiles sunning themselves on a river bank or log.

On the other hand, warm-blooded animals keep their body temperature constant. To keep themselves warm, they do not "sun themselves," but they do have to eat constantly. Some big cats, for example, must eat their own body weight in food every ten days. Cold-blooded animals eat far less; some reptiles need less than one-tenth of their weight in food every ten days.

Because their need for food is so immense, warm-blooded animals tend to take over any area they move into. For millions of years, dinosaurs were the most dominant form of life on earth, and if dinosaurs were cold-blooded, a hungrier, warm-blooded animal should have taken over the dinosaur's world.

Because warm-blooded animals require more food to stay warm and survive, the natural balance of species provides their food. Nature provides more prey for warm-blooded animals; there are many more deer for each wolf than there are frogs for each snake. The cold-blooded animal simply does not require quite so much food for survival, so nature, always efficient, does not waste time providing it. By examining fossil teeth, dinosaurs can be classified as predator or prey. The predators have sharp, knife-like teeth to cut and tear meat; the animals preyed upon lack this equipment, for they ate mostly vegetation. And there are many more prey dinosaurs than predator dinosaurs, suggesting that meat-eating dinosaurs were warm-blooded and required gigantic amounts of food.

In 1964 a new species of dinosaur was discovered. Until this discovery, only one species of dinosaur, the *Tyrannosaurus rex* (tĭ răn ə sôr′ əs rĕx), was thought to be a meat eater. But the new dinosaur had an enormous, crescent-shaped claw on each foot. From its skeleton, scientists could tell that *Deinonychus* (dā nŏn′ ĭ kŭs), whose name means "terrible claw," ran on two legs, enabling it to move quickly and to cut its prey with its enormous claws. The discoverers of this dinosaur even suggested that it hunted, like warm-blooded animals, in groups. More scientists came to support this theory when a similar dinosaur was discovered with its fossilized talons deep in the belly of the remains of a much smaller dinosaur.

The more we learn about these animals, the more we discover that our early ideas about dinosaurs were probably much too simple. Dinosaurs weren't all lizards, and their behavior was as complex as that of any species alive today.

▲ (652 WORDS) ▲

PASSAGE 3-15

Circle the correct answer:

1. The main idea of this passage is that
   a. dinosaurs required a great deal of food.
   b. cold-blooded animals are vastly different from warm-blooded animals.
   c. dinosaurs were called "terrible lizards."
   d. the facts about dinosaurs have been misunderstood by scientists.

2(a) According to the passage, which of the following statements is not true?
   a. The first fossilized dinosaur bones were discovered in the late 1700s.
   b. Dinosaurs were huge, stupid, scaly lizards.
   c. Some dinosaurs may have been small, almost birdlike.
   d. Cold-blooded animals do not really have cold blood.

2(b) Lizards, snakes, and crocodiles are
   a. cold-blooded
   b. lizards
   c. warm-blooded
   d. dangerous

3. We can conclude from the passage that
   a. dinosaurs still live in some areas of the world.
   b. fossils that have been found indicate that all dinosaurs were predators.
   c. fossil remains provide us with invaluable information about dinosaurs.
   d. warm-blooded animals are less vicious than cold-blooded animals.

4(a) The passage suggests that
  a. most scientists underestimated the complexity of dinosaurs.
  b. original research about dinosaurs has proved accurate.
  c. *Tyrannosaurus rex* was the only meat-eating species among the dinosaurs.
  d. only cold-blooded dinosaurs were predators.

4(b) The author's tone is
  a. satirical
  b. ironic
  c. negative
  d. objective

5(a) As used in this passage, the word *fossilized* means
  a. imprinted in the earth's crust
  b. living
  c. modern
  d. useless

5(b) As used in this passage, the word *diligently* means
  a. carelessly
  b. painstakingly
  c. quietly
  d. cheaply

5(c) As used in this passage, the word *immense* means
  a. awkward
  b. limited
  c. large
  d. slight

5(d) As used in this passage, the word *vegetation* means
  a. fish
  b. dirt
  c. plants
  d. animals

5(e) As used in this passage, the word *crescent* means
  a. beautifully
  b. blunt
  c. angular
  d. sickle

5(f) As used in this passage, the word *talons* means
  a. claws
  b. aptitude
  c. appetite
  d. wax

PASSAGE 3-16   SUBJECT:
Science Fiction Writers

Scientists and writers of science fiction have long predicted that humans will live in colonies in outer space. Some of the predictions sounded <u>outlandish</u> at first, and they still are. But in this era of space shuttles and manned <u>exploration</u>, some of the predictions are becoming very possible.

For example, one of the more outlandish predictions has been stated by Brian Aldiss, Britain's most popular science fiction writer. In his book *Who Can Replace a Man?* he predicted that the planet Venus would become Earth's first colony. In the year 2500, Venus would be moved into orbit around the Earth. The two planets would travel in circles around each other forever, and people would begin transforming Venus. Its atmosphere would become breathable, and its temperatures would become tolerable. Humans would make Venus a paradise for vacations.

Slightly more probable are the predictions of M. E. Davies, a space scientist and author. Davies predicts that the first colony will be on the planet Mars. This is logical enough, for Mars seems to be the planet attracting most exploration. But the entire atmosphere of the planet Mars would have to be altered before human beings could live there. Nevertheless, Davies maintains that both the pressure and the composition of the Martian "air" can be made suitable for humans. He predicts humans will walk on the Martian surface by 2010, that the first colony will exist by 2040, and that human cities will thrive on Mars twenty years later.

Both Davies' and Aldiss' predictions of space colonies seem difficult to imagine; both depend upon the invention of technology that we do not now possess.

The predictions of Gerard K. O'Neill appear much more likely to us. O'Neill's predictions are the efforts of a physicist; they are <u>systematic</u>, they are possible, and they are designed to produce profit.

In his book *The High Frontier,* O'Neill shows how space shuttle flights can lead to building a space colony. Shuttle flights can deliver the materials necessary to build a small, temporary colony for workers. O'Neill thinks the colony should be built midway between Earth and the moon. Once temporary quarters are established, the materials for building the larger, permanent quarters can be mined from the moon's surface. Because the moon has one-sixth the gravity of Earth, huge quantities of minerals can be mined cheaply. O'Neill claims that these minerals can be hurled into space by the use of a mass driver, a device he has already invented.

The colony itself, "Island One," has been described as having various shapes; O'Neill is still refining his designs. Whether <u>spherical</u> or shaped like a huge can, the colony would rotate slowly to create a gravity force. The colony would be a mile around and would house 10,000 workers. Inside the colony would be a near-copy of

Earth's environment; mirrors would let in sunshine, and the illusion of night could be created by screens. Crops could be grown outside in greenhouses; industry also might be located outside the colony itself, where there would be no gravity.

Although low or zero gravity would allow industrial processes to be speeded up and made more efficient, it would also have interesting effects on the occupants. New sports, new dances—all might be enhanced by the freedom allowed by a lower force of gravity. People with heart problems or high blood pressure might live longer; people with physical handicaps would find movement much easier.

But the important thing about O'Neill's ideas is that the colonies he envisions have a purpose. The greenhouses would provide food for the workers, and the industries would provide both profit to pay for the expense of construction and materials to begin building the next colony. The most profitable idea of all is that every colony could house a collector to draw energy from the sun. This pollution-free solar energy could be beamed back to Earth at great profit for any company willing to put up its own colony.

▲ (660 WORDS) ▲

PASSAGE 3-16

Circle the correct answer:

1(a) A good title for this passage might be
    a. Science Fiction and Space
    b. Myths About Space
    c. Space Patrol
    d. Space Colonies of the Future

1(b) This passage is mainly about
    a. the accuracy of science fiction writers' predictions.
    b. space exploration beyond our solar system.
    c. the feasibility of one of the many predictions that have been made by writers.
    d. science fiction writers.

2. Which of the following statements is true?
    a. Aldiss believes that people will colonize Venus.
    b. Davies believes that humans will learn to breathe the existing air on Mars.
    c. Gerard O'Neill wrote *Who Can Replace a Man?*
    d. Davies predicts a "city" on Mars by the year 2010.

3. We can conclude from the passage that
    a. foods grown in outer space will be larger because of the intake of excessive amounts of nitrogen.

b. our planet's gravity is caused by the rotation of the planet as it orbits the sun.
  c. coal will probably be mined on the moon by the year 2500.
  d. the greatest danger to a space colony would be radiation poisoning.

4. The author feels that
  a. science fiction writers are better predictors of the future than scientists.
  b. there is life on other planets outside of our universe.
  c. of the three predictions he discusses, O'Neill's is most important because it has a purpose.
  d. pollution will drive humans into space colonization in the next century.

5(a) As used in this passage, the word *outlandish* means
  a. fantastic
  b. superficial
  c. feasible
  d. gruesome

5(b) As used in this passage, the word *systematic* means
  a. accurate
  b. organized
  c. scientific
  d. proven

5(c) As used in this passage, the word *spherical* means
  a. circular
  b. elliptical
  c. oval
  d. oblong

5(d) As used in this passage, the word *illusion* means
  a. coolness
  b. darkness
  c. equivalent
  d. appearance

PASSAGE 3-17

SUBJECT: Roller Skating

Roller skating was invented, as you might suspect, in rural Holland. Ice skating had been a popular sport in Northern Europe for centuries, but even in the extreme northern sections of Europe, the ice eventually thaws. To continue the sport through the warm months, someone—no one knows who—invented some heavy, nonsteering roller skates by attaching thread spools to ice skates.

There were several attempts to popularize the new sport in the rest of Europe. One showman, a musician named Joseph Merlin, skated into a concert hall playing a new violin; when he crashed through a gigantic mirror, the new invention, roller skating, took a great leap backward. In the early eighteenth century, inventors began to try to improve the bulky Dutch skates. A French enthusiast obtained the first patent for a skate; his skate had only a single row of wheels, and only experts could skate on them at all. In 1823 the first really practical skate, invented by John Tyers, began to sell in huge quantities when expert ice skaters began to use Tyers' roller skates in exhibition performances. Soon the novelty of roller skating began to catch on. Waitresses in German beer gardens began skating up to their tables, and in Paris an opera on roller skates was written and performed. In the mid-1850s, the first public rink was opened in London, and the very daring—and the very muscular—tried out the Tyers skates.

Roller skating captured public attention in America after an inventor named Plimpton designed the first modern skate. The wheels on the Plimpton skate turned when the skater's foot tipped to the side; this principle is still in use today. More importantly, at last there was a steerable roller skate, which did not require nearly superhuman balance and strength. In addition to his engineering skill, Plimpton knew the status game. He built very large, specially decorated skating rinks in New York and in Newport, Rhode Island; the wealthy and the socially prominent took to skating immediately. Once skates began to be mass-produced, the sport became inexpensive enough to allow the working class to take up the sport. Eventually, skating rinks began to appear all over America; for a quarter (the price included skate rental) anyone could join in the fun.

During this popularization of the sport, many small improvements were made to the basic design of the skate. Better bearings were invented, making the skates even faster. But the wooden wheels, which were affected by changes in the weather and weren't very durable, were a problem. Aluminum wheels stained the maple floors of the rinks; the best wood, Turkish boxwood taken from the holds of Turkish ships, was hard to obtain and was supplanted by hard maple. Plastic was too slippery to be used in the wheels; synthetic rubber and carbon compounds became the standard for wooden rinks. Strangely, speed skaters have found that wooden wheels are still the fastest wheel; pine and sycamore wood are the favorite woods now, with metal inserts around the bearings.

Since its beginnings, the sport has supported competition of all sorts; few devoted skaters could be satisfied simply traveling around in a circle at the local rink. Speed competition and long distance runs were held at the beginning of the century and were very popular as a spectator sport. Figure skating and "roller polo" were popular in the early days of the sport, but only competitive figure skating has held its own as an organized sport. Roller hockey, a refinement of roller polo, is now gaining in popularity.

But roller skating doesn't really lend itself to team competition. Skate dancing and roller disco are becoming popular despite the demands these sports place on the skater. Thousands of people are trying outdoor skating for exercise and for fun. The most daredevil group are the "radical terrain" skaters. These enthusiasts use drainage pipes, storm drains, or special concrete "bowls" in skating parks to perform the same moves that skateboard riders perform on these radical surfaces. Whether enjoying these exciting jumps and turns, dancing, "jogging" on skates, or recapturing the freedom of childhood by just skating down a sidewalk, roller skaters all agree that their sport lures them just "for the fun of it."

▲ (707 WORDS) ▲

PASSAGE 3-17

Circle the correct answer:

1(a) This passage is mainly about
    a. competitive roller skating.
    b. John Tyers' invention of the modern skate.
    c. the invention of roller skates.
    d. the history of roller skating.

1(b) A good title for this passage might be
    a. How to Win on Skates
    b. John Tyers, Inventor of the Roller Skate
    c. Skating in Holland
    d. The Rise of the Roller Skate

2(a) Speed skaters still use wheels made from
    a. sycamore
    b. maple
    c. synthetic rubber
    d. carbon compounds

2(b) According to the passage, which of the following statements is not true?
   a. Roller skating was invented in rural Holland.
   b. Joseph Merlin obtained the first patent for a skate.
   c. John Tyers invented the first practical skate.
   d. An inventor named Plimpton designed the first modern skate.

3. We can conclude from the passage that
   a. improved technology has helped make the roller skate popular.
   b. wooden skates are no longer used because they aren't durable.
   c. roller skating is now more popular than ice skating.
   d. roller skating's popularity has declined since the mid-1850s.

4(a) The passage suggests that
   a. most people roller-skate purely for entertainment.
   b. most people roller-skate for exercise.
   c. most people roller-skate because it's adventurous.
   d. most roller skaters hope to become racers eventually.

4(b) The author's tone is
   a. sarcastic
   b. subjective
   c. ironic
   d. positive

5(a) As used in this passage, the word *novelty* means
   a. usefulness
   b. unusualness
   c. benefit
   d. awkwardness

5(b) As used in this passage the word *supplanted* means
   a. derived
   b. repaired
   c. replaced
   d. destroyed

5(c) As used in this passage, the word *standard* means
   a. exception
   b. basis
   c. custom
   d. safeguard

5(d) As used in this passage, the word *radical* means
   a. nontraditional
   b. smooth
   c. acrobatic
   d. common

PASSAGE 3-18 SUBJECT:
Mormonism (môr′ mən ĭzəm)

One of the most shameful—and puzzling—events in our past is the persecution and mistreatment of the early Mormon church. In a country noted for its religious freedom, it is awkward to explain all the burning, looting, beating, and even murders committed by anti-Mormon mobs.

The Mormon faith began with a religious vision given to Joseph Smith in New York in 1823. Immediately he began to call for believers and converts to turn to the new religion. Within ten years, Smith had his band of followers. But almost immediately after his claim to have received his revelation, his neighbors in Palmyra (păl mī′ rə), New York, began to attack his character and to revile him in public.

Many people, no doubt, were offended by Smith's claim to have been selected to talk with angels. But documents surrounding Smith's revelation read almost like accusations made during the Salem witch-hunts. Seventy-two signed statements exist that consist almost entirely of personal attacks on Smith. The founder of what may be the most successful branch of religion in America was described as "destitute of moral character." Other people in Palmyra accused the prophet of laziness and drunkenness. Some say he was a "glass looker"—rather like someone claiming to use a crystal ball to reveal the unknown. Others accused him of digging for buried treasure; both "money-digging" and "glass looking" were criminal offenses in the 1820s. Though historians have disproved these claims, the accusations may have been quite effective in slowing the development of the Mormon church.

As Smith and his followers fled the hostile atmosphere of New York, the reactions to Smith's religion became more and more violent. In Hiram (hī′ rəm), Ohio, in 1832, Smith himself was attacked by a dozen men. Smith was beaten and choked, then stripped; at first, the mob apparently intended to kill Smith, but eventually they decided to tar Smith instead. After covering his body with steaming tar, the mob left Smith to crawl to the home of a recent convert to Mormonism, who treated Smith's wounds.

In Independence, Missouri, in 1833, a Mormon bishop was tarred and feathered by a mob of three hundred men. The same mob forced other Mormons, mostly women and children, from their homes, and destroyed the congregation's printing press. Near Nauvoo (nô′ voo), Illinois, in 1845, an entire Mormon settlement was burned to the ground during a two-day raid. Mounted raiders burned barns, homes, and crops as frightened Mormons hid in the surrounding forests.

But by far the worst example of violence directed against Mormons occurred at Hann's Mill, a tiny settlement in Missouri, in 1838. A group of about thirty families had recently migrated from the East. They were camped at a mill, near the homes of settled Mormons in the area. All the Mormons were nervous because a "militia" group had been active in the Hann's Mill area. On the afternoon of October 30, over two hundred militiamen rode into the encampment, firing from military formation and without warning. The Mormons surrendered immediately, but the militia continued to fire. Twenty-nine Mormons were killed or wounded, including an old man and a nine-year-old boy; houses and tents were looted, the dead and wounded stripped, and the horses and wagons stolen.

The methods of these militia or vigilantes were the typical methods used by frontier settlers to protect themselves against danger. Though these vigilantes were often local leaders, some ruffians were certainly among the Mormon persecutors. The real conflict, though, may have been more economic and political than religious. The Mormons wanted a separate culture. Their land was passed on only to other Mormons. Their supplies and goods were bought from other church members. Mormons voted for leaders who supported Mormon causes. Other settlers naturally saw self-contained Mormon settlements as threats, though surely this is no excuse for beatings or murders. But it is true that this conflict and persecution continued as the Mormons migrated farther and farther to the West. Finally, in 1847, when the Mormons arrived in Utah, the persecutions eventually stopped. In Utah, Mormons were the majority at last; *they* were the old settlers. Here they could at last welcome migrants from the East, along with converts from Europe, to the society Joseph Smith had planned.

The prophet, however, never saw his society realized. Like many great leaders, he was doomed never to see the results of his work. In 1844 Smith—along with his brother—was assassinated while in the custody of the police in Carthage (Kâr′ thĕj), Illinois.

▲ (746 WORDS) ▲

PASSAGE 3-18

Circle the correct answer:

1. The main idea of this passage is that
   a. Joseph Smith founded his church on his religious visions.
   b. Mormonism is uniquely American.
   c. the Mormons have been one of the most persecuted religious groups in American history.
   d. Joseph Smith was a true prophet.

2. According to the passage, which of the following statements is not true?
   a. Mormonism began in New York.
   b. The Mormons migrated primarily to the South.
   c. Joseph Smith was accused of using a crystal ball.
   d. The Mormons arrived in Utah in 1847.

3(a) We can conclude from the passage that
- a. Joseph Smith was a wizard.
- b. Joseph Smith was a "glass looker."
- c. Jospeh Smith was a "money-digger."
- d. Joseph Smith was a unique religious thinker.

3(b) Which of the following conclusions does the passage support?
- a. The persecution of the Mormons increased as they moved into Utah.
- b. The Mormons faced more violent persecution in Missouri than in New York.
- c. It took Joseph Smith twenty years to gather a following.
- d. The charges against Joseph Smith for being a "money-digger" have never been disproved.

4. The passage suggests that
- a. economics and politics had little to do with the persecution of the Mormons in Missouri.
- b. the people of New York persecuted the Mormons because of their belief in polygamy.
- c. Joseph Smith gained a following quickly.
- d. many people believed in Joseph Smith's revelations.

5(a) As used in this passage, the word *revelation* means
- a. vision
- b. idea
- c. hope
- d. fanaticism

5(b) As used in this passage, the word *revile* means
- a. respect
- b. tease
- c. denounce
- d. avoid

5(c) As used in this passage, the word *branch* means
- a. rebirth
- b. division
- c. belief
- d. mockery

5(d) As used in this passage, the word *destitute* means
- a. devoid
- b. filled with
- c. representative
- d. frightened

5(e) As used in this passage, the word *hostile* means
- a. surprising
- b. placid

    c. friendly
    d. unfriendly

5(f) As used in this passage, the word *migrated* means
    a. fled
    b. arrived
    c. transmuted
    d. moved

5(g) As used in this passage, the word *ruffians* means
    a. politicians
    b. criminals
    c. Protestants
    d. mercenaries

PASSAGE 3-19

SUBJECT:
Obesity (ō bē′ sə tē)

Far too many people are overweight. Obesity may be the most serious health problem facing Americans today. Other problems are more serious. No one would suggest that fat is more deadly than heart problems, diabetes, or cancer. But seventy million Americans are overweight right now, so the disease—or condition—of overweight affects more people than any other health problem.

Overweight is also serious because it is a contributing cause to so many other health problems. Heart and artery system disease, diabetes, high blood pressure, and arthritis are more common in people who are overweight. Extra weight causes problems with muscles and joints. Many studies are beginning to link cancer with obesity, for cancer cells are more likely to be found in fat tissue than in muscle.

In addition to their health problems, overweight people may suffer psychologically. Our culture teaches us that "slim is beautiful," so where does that leave obese people? People who are overweight find it difficult to buy clothes. People who are significantly overweight find public facilities such as airline seats or waiting room chairs too small. Some obese people say they feel humiliated by their condition, so they avoid going out in public. Some overweight people avoid exercise because their extra weight makes exertion difficult. As their activity decreases, it becomes easier to gain weight, for exercise would have "burned off" at least some calories.

Overweight is always caused by people's consuming too many calories for their bodies' needs. Glandular (glăn′ jə lər) and metabolic (mĕt ə bŏl′ ĭk) conditions may cause the body to need fewer calories, but only a very few cases of obesity can be explained by metabolism (mə tăb′ ə lĭz əm) or hormone (hôr′ mōn) imbalance. Some people gain weight because their diet is rich in very high calorie foods like desserts, but this, too, is rare. Others claim they gain weight because they eat when they're nervous and depressed, but this is simply an excuse. People gain weight and become obese because they simply eat too much. Almost everyone who is overweight has a huge appetite.

The roles of hunger and taste in causing overweight are beginning to receive attention. At the University of Pennsylvania, scientists found a way to feed rats directly into the stomach. With taste, smell, and texture absent, normal rats ate just enough to maintain their weights. Similarly, a New York University experiment showed that rats eat less when their tongues are anesthetized (ə nĕs′ thə tīzd), dulling the sense of taste.

Similar experiments have been performed with human subjects, professional tasters in fact. These tasters described the tastes of several liquids before and after chewing an anesthetic (ăn ĭs thĕt′ ĭk) gum. As expected, an anesthetized tongue reduces the sensation of taste. The nerves inside the tongue are only one set of several forming the trigeminal (trī jĕm′ ə nəl) nerve system. This system provides information to the brain about temperatures and textures in the mouth and on the surface of the face. It is the trigeminal nerve system that makes the temperature of baked Alaska or the texture of salad tempting. Pigeons and chimpanzees that have had damage to the trigeminal nerve lose their appetites; but damage to the brain does not cause a lack of appetite. Hunger is located in the brain, but the urge to have food in the mouth, stimulating the trigeminal nerve, is what causes appetite.

Taste and texture <u>compel</u> overweight individuals to overeat. In 1968 an experiment by R. E. Nisbett showed that overweight people are more sensitive to taste than normal people. Two groups of people, one group normal and one group overweight, were supposedly testing ice cream, and all tasters were told to eat as much as they wanted, and, of course, the overweight tasters ate more. Gradually, the taste of the ice cream was <u>modified</u> with very bitter flavoring. Both groups ate less after modification, but the <u>overweight</u> group consumed substantially less. Their ice-cream consumption became exactly like the normal group's once the taste was made less pleasant.

In a famous experiment performed at St. Luke's Hospital in New York, completely tasteless food was given to two groups of patients. Throughout the experiment, the normal group ate just enough to maintain their health. When the overweight patients were fed through tubes, they wanted less than a tenth of the amount they previously demanded. Being fed in a paper container caused the overweight group to double consumption immediately. The amount they ate doubled again when the food was served in attractive crystal dishes; when candlelight was added, their <u>intake</u> doubled again. Lean people eat the necessary amount, regardless of external <u>factors</u>. Overweight people consume less as their enjoyment is eliminated—in other words, they eat because it feels good; they are simply more aware of taste.

▲ (778 WORDS) ▲

PASSAGE 3-19

Circle the correct answer:

1. The main idea of this passage is that
    a. obesity is a serious problem caused by overeating.
    b. overweight people may suffer psychologically.
    c. people suffer psychologically when they are obese.
    d. obese people eat more than people of normal weight.

2(a) The trigeminal nerve system
    a. includes the nerves in the tongue.
    b. provides information about temperature and texture in the mouth.

  c. provides information about temperature and texture on the surface of the face.
  d. all of the above.

2(b) According to the passage, which of the following statements is not true?
  a. Feeding obese people on paper containers halved their consumption.
  b. Overweight patients fed through tubes wanted less than a tenth of the amount of food they previously demanded.
  c. The use of attractive crystal dishes doubled the consumption of obese people.
  d. Candlelight also doubled the consumption of obese people.

3(a) We can conlcude from the passage that
  a. some people gain weight even if they don't exceed the caloric needs of their body.
  b. all overweight people are emotionally disturbed.
  c. obesity causes cancer.
  d. obesity is dangerous because of its effects on the body.

3(b) Which of the following conclusions does the passage support?
  a. The experiments discussed were biased because they did not use a large enough sample.
  b. The experiments discussed were inconclusive.
  c. One of the experiments discussed indicates that environment affects appetite.
  d. Both experiments were based on animal studies.

4. The passage suggests that
  a. all overweight people are depressed by their condition.
  b. obesity is the primary cause of heart attack.
  c. the way food is served affects the appetites of overweight people.
  d. most overweight people are genial extroverts.

5(a) As used in this passage, the word *obesity* means
  a. heart problems
  b. overweight
  c. cancer
  d. diet

5(b) As used in this passage, the word *humiliated* means
  a. exhausted
  b. frustrated
  c. embarrassed
  d. ridiculed

5(c) As used in this passage, the word *anesthetized* means
  a. removed
  b. numbed
  c. stimulated
  d. sensitized

5(d) As used in this passage, the word *compel* means
   a. force
   b. implore
   c. restrain
   d. effect

5(e) As used in this passage, the word *modified* means
   a. improved
   b. infused
   c. spoiled
   d. changed

5(f) As used in this passage, the word *intake* means
   a. greed
   b. appetite
   c. heart rate
   d. consumption

PASSAGE 3-20   SUBJECT:
Definitions of Love

An old rock-and-roll lyric from the 1950s <u>plaintively</u> repeats the question, "Why do fools fall <u>in love</u>?" Not all people who fall in love feel that love has made them look like idiots, but no one can offer satisfying explanations for the phenomena (fĭ nŏm' ə nə) we call love.

I use the plural form, phenomena, because all love is certainly not similar; there probably are many different types of love. We all know people who married on a moment's impulse or after a courtship of only a few days or weekends, and most of us can also refer to people whose love or whose marriage seems to be based on very practical matters. The newspapers regularly carry tales of people who love each other deeply but are divorced and remarried each year to save money on their taxes or to increase their pension benefits. It is a part of the myth surrounding love that every ambitious young man wants "to marry the boss's daughter." Similar tales <u>abound</u> of young women who attend college only to meet suitable young men for marriage or of women who become nurses solely to meet future doctors. As hard as it might be to point out a single instance of these single-minded pursuits, the idea apparently persists.

Until this century, marriage and love were, in fact, viewed as practical matters. The rulers of Sparta, for example, had to encourage population growth to provide soldiers for their military machine, so bachelors were considered almost as traitors by the government. They were ridiculed in public and were sometimes forced by the authorities to pick a mate among a group of women gathered up and forced into a dark room. Among the Incas, a priest lined up unwed men and women in two rows during an annual ceremony. After a short prayer, he assigned each woman a husband.

By the Middle Ages, love and marriage had become an established way of gaining new lands or settling disputes. Marriages were used to combine kingdoms when a king and queen combined their lands. Daughters were given in marriage to powerful rulers who might otherwise become an enemy; even then, it was bad form to fight with in-laws. Treaties were sealed by marriages that interlocked the former enemies in ties much stronger than greed, ambition, or hatred. Arranged marriages have been the most common type of relationship historically. Only recently did the custom lose its popularity, and it is still a convenient way of choosing a mate in some Oriental societies.

The modern explanation of love is simply a mutual attraction. But what is that attraction? Theodor Reik (rīk), a psychoanalyst, claims that the attraction is selfish, that we see our weaknesses and are attracted to personalities who have the qualities we lack. A similar theory is advanced by Erich Fromm (ĕ rĭk frŏm), a popular philosopher, who maintains that all of us have an inborn fear of loneliness and that we instinctively choose a partner who will help keep this fear away.

In the 1900s, one thinker proposed the "law of affinity." This "law" claimed that people fell in love because of an attraction between the chemicals in the lovers' bodies. Another theorist said love was caused by a chemical in the brain that, once it was released, began to cause madness by altering the tissue in the brain. Once the disease had begun, the sufferer fell in love with the next person he or she met.

A number of theories explaining love involve the idea of a "love type." In the 1890s, a Frenchman named Danville suggested that all of us have an image of our perfect mate already in our minds. During adolescence, when people are first interested in sex, our minds are imprinted by idealized versions of love, including sights, sounds, and smells, so when we meet a person who closely matches the resulting image in our unconscious, we fall helplessly, romantically in love. A modern version of this theory was reported in the *Los Angeles Times*. The terms differ from Danville's, but the idea is essentially the same. We are programmed in our childhoods to value certain physical and mental traits. The nerve circuits are locked—we do not know the information in them—until they are stimulated by our meeting a person who matches our nerve circuits. Sounds rather mechanical, doesn't it?

The most unromantic of modern theories results—as unromantic explanations often do—from our knowledge of animals. Many animals, particularly mammals and insects, use scents to attract mates. A substance called pheromone (fĕr′ ə mōn) creates a scent that attracts the attention of possible mates; certain female moths, for example, secrete a pheromone that can be detected by the males of the species even at half a mile. So far, no biologist has been able to identify substances like this that trigger affection in the human species, but many people are attracted by the possibility that human pheromones exist. If scientists discover that the complex reactions and behaviors we call "love" really are triggered by pheromones, we'll have to change our language along with our ideas. Does "love at first smell" sound romantic to you?

▲ (853 WORDS) ▲

PASSAGE 3-20

Circle the correct answer:

1. The main idea of this passage is that
    a. love is based on mutual attraction.
    b. love and marriage should be considered practical matters.
    c. there have been several differing theories offered to explain what "love" is.
    d. love is probably based on a chemical reaction in the lovers' bodies.
2. According to the passage, which of the following statements is not true?
    a. Some people believe women attend college only to find a husband.

  b. Most marriages are based on convenience.
  c. Until this century, marriage was viewed as a practical matter.
  d. In the Middle Ages, marriages were used to settle disputes.

3(a) We can conclude from the passage that
  a. no one really understands what causes people to fall in love.
  b. practicality is the best reason for a marriage.
  c. chemical imbalances cause us to fall in love.
  d. "love" isn't as romantic today as it was in the past.

3(b) Which of the following conclusions does the passage support?
  a. Most theories support a romantic view of love.
  b. Respect is the most important ingredient in a successful marriage.
  c. Most doctors believe love is caused by a chemical attraction.
  d. Some theorists try to define "love" as the attempt to satisfy a need.

4. The passage suggests that
  a. we are close to discovering what causes "love."
  b. love is not particularly important in a marriage.
  c. love may simply be a chemical attraction between people as it is in other animals.
  d. love is too complex to be simply a chemical attraction.

5(a) As used in this passage, the word *plaintively* means
  a. happily
  b. mournfully
  c. sarcastically
  d. often

5(b) As used in this passage, the word *abound* means
  a. are scarce
  b. are ridiculous
  c. are plentiful
  d. are shameful

5(c) As used in this passage, the word *traits* means
  a. disorders
  b. characteristics
  c. appearances
  d. movements

5(d) As used in this passage, the word *secrete* means
  a. hide
  b. display
  c. attract
  d. manufacture

SECTION 4 | READING PASSAGES

DIRECTIONS: Read all of the passages that your instructor has assigned in this section. Answer the comprehension items that have been assigned on your Student Score Sheet. Be sure to read each passage carefully and to refer to the passage to check your answers to the comprehension questions.

PASSAGE 4-1

SUBJECT: The Western

The western has been the favorite type of American adventure story since the nineteenth century. While the American West was being settled, newspapers and "dime novels" could depend on stories of the frontier settlements and tall tales about living in the untamed wilderness to sell. The public back East was eager to read about the West, even if the stories were more fiction than fact.

In 1902, Owen Wister published his novel *The Virginian,* which was one of the first novels to treat the western as a serious literary form; the novel still sells well and has inspired several movies and a television series. In 1905, Bertha H. Bower and Zane Grey published their first novels, and the popular western novel has continued to flourish from that day on, with current novels by Luke Short, Max Brand, and Louis (Loo′ ē) L'Amour (Lă mōr′) carrying on the tradition.

The first western movie appeared even earlier than these serious western novels. Before the turn of the century, an associate of Edison's had filmed *Cripple Creek Barroom Scene,* a few seconds of film showing the inside of a saloon, to help publicize the invention of the movie camera. In 1903 the Edison company filmed the first "full-length" western, *The Great Train Robbery.* The film lasts less than fifteen minutes, but a story is told in its entirety. In the movie, bandits rob a train and its passengers, killing the engineer, and find themselves tracked down by a posse (pŏs′ sē). Audiences loved the movie. Some theaters were actually opened for the single purpose of showing *The Great Train Robbery* and only later realized that they could do equally well showing other movies. The film was so successful that other companies, and finally even the Edison company itself, began producing copies and other versions of *The Great Train Robbery.* Ironically, in an era when the West was still very real—Arizona, New Mexico, Oklahoma were all territories rather than states in 1903—*The Great Train Robbery* was filmed in New Jersey.

▲ (332 WORDS) ▲

PASSAGE 4-1

Circle the correct answer:

1. The purpose of this passage is to
    a. discuss the making of the movie *The Great Train Robbery.*
    b. discuss the early western novels.
    c. discuss the art of movie making.

d. trace the development of the western as an American adventure story tradition.

2. Zane Grey was a
   a. novelist
   b. actor
   c. cowboy
   d. movie producer

3. We can conclude from this passage that
   a. people lost interest in the West after 1903.
   b. Owen Wister was an ex-cowboy.
   c. New Jersey was still "untamed wilderness" in 1903.
   d. films were fairly uncommon at the time *The Great Train Robbery* was made.

4. The passage suggests that
   a. Edison's invention of the movie camera happened by accident.
   b. movie houses didn't make much money in the early days.
   c. Easterners were fascinated by the "wild West."
   d. *The Great Train Robbery* was poorly received by the public because it lacked a plot.

5(a) As used in this passage, the word *untamed* means
   a. barren
   b. wild
   c. unhealthy
   d. rich

5(b) As used in this passage, the work *literary* means
   a. humorous
   b. financial
   c. appropriate to literature
   d. amateur

5(c) As used in this passage, the word *flourish* means
   a. change
   b. deteriorate
   c. thrive
   d. weaken

5(d) As used in this passage, the word *tradition* means
   a. practice
   b. farce
   c. area
   d. falsehood

5(e) As used in this passage, the word *era* means
   a. place
   b. moment
   c. area
   d. time

PASSAGE 4-2

SUBJECT: Foxfire

In 1966, Eliot Wigginton left Cornell University for a career in teaching. He had a bachelor's degree in English and a master's degree in teaching, and, in his words, he thought he "was a force to be reckoned with." Wigginton's first teaching job was at Rabun Gap—Nacoochee (nə koo' chē) School, in Rabun Gap, Georgia, a school with fewer than three hundred pupils. Rabun Gap is in north Georgia in the Appalachian (ăp ə lā' chē ən) Mountains; Wigginton tried to ignore the breathtaking scenery and concentrate on teaching English and geography to his ninth and tenth grade pupils.

After about six weeks of trying to teach Shakespeare, among other things, Wigginton realized that he was boring his students and not really communicating with them. Rabun Gap students, despite the gorgeous mountain wilderness surrounding them, were no different from students in Chicago or Los Angeles who are bored by dull lectures. No one has ever been convinced that English will be important after school merely because a teacher *said* the skills of communication might someday be necessary.

Wigginton decided to throw away his textbooks and involve his students, all of them, in the day-to-day work of producing their own magazine. At first the students sold advertisements to local merchants to raise money for their magazine, but after the first issue the magazine sold enough copies to support itself. The students wrote poems, took pictures, wrote letters, and edited copy for the magazine. Famous poets' work appeared with the work of Wigginton's students. The students began to use spelling, grammar, and writing skills. Most importantly, they were using these skills to preserve the mountain ways that were starting to die out because the younger people were not seeking them out. The magazine, *Foxfire*, gained a national reputation and circulation for the students' interviews with the Rabun Gap mountain people. Every issue of *Foxfire* contains new articles about cabin building, quilt-making, soap-making, and preserving and cooking mountain foods; with their now-famous magazine, Wigginton and his once-bored students have helped keep this mountain lore alive for the next generation, too.

▲ (339 WORDS) ▲

PASSAGE 4-2

Circle the correct answer:

1. The purpose of this passage is to
   a. compare rural and urban education.

b. provide a short account of Eliot Wigginton's attempts to teach Shakespeare.
   c. describe the development of the magazine *Foxfire*.
   d. discuss mountain life.

2. *Foxfire* contains articles about
   a. quilt-making
   b. preserving
   c. soap-making
   d. all of the above

3. We can conclude from this passage that
   a. *Foxfire* demonstrated to the students the need for communication skills in the real world.
   b. *Foxfire* developed into a nationally circulated magazine because it taught grammar, spelling, and writing skills.
   c. the educational level of the students in Rabun Gap was below the national norm.
   d. Wigginton's students never did learn to understand Shakespeare.

4. The passage suggests that
   a. Wigginton's students didn't respond to him at first because they had trouble understanding his accent.
   b. Wigginton felt that the important thing in teaching English was to teach students to communicate.
   c. Wigginton no longer teaches in Rabun Gap.
   d. the parents were suspect of Wigginton's project at first.

5(a) As used in this passage, the word *breathtaking* means
   a. tiring
   b. awe-inspiring
   c. altitude
   d. polluted

5(b) As used in this passage, the word *merely* means
   a. despite
   b. needlessly
   c. simply
   d. usually

5(c) As used in this passage, the word *preserve* means
   a. save
   b. destroy
   c. alter
   d. modernize

5(d) As used in this passage, the word *lore* means
   a. falsehood
   b. popularity
   c. superstition
   d. tradition

PASSAGE 4-3

SUBJECT: Game Ranches

Is raising a herd of buffalo or moose any different from raising herds of other livestock? A group of ranchers in the West are raising exotic game animals on what used to be cattle and livestock ranches, and many environmentalists are objecting.

In Montana, there are currently 230 licensed game ranches; some of these are just a collection of enclosures where wild livestock is raised as a curiosity, but several of these game ranches are enormous, fenced ranches of a thousand acres or more. At many of these ranches, hunters can shoot elk, moose, bison (bī′ sən), deer, or sheep after paying a fee. It's easy to realize why game farming raises such a controversy; opponents of this sort of hunting believe that there's not much genuine hunting involved. Clients pay substantial fees, which may range upwards to almost $5,000 for the privilege of bagging an elk, and are able to hunt on the private ranches without bothering to obtain licenses or permits. About the only method by which the hunting can be made sporting is by insisting on making one's shots at long range.

Elk, in particular, are being raised for another reason many people find objectionable. Their antlers are prized as a medicine in the Oriental drug market. Black-market prices for elk antlers usually range from $8 to $80 a pound, depending on the grade. Not too many people object to the harvesting of mature antlers, though it is illegal to gather antlers on federally controlled land, because the mature antlers are shed each winter by the elk; but the most valuable antlers are the immature antlers that are covered in a velvety skin, also harvested for boiling as "medicine." Many people, even some of the game ranchers, think it is wrong to cut the antlers in this stage. The elk are not hurt by the cutting operation, but opponents of game farming object to the practice on the aesthetic grounds. Elk were meant to have antlers, they say, and not to live shut up behind fences.

▲ (338 WORDS) ▲

PASSAGE 4-3

Circle the correct answer:

1. The purpose of this passage is to
   a. compare traditional farming and game farming.

b. show how people have destroyed the natural environments of animals.
   c. discuss the practice of game farming.
   d. discuss the commercial uses of elk antlers.

2. According to the passage, which of the following statements is not true?
   a. There are 230 licensed game farms in Montana.
   b. Some game farm clients pay $5,000 to hunt there.
   c. Elk antlers sometimes sell for $80 a pound.
   d. Elk are seriously injured when their antlers are cut.

3. We can conclude from the passage that
   a. the claim that cutting the antlers of elk for sale is cruel and painful is largely unfounded.
   b. elk are more easily raised than other animals.
   c. elk do not live long in captivity.
   d. elk antlers have no beneficial medical effects on man.

4. The passage suggests that
   a. most of the critics of game farming are vegetarians.
   b. many people find raising animals for food less objectionable than raising them for hunting.
   c. hunting on game farms is more difficult than hunting in the wild.
   d. Montana is considering banning the practice of game farming.

5(a) As used in this passage, the word *exotic* means
   a. dangerous
   b. vicious
   c. unusual
   d. timid

5(b) As used in this passage, the word *bagging* means
   a. chasing
   b. petting
   c. seeing
   d. killing

5(c) As used in this passage, the word *mature* means
   a. grown
   b. new
   c. small
   d. young

5(d) As used in this passage, the word *aesthetic* means
   a. political
   b. naturalistic
   c. illegal
   d. necessary

PASSAGE 4-4   SUBJECT:
Isabella Stewart Gardner

In Boston, during the later part of the nineteenth century, $6 or $7 million dollars was not really a very impressive fortune to control, but Mrs. Jack Gardner knew how to spend money and how to have a wonderful time doing it.

She was certainly never <u>awestruck</u> by the money of other people, however. Once when Mrs. Gardner was being shown the solid gold tableware of one of her social rivals, she <u>coyly</u> asked, "What do you use when you have company?" To showcase her personal fortune, she purchased the mansion next door to the mansion she already owned; this second mansion she ordered entirely redecorated to serve merely as an entertainment area.

And she certainly entertained well: in the adjoining mansion, Pavlova (păv lō′ və), the leading ballet artist of the day, danced as Paderewski (pă də rōō′ skē), already a legend, played the piano for her. Strauss (strous), Brahms (brömz), and Liszt (lĭst) all visited her here and helped her turn the second mansion into a concert hall; Henry James and Henry Adams both wrote Mrs. Gardner <u>fervent</u> letters. She was the leading figure in Boston during a period when only Boston was thought to be <u>civilized</u>.

The Isabella Stewart Gardner Museum in Boston shows another side of this remarkable woman. She loved paintings from the Renaissance (rĕn′ ə zŏns′) and filled her museum with them. She was also capable of being very business-minded about art, though, for all the paintings were bought at bargain prices; some famous and very desirable paintings she simply refused to buy because the price was unreasonable. Her very personal taste in art shows in the museum still.

She had one other consuming passion. After selecting the site and designing the building, she supervised each step of the construction and sometimes showed up with her own lunch pail and called the workmen together by blowing loudly on a trumpet. But what she really wanted from them was some serious conversation about her real passion—baseball. She was a lifelong, enthusiastic, and knowledgeable fan of the local teams, even to the point of wearing a beaded headband <u>emblazoned</u> "Go Red Sox" to symphony balls.

▲ (345 WORDS) ▲

PASSAGE 4-4

Circle the correct answer:

1. The purpose of this passage is to
    a. provide a brief biography of Isabella Stewart Gardner.
    b. describe the life-style of the wealthy.
    c. discuss the cultural atmosphere of nineteenth-century Boston.
    d. compare Mrs. Gardner's two distinctly different interests.

2. Mrs. Gardner numbered among her friends
    a. Brahms
    b. Henry James
    c. Paderewski
    d. all of the above

3. We can conclude from the passage that
    a. Mrs. Gardner was a frustrated artist.
    b. Mrs. Gardner died impoverished.
    c. Mrs. Gardner used her wealth to enjoy life.
    d. Mrs. Gardner later married Henry Adams.

4. The passage suggests that
    a. Henry James and Henry Adams were interested in Mrs. Gardner because of her wealth.
    b. Mrs. Gardner had little interest in things not associated with "culture."
    c. Boston is no longer the cultural center of the United States.
    d. Mrs. Gardner was a woman of varied interests and tastes.

5(a) As used in this passage, the word *awestruck* means
    a. deeply impressed
    b. frightened
    c. bought
    d. greedy

5(b) As used in this passage, the word *coyly* means
    a. insolently
    b. bravely
    c. strangely
    d. deviously

5(c) As used in this passage, the work *fervent* means
    a. passionate
    b. boring
    c. obscene
    d. threatening

5(d) As used in this passage, the word *civilized* means
   a. cultured
   b. acclimated
   c. sturdy
   d. populated

5(e) As used in this passage, the word *emblazoned* means
   a. refuting
   b. displaying
   c. disguised
   d. hoping

PASSAGE 4-5 SUBJECT:
Tennessee Valley Authority

Any talk of the energy needs of the United States should include a discussion of the Tennessee Valley Authority, a successful but sometimes quiet federal agency.

The Tennessee Valley Authority began life in 1933 as one of the public works agencies designed to help fight the Great Depression. The TVA was first meant to employ thousands of men to build a chain of dams down the Tennessee River. These dams were to include electric plants for generating electricity to provide cheap power for the rural land in the valley area.

Within ten years, most of the homes in the TVA area had electricity. In twenty years, there were four times as many homes in the area with power. At first, TVA electricity cost a penny per kilowatt (kĭl' ə wŏt). Many homes in the area relied on electricity for heating. This results in criticism now that electricity is more like three pennies per kilowatt.

Other criticism has been aimed at the TVA's other methods of generating power. In 1975, the Authority was sued for polluting the air with its coal-generating plants. Antinuclear groups point out that the TVA would soon have a total of seventeen atomic reactor plants supplying power for its service area.

But the Tennessee Valley Authority has adjusted to the new times. It quickly became a model for pollution control at its coal plants. Just as quickly the TVA found itself an energy conserver as well as a producer. The TVA conducts free home energy consultations and offers cheap loans to consumers who want to install insulation, storm windows, solar energy equipment, or woodburning stoves. The resulting decrease in demand has allowed the TVA to postpone or delay construction of two nuclear reactors.

Instead, the Authority is building a plant to extract coal gas from low-grade coal. Their first step will be to use the coal gas to make an ammonia (ə mōn' ē ə) fertilizer for farmers in the TVA service area. Their ultimate goal is to produce a synthetic fuel from the coal gas; the TVA will then be once again producing a cheaper source of energy and helping solve the nation's problems, several at a time.

▲ (356 WORDS) ▲

PASSAGE 4-5

Circle the correct answer:

1. The main idea of this passage is that
   a. electricity purchased by TVA's customers has tripled in price.
   b. the TVA has not served its function well.
   c. The TVA is dangerous to the environment.
   d. the TVA has always been a pioneer in the energy field.

2. According to the passage, which of the following statements is not true?
   a. The Tennessee Valley Authority was created in 1933.
   b. The TVA's initial function was to provide work for the unemployed.
   c. The TVA has forged steadily ahead in decreasing the number of nuclear reactor plants it depends on.
   d. The TVA is interested in producing coal gas from low-grade coal.

3. We can conclude from the passage that
   a. the TVA no longer supplies electricity for heating.
   b. before the TVA, few homes in the Tennessee Valley had electricity.
   c. the TVA hasn't had to rely on atomic reactors for its power.
   d. coal gas is expensive to produce.

4. The passage suggests that
   a. the TVA is now privately owned.
   b. the TVA is more interested in what is good for the nation than in making money.
   c. synthetic fuel is cheaper to produce than electricity.
   d. ammonia fertilizers are nonpolluting.

5(a) As used in this passage, the word *generating* means
   a. using
   b. producing
   c. wasting
   d. storing

5(b) As used in this passage, the word *rural* means
   a. vacant
   b. hostile
   c. country
   d. city

5(c) As used in this passage, the work *extract* means
   a. burn
   b. reshape
   c. defy
   d. remove from

222

5(d) As used in this passage, the word *synthetic* means
 a. artificial
 b. dangerous
 c. expensive
 d. inexpensive

PASSAGE 4-6   SUBJECT:
Mary Church Terrell and Ralph Bunche

Mary Church Terrell was born in 1863, the year in which Lincoln signed the Emancipation Proclamation to free the slaves. Ms. Terrell was the daughter of an ex-slave who had gone on to achieve wealth, and she spent her life in the fight for equality. She became an author, a speaker, and an activist, living in segregated Washington, D.C.

In 1895, Mary Terrell became a Washington, D.C., School Board member. In 1896 she was a charter member of the National Association for the Advancement of Colored Women. In 1890 she joined the year-old National Association for the Advancement of Colored People. She organized and led Washington campaigns for women's rights and the fight to integrate Washington restaurants and organized Delta Sigma Theta Sorority in 1913.

She was often sent as the U.S. delegate to international conferences. At the International Council of Women at Berlin, she astounded her audience by giving her speech in German, English, and French. In 1953, at the age of eighty-nine, Mary Terrell lost a court case that found that segregation was valid. In 1954 she died in Annapolis (ə năp′ ə lĭs), but not until a few months after the Supreme Court's decision making discrimination by race illegal.

Ralph Bunche was born in Detroit and educated at UCLA and Harvard. He taught government at Howard University until World War II. Bunche is remembered now for his part in the civil rights struggle, having marched in Selma and Montgomery. But he, too, like Mary Church Terrell, served his government at very high levels.

Bunche worked first for the War Department as an African and Far Eastern specialist, and later he worked as head of the colonial affairs division at the State Department. In 1945 he helped form plans for the United Nations, and in 1947 he became a director of the United Nations Trusteeship division. In 1950 he received the Nobel (nō bĕl′) Peace Prize for his part in the armistice talks, and he also received our highest civilian award, the Medal of Freedom.

Just before his death in 1971, Bunche retired from the United Nations after twenty-five years of service. Having also been a board member of the NAACP for over twenty years, he had a long career of admirable service to both his country and his race.

▲ (376 WORDS) ▲

PASSAGE 4-6

Circle the correct answer:

1. The main idea of this passage is that
    a. Mary Terrell and Ralph Bunche were two very important Americans.
    b. Mary Terrell and Ralph Bunche were influential only in international affairs.
    c. Mary Terrell and Ralph Bunche helped found the NAACP.
    d. Mary Terrell and Ralph Bunche both served in the U.S. government.

2(a) Of which two organizations was Mary Church Terrell a charter member?
    a. National Association for the Advancement of Colored People.
    b. Delta Sigma Theta Sorority.
    c. International Council of Women.
    d. National Association for the Advancement of Colored Women.

2(b) In 1947, Ralph Bunche became
    a. an African and Far Eastern specialist for the War Department.
    b. a Nobel Peace Prize recipient.
    c. a director of the United Nations Trusteeship division.
    d. a board member of the NAACP.

3. We can conclude from this passage that
    a. *both* Bunche and Terrell were well-educated.
    b. Bunche and Terrell served both their country and their race admirably.
    c. Bunche and Terrell involved themselves in their various activities to help their race.
    d. both Bunche and Terrell were proudest of the achievements they made in the area of civil rights.

4. The author's tone is
    a. subjective
    b. sarcastic
    c. indifferent
    d. admiring

5(a) As used in this passage, the word *charter* means
    a. unwilling
    b. minority
    c. founding
    d. protesting

5(b) As used in this passage, the word *astounded* means
    a. amazed
    b. insulted
    c. captured
    d. depressed

5(c) As used in this passage, the word *valid* means
   a. desired
   b. effective
   c. true
   d. legally sound

PASSAGE 4-7

SUBJECT:
Black Americans in the Military

Black Americans have served with honor in every American military action, though this fact is often omitted in history books. Even though black men almost had to beg to be allowed to serve in the Revolutionary War, they went on to serve well. Two black men, Oliver Cromwell and Prince Whipple, were with Washington when he crossed the Delaware on Christmas Day, 1776, to attack the British at Trenton. A black man named Prince Estabrook (ĕs′ tə brŏŏk) captured the Royal Army's General Prescott Newport, and Peter Salem, a black, killed Major Pitcairn (pĭt kârn′) as he was savoring his expected victory at Bunker Hill.

Even though they were forced to serve in segregated units, black soldiers distinguished themselves in combat; this was despite the fact that whites had long believed that blacks could neither command nor use firearms. In 1863, William Carney of the Massachusetts Colored Infantry received the Congressional Medal of Honor for his role in battles with the Plains Indians. Isaiah Dorman (ī zā′ ə dôr′ mən), Custer's black scout, served and died at the Little Big Horn in 1876. Henry Flipper was the first black graduate of West Point in 1877.

In World War I, 40,000 black American combat soldiers served with the French command. Neither U.S. nor British commanders would use these men. But Henry Johnson and Needham Roberts, soldiers in the 369th Infantry's black "Hellfighters" were still the first Americans to win the Croix de Guerre (krwä′ də gâr′), France's top military award.

During World War II over 1,400,000 black men and women served in the armed forces, including some 500,000 who served overseas. Dorie (dō′ rē) Miller, a black mess attendant in the navy, was one of our first heroes in this war. At Pearl Harbor during the Japanese sneak attack, he manned a machine gun and shot down four planes. The black fighter pilots of Benjamin Davis, Jr., distinguished themselves throughout the war. They served most courageously during the Italian campaign.

During the war in Vietnam, mainly because of civil rights pressures in America but also owing to the fine record of black military units, all American forces were fully integrated. Once again blacks played vital roles. And 13.2 percent of all war deaths were of blacks, even though blacks constitute only 11 percent of all Americans. Black American soldiers continue to serve their land well.

▲ (380 WORDS) ▲

PASSAGE 4-7

Circle the correct answer:

1. The main idea of this passage is that
    a. black Americans served admirably during the Revolutionary War.
    b. black Americans have served their country admirably in at least five wars.
    c. black Americans served under the French in World War I.
    d. black Americans constituted a larger portion of war deaths in Vietnam than did any other minority group.

2. Benjamin Davis, Jr., was
    a. commander of a group of black fighter pilots during World War II.
    b. awarded the Croix de Guerre, France's highest military award.
    c. one of the soldiers who crossed the Delaware with Washington in 1776.
    d. a scout for Custer and died at the Little Big Horn.

3. We can conclude from the passage that
    a. blacks make excellent scouts.
    b. blacks were instrumental in the successful defense of Pearl Harbor.
    c. blacks never rose to hold high ranks in the military.
    d. blacks have always felt a sense of patriotism for their country.

4. The passage suggests that
    a. black slaves were forced to fight in the Revolution.
    b. blacks went into the military because they had difficulty securing civilian jobs.
    c. blacks received only menial assignments in the military.
    d. history has kept Americans ignorant of the role that blacks have played in America's military history.

5(a) As used in this passage, the word *savoring* means
    a. demanding
    b. exploiting
    c. assured of
    d. enjoying

5(b) As used in this passage, the word *segregated* means
    a. racially mixed
    b. sexually separated
    c. racially separated
    d. sexually mixed

5(c) As used in this passage, the word *campaign* means
    a. advertisement
    b. battles
    c. peace
    d. loss

5(d) As used in this passage, the word *vital* means
    a. important
    b. lively
    c. insignificant
    d. trivial

PASSAGE 4-8

SUBJECT:
Superman

We're all familiar with the story; just before Krypton (krĭp′ tŏn), a planet that <u>revolved</u> around a red sun, exploded, a scientist placed his infant child in a rocket that eventually carried the boy away from the doomed planet and into the atmosphere of the planet Earth.

Martha and Jonathan Kent discovered the little boy in the wreckage of his rocket; they adopted him and named him Clark. But the little fellow was strangely affected by Earth's atmosphere, particularly its yellow sun. Earth's much weaker gravity made Clark's muscles fantastically powerful. Not only could he bend steel in his bare hands—he could move an airliner with one fingertip or push a supertanker with just one hand. His legs were so strong that he could "leap tall buildings in a single <u>bound</u>"; in fact, he could literally fly around the Earth with one single leap.

The rays from the yellow sun hardened the infant's skin to the toughness of metal and developed his <u>immunity</u> to all diseases, in addition to producing X-ray vision capability in Earth's atmosphere, enabling him to see through walls. His enormous muscles allowed him to perform any action at superspeed, and incredible lung power gave him superbreath, so he could blow the snow from an entire mountain range with one breath.

The hero described here is Superman, of course—the most popular <u>fictional</u> character in the twentieth century. The cartoon was created by Jerry Siegel (sē′ gəl) and Joe Shuster (shoo′ stər), two science fiction fans who grew up in a rough neighborhood in Cleveland: One could write and the other drew pictures, and together they dreamed up stories of an imaginary hero who feared no one and who <u>waged</u> war on crime and corruption. The two of them wrote Superman's adventures for six years before the first story was published in *Action Comics* in 1938; no one could have guessed how popular the character would become.

Superman soon got a comic book of his own, a comic still being published today. A television series based on his comic book adventures was begun in 1955 and is still being shown in syndication today. A feature-length movie made in the late seventies drew enormous audiences and made millions of dollars. Even today the adventures of Superman are known in thirty-five languages. Siegel and Shuster's daydreams have become a fixture of human culture around the world.

▲ (392 WORDS) ▲

PASSAGE 4-8

Circle the correct answer:

1. The purpose of this passage is to
    a. discuss the most popular fictional character in the twentieth century.
    b. describe the development of Superman's powers.
    c. show how Siegel and Shuster developed their character.
    d. explain the appeal of the Superman character in other nations.

2. Superman's muscles were affected by
    a. the explosion of Krypton.
    b. the Earth's atmosphere.
    c. the Earth's gravity.
    d. the rays of a yellow sun.

3. We can conclude from the passage that
    a. the fictional character of Superman was based on an old legend.
    b. Siegel and Shuster never gave up on their character creation.
    c. Superman is no longer popular in the United States.
    d. Siegel and Shuster made very little money from their character.

4. The passage suggests that
    a. Superman was based on a real-life character known to Siegel and Shuster when they were children.
    b. Siegel and Shuster founded *Action Comics*.
    c. Superman was not very popular as a television series.
    d. people all over the world are attracted by a character who fights crime and corruption.

5(a) As used in this passage, the word *revolved* means
    a. sped
    b. hung
    c. fell
    d. orbited

5(b) As used in this passage, the word *bound* means
    a. second
    b. leap
    c. instance
    d. place

5(c) As used in this passage the word *immunity* means
    a. allergy
    b. fear
    c. resistance
    d. susceptibility

5(d) As used in this passage, the word *fictional* means
   a. real
   b. heroic
   c. nonreal
   d. famous

5(e) As used in this passage, the word *waged* means
   a. engaged in
   b. avoided
   c. dreamed of
   d. paid for

PASSAGE 4-9 SUBJECT:
Passports and Visas (vē′ zəz)

Your passport is your official identification as an American citizen. In America, most people never consider obtaining a passport unless they are planning a trip out of the country. In Europe, where travel from one country to another is much more common, almost everyone carries a passport. A passport is final proof of identity in almost every country in the world.

In 1979 almost 15 million Americans held passports. Most of these passports were obtained to travel outside the country because, except for a few Western nations, passports are required to enter every country. And if you travel abroad, you must have a valid passport to reenter the country.

When traveling abroad, you will need a passport for identification when exchanging dollars for francs or marks or other foreign currency. You may also need your passport to use a credit card, buy an airplane ticket, check into a hotel or casino (kə sē′ nō). As a passport is an official U.S. document, it is valuable as identification in any emergency overseas, such as floods, fires, or war.

Don't confuse passports and visas. Whereas a passport is issued by a country to its citizens, a visa is official permission to visit a country granted by the government of that country. For some years, many countries were dropping their visa requirements, but that trend has reversed. Argentina, Brazil, and Venezuela now require visas from U.S. citizens. They may be obtained from the embassy of the country you wish to visit.

Passport applications are available at passport agency offices in large cities like Boston, New York, or Chicago. In smaller cities, applications are available at post offices and at federal courts. To get your first passport, you must submit the application in person, along with a birth certificate and two pictures.

Maybe because most Americans use their passports only when traveling and because they are good for five years, many people lose their passports. Last year, more than 25,000 passports were stolen. And every passport is worth thousands of dollars to smugglers or criminals who desire to enter this country illegally or assume a false identity. Travelers should keep their passports in their pockets or pocketbooks at all times; never pack them or leave them in a room or automobile; when you arrive back home, store your passport in a safe or safety deposit box. And report a lost or stolen passport immediately; it is literally your identity.

▲ (404 WORDS) ▲

PASSAGE 4-9

Circle the correct answer:

1. The main purpose of this passage is to
    a. discuss traveling in other countries.
    b. distinguish between passports and visas.
    c. discuss the financial uses of a passport.
    d. provide information about passports.

2. Passports are beneficial for
    a. exchanging currency.
    b. using a credit card.
    c. checking into hotels.
    d. all of the above.

3. We can conclude from the passage that
    a. passports are more important than visas.
    b. visas and passports are the same thing.
    c. foreign governments issue visas instead of passports.
    d. visas are required to obtain passports.

4. The passage suggests that
    a. most people don't realize how important passports are.
    b. passports aren't important once you are in the country you've chosen to visit.
    c. passports are simple to obtain through the mail.
    d. passports are obtained at the embassy once you enter a country.

5(a) As used in this passage, the word *valid* means
    a. foreign
    b. legal
    c. monetary
    d. illegal

5(b) As used in this passage, the word *trend* means
    a. tendency
    b. flow
    c. law
    d. vocalization

5(c) As used in this passage, the word *assume* means
    a. discover
    b. steal
    c. adopt
    d. smuggle

234

PASSAGE 4-10

SUBJECT: Microwaves

Microwaves are a type of electromagnetic radiation; they are a very mild form of electrical or magnetic wave that moves through space. Unlike X rays and gamma (găm' mə) rays, which are very powerful waves of radiation, microwaves are rather weak and are much more like the waves of radiation used in radio broadcasting.

In microwave ovens, the use of microwaves with which most people are familiar, the waves are produced by an electronic tube called a magnetron (măg' nə trŏn). Microwaves produce heat in any food placed inside the oven by causing the water in the food to vibrate rapidly and thus heat up. Food that have more water in them take less time to cook and probably have more of their nutrients left intact when cooked in a microwave oven.

Microwaves do not pass through metal, so the microwaves are retained inside the oven. Microwaves pass immediately through glass, paper, and plastic with no effect on these materials or on the microwaves; nothing inside a microwave is heated except the food itself, so the cooking process is much more efficient than in conventional ovens. Sometimes a pan or container is heated because it is touching the hot food, though; some users of microwave ovens have been burned by hot food, by hot pans, or steam escaping from the food. No documented case of radiation burns from a microwave oven has ever been reported.

Actually, we know very little about how microwave radiation might affect human beings. Obviously, if microwaves can cook a roast by exciting the water molecules (mŏl' ə kyoolz) in the meat, they could do the same thing to human flesh. Human beings could be burned by prolonged exposure to high levels of microwaves. But scientists are more concerned about the effects of low-level microwave exposures, such as might result from a leaking microwave oven.

No research has yet been performed on people who have been exposed to low-level microwave radiation. Some experiments have been performed on animals, but the results are difficult to interpret. As the eyes are particularly sensitive, rabbits exposed to low-level microwaves were checked for the growth of cataracts (kăt' ə răks), and none were found. On the other hand, some animals seem able to sense microwave radiation and try to escape from it immediately. In others, microwave radiation causes the body to react as if defending itself against a disease. These responses lead some scientists to think that microwave radiation is harmful, though in some yet-undiscovered way.

▲ (405 WORDS) ▲

PASSAGE 4-10

Circle the correct answer:

1. The purpose of this passage is to
   a. discuss the beneficial use of microwaves.
   b. discuss the harmful effects of microwaves.
   c. discuss modern methods of cooking.
   (d.) discuss the use and possible harmful effects of microwaves.

2. Microwaves are
   a. absolutely safe at low levels.
   (b.) very efficient for cooking.
   c. cancer-causing in people with weak eyes.
   d. completely understood by scientists.

3. We can conclude from the passage that
   a. the heat created in microwave ovens is difficult to control.
   b. food tastes better when it has been cooked in a microwave oven.
   (c.) food cooked in a microwave oven is probably more nutritious than food cooked in more conventional ways.
   d. most research on the effects of microwaves on humans has been restricted to the study of low-level microwave radiation.

4. The author's tone is
   (a.) objective
   b. sarcastic
   c. negative
   d. skeptical

5(a) As used in this passage, the word *intact* means
   a. useless
   b. burned
   c. tasteless
   (d.) whole

5(b) As used in this passage, the word *retained* means
   a. bounced
   b. lost
   (c.) kept
   d. dispersed

5(c) As used in this passage, the word *conventional* means
   a. gas-operated
   (b.) customary
   c. radical
   d. sublime

5(d) As used in this passage, the word *documented* means
   a. numbered
   b. recorded
   c. legal
   d. believable

5(e) As used in this passage, the word *prolonged* means
   a. extended
   b. brief
   c. dangerous
   d. fatal

PASSAGE 4-11   SUBJECT:
George and John Johnson

Two of the wealthiest black men in America live in Chicago, with its large black middle-class community; because both men are named Johnson, their names and businesses are sometimes each confused with the other, aggravating both men. Each is justifiably proud of the business he has created for himself and the position it gives him in black cultural, social, and business life.

George Johnson is the founder of Johnson Products Company, which manufactures cosmetics. The Johnson Products Company is one of the largest black-owned companies in the United States, and it is also one of the most successful. Its founders and its corporate officers are proud of the company's position. They also feel a certain pride because the Johnson Products Company was among the first companies to realize that blacks in America were a distinct market group, with distinct needs, and with the affluence to buy and support products aimed at meeting their needs. The Johnson Products cosmetics are all designed for the needs of blacks. Ultra-Sheen and Afro-Sheen were for many years unique until companies saw Johnson's success and began to bring out rival cosmetics.

John Johnson is the founder of Johnson Publishing Company, the largest black-owned publishing company in the nation. As an office boy at Supreme Life Insurance, Johnson was assigned to maintain a file of news clippings about the achievements of blacks, and he noticed that there was no national newspaper or magazine devoted to coverage of black news. He borrowed the printing equipment at the life insurance offices, and he raised money for advertisements by mortgaging his mother's furniture. He knew he was going to make it when $6,000 worth of subscriptions poured in for his first issue. His monthly *Negro Digest* made him wealthy enough to launch a second publication, *Ebony,* which was even more successful than his first. *Ebony* has one and a third million subscribers. Mrs. Johnson, needless to say, was able to keep her furniture; today the Johnson Publishing Company has annual sales figures of around $40 million. The company, if it were ever sold, would probably be worth more than $60 million because the company has branched into real estate, banking, and insurance. The officers and owners are proud that this success has come from serving the black community, once again proving its power as a market. *Life* magazine, which *Ebony* followed in its use of large photographs, has ceased publication, but *Ebony* keeps rolling off the presses every week.

▲ (412 WORDS) ▲

PASSAGE 4-11

Circle the correct answer:

1. The purpose of this passage is to
    a. provide a short biography of George Johnson.
    b. provide a short biography of two of the wealthiest black men in America.
    c. discuss the buying power of the black community.
    d. provide a short biography of John Johnson.

2. According to the passage, which of the following statements is not true?
    a. *Ebony* magazine provided Johnson with the capital to start *Negro Digest*.
    b. The Johnson Products Company is one of the largest black-owned companies in the United States.
    c. John Johnson started out as an office boy.
    d. *Ebony* has over a million subscribers.

3. We can conclude from the passage that
    a. *Ebony* imitated *Life* magazine in an attempt to appeal to white audiences.
    b. there aren't enough affluent blacks to support a product aimed at them only.
    c. *Life* magazine began to imitate *Ebony* in order to enlarge their audience.
    d. both George and John Johnson believed there was a product market in the black community.

4. The passage suggests that
    a. Johnson Publishing Company is the third largest publishing house in the United States.
    b. Johnson Publishing Company publishes only books by black authors.
    c. most white-owned companies had ignored the black buyer prior to the Johnsons' success.
    d. white-owned companies have taken over the cosmetic field first tapped by the Johnson Products Company.

5(a) As used in this passage, the word *distinct* means
    a. separate
    b. poor
    c. divided
    d. problem

5(b) As used in this passage, the word *affluence* means
    a. wealth
    b. credit
    c. knowledge
    d. rationale

5(c) As used in this passage, the word *rival* means
    a. duplicate
    b. better

c. more expensive
  d. competing

5(d) As used in this passage, the word *devoted* means
  a. able
  b. qualified
  c. supportive
  d. dedicated

PASSAGE 4-12

SUBJECT:

Sugar has acquired a bad reputation in recent years. Sugar is often, for example, listed as a cause of obesity (ō bē′ sə tē) and other problems.

Actually, sugar has no more calories than other substances in foods. Sugar has four calories per gram, but then so does protein, the mainstay of most reducing diets. Sugar may contribute to overweight, but usually as only one of several contributing factors. Generally, of course, overweight is caused by the consumption of too many calories. Usually, an overweight person will find that these surplus calories are found in a high carbohydrate (kär bō hī′ drāt) diet, and sugar is one of many carbohydrates.

Doctors often tell dieters to cut sugar from their diets. Sugar can be eliminated. This cuts out some calories without losing any nutritional value. Sugar calories are often called "empty calories" because there are no vitamins or minerals in sugar. It is a simple matter for an overweight person to eliminate these empty calories; it is equally simple for an underweight person to add these empty calories to gain weight. And most dietitians agree that the empty calories are fine as long as the person consuming them is not overweight or allowing the sugar to prevent the eating of nutritional food.

Some research had indicated that sugar can cause a child to suffer from hyperactivity; not so, according to Dr. A. T. Murphey, a fellow of the American Diabetes Association. "It has been theorized, but I don't know that there's any proof of it." Children often prefer sweets, possibly because sweets are sometimes used as rewards, but most children learn to like other foods.

And sugar is not an addicting substance, despite some dietitians claims. It is a habit, an acquired preference; if people eliminate sugar from their diets, there will be no "withdrawal" symptoms.

Sugar isn't even a source of quick energy as many people think. Those people who eat a candy bar for a quick lift when they feel tired are just fooling themselves; the feeling of energy some claim to experience after a candy bar or cola may be due to the caffeine (kă fēn′), but it's certainly not because of sugar. The body uses the sugar, but only after adrenalin (ə drĕn′ əl ĭn) has stimulated the liver to release sugar into the bloodstream.

In fact, the only disease associated with sugar is tooth decay, and even tooth decay isn't caused by sugar, but by bacteria that grow and thrive in sugar. In other words, if you brush your teeth frequently, even this ill-effect of sugar is just another myth.

▲ (420 WORDS) ▲

PASSAGE 4-12

Circle the correct answer:

1. This passage is mainly about
    a. the effect of sugar on weight control.
    b. the myths that surround sugar.
    c. the effect of sugar on activity levels in humans.
    d. the ill-effects of sugar consumption.

2. Sugar calories are often called "empty calories" because they
    a. negate the effect of nutritional foods.
    b. contain no vitamins or minerals.
    c. are the first calories cut from a diet.
    d. provide no energy.

3. We can conclude from the passage that
    a. despite belief to the contrary, sugar doesn't contribute to obesity.
    b. sugar is less dangerous to people than are saturated fats.
    c. sugar is not the dietary "culprit" we think it is.
    d. sugar is the only carbohydrate that affects weight.

4. The passage suggests that
    a. sugar's effect on activity level is widely misrepresented.
    b. reducing the amount of sugar consumed is the most effective diet.
    c. protein is also called an "empty calorie" source.
    d. the danger sugar consumption represents to teeth is sufficient reason to eliminate it from the diet.

5(a) As used in this passage, the word *obesity* means
    a. underweight
    b. normal weight
    c. loss of weight
    d. overweight

5(b) As used in this passage, the word *mainstay* means
    a. harmful element
    b. central ingredient
    c. only ingredient
    d. nemesis

5(c) As used in this passage, the word *surplus* means
    a. excess
    b. vital
    c. dangerous
    d. fatty

5(d) As used in this passage, the word *addicting* means
    a. pain-relieving

b. beneficial
   c. habit-forming
   d. damaging

5(e) As used in this passage, the word *myth* means
   a. false belief
   b. fear
   c. fairy tale
   d. fact

PASSAGE 4-13

SUBJECT: Vitamin E

Is vitamin E a cure for baldness? Will it cure acne (ăk′ nē)? Can vitamin E relieve the pain of arthritis or prevent ulcers? These are only a few of the uses some people claim for vitamin E, but for many years no scientific proof has been possible for any of these claims.

Vitamin E is not a rare substance by any means; it is present in vegetable oils and in grains, but in most diets the main source of vitamin E is leafy vegetables. Some vitamin E is lost in the cooking process, but not a really significant amount; a good balanced diet will, according to critics of "vitamin medicine," supply all the vitamin E anyone needs.

In animals, shortage of vitamin E causes sudden and obvious changes. Chickens deprived of E develop muscular weakness. Calves whose diet contain inadequate amounts of E develop heart disease. Rats who are deprived of E develop liver degeneration. Nor do they grow as quickly as healthy rats.

But in humans, with one exception, there are no symptoms of any kind associated with a vitamin E deficiency. Premature infants who lack proper amounts of vitamin E sometimes develop anemia (ə nē′ mē ə) or skin rashes, but any symptoms caused by this deficiency in adult humans are either too insignificant to appear in normal tests or are simply nonexistent. A study in Elgin, Illinois, followed subjects maintained on low vitamin E diets for six years and could discover no effects of the diet on the subjects at all.

Some studies, such as a study performed by three Canadian doctors in the late 1940s, have found vitamin E helpful in treating specific diseases, such as angina pectoris (ăn jī′ nə pĕk′ tə rĭs), a type of heart disease. But other studies have tried to duplicate these findings and failed. So there is no absolutely undeniable evidence that vitamin E will prevent or cure disease.

Claims for the cosmetic use of vitamin E continue to multiply, however. Creams and ointments containing vitamin E appear on the market almost daily, to help remove skin blemishes, to help soften dry skin, to control skin wrinkles. Vitamin E is even used in deodorants. E itself is a preservative, an antioxidant, so the producers' thinking is that vitamin E will prevent odor by preventing bacteria from oxidizing perspiration. But no study or medical proof ever appeared to prove any of these cosmetic claims completely.

You can add vitamin E pills to your morning routine if you like, but unfortunately no one has ever been able to demonstrate conclusively any reason why you should.

▲ (424 WORDS) ▲

PASSAGE 4-13

Circle the correct answer:

1. The main idea of this passage is that
   a. taken as a preventive measure against disease, vitamin E can be harmful.
   b. although vitamin E has not been proved effective in fighting disease, it does have some cosmetic value.
   c. most of the medical and cosmetic claims about vitamin E are not supported by research.
   d. advertisers are attempting to mislead the public with their claims about vitamin E.

2. In animals, vitamin E deficiency is associated with all of the following disorders except
   a. heart disease
   b. diabetes
   c. liver degeneration
   d. muscular weakness

3(a) We can conclude from this passage that
   a. a balanced diet is probably preferable to vitamin supplements.
   b. the American public is gullible.
   c. vitamin supplements can be useful for farm stock.
   d. the FDA should supervise advertisers more closely.

3(b) Which of the following conclusions is not supported by the passage?
   a. Vitamin E deficiency is less harmful to humans than to other animals.
   b. Vitamin E may be helpful in treating angina pectoris.
   c. Vitamin E is more useful cosmetically than medically.
   d. Vitamin E is fairly abundant in a balanced diet.

4. The passage suggests that
   a. little research has been done to protect consumers.
   b. the public regards vitamin E as a "wonder" drug.
   c. advertising is basically a business of deception.
   d. some research that has been reported has been proved false.

5(a) As used in this passage, the word *degeneration* means
   a. ailment
   b. deterioration
   c. deviance
   d. maturation

5(b) As used in this passage, the word *premature* means
   a. born later than normal
   b. stillborn
   c. born earlier than normal
   d. unaware

5(c) As used in this passage, the word *duplicate* means
   a. erase
   b. disprove
   c. falsify
   d. reproduce

5(d) As used in this passage, the word *cosmetic* means
   a. medical
   b. beautifying
   c. damaging
   d. degenerative

PASSAGE 4-14

SUBJECT: The Poles and American History

Legends about Polish sailors aboard Columbus's ships and of Polish explorers who sailed to America before Columbus link the Polish and American people even before there was a country called America. Many early settlers in the New World were Polish craftsmen, explorers, or soldiers.

Perhaps two of the best-known Poles connected with America's past are Count C. Pulaski (pōō lăs′ kē) and General T. Kosciuszko (kŏs ē ŭs′ kō). Both these men fought in the American Revolution. Pulaski was an idealist who volunteered to fight for freedom, even for the freedom of another country. He was flamboyant, but brilliant and a very hard worker. He put together the American cavalry force that led to many American victories, and he created this American cavalry at a moment when even the American commander, George Washington, was beginning to become indecisive and discouraged. He may, in fact, have been Washington's major military planner.

General Kosciuszko aided the Continental Army in quite another way. He was an engineer, building forts and fortifications. Kosciuszko was a genius at using the terrain of an area as a fortification. He could dig trenches, cut trees, and use natural barriers to make a fortress out of any camp. He helped the American army countless times in just this manner. His use of terrain was primarily responsible for the American victory at Saratoga (sărə tō′ gə), which brought the French into the war on America's side.

Throughout the 1800s immigration of Poles to America was steady. By the early 1900s, two and a half million Polish peasants had come to America. They were often a source of cheap, unskilled labor, forced into ethnic "neighborhoods." But within one generation, partly because of hard work and the value they placed on education and financial independence, Poles began to excel in the professions, the arts, and the sciences. Helena (hĕ′ lĕ nə) Modjeska (mə jĕs′ kə), a Polish actress, was probably the finest Shakespearean actress in the world at the turn of the century. And few people realize that Madame Curie (kyōōr′ ē), who discovered radium (rā′ dē əm), was actually Marie Curie-Sklodowska (sklə dō′ skə), a Polish scientist who had married a French scientist. Mme. Curie traveled to America to aid in establishing Polish-American educational institutions.

Polish-American names are now familiar in almost every range of U.S. life. Many Polish-Americans continue to work in the creative fields, among them Arthur Rubinstein (rōō′ bən stīn), the great pianist, and Charles Bronson and Jack Palance, leading Hollywood "character" actors. Many are sports stars. John Matuszak (mə tōō′ săk) of the Oakland Raiders, Carl Yastrzemski (yə strĕm′ skē) of the Boston Red Sox, and

247

Hank Stram (străm), ex-coach of the New Orleans Saints are examples. No area is as resistant to the growth of "outsiders" as politics, but Polish-Americans like Barry Goldwater, Senator Edmund Muskie, and former National Security Council Chairman Dr. Zbigniew Brzezinski (zvĭg' noo brŭ zĭn' skē) are proof that the intermingling of these two countries continues and is as thorough as ever.

▲ (462 WORDS) ▲

PASSAGE 4-14

Circle the correct answer:

1. The main idea of this passage is that
   a. the Poles helped America win the Revolutionary War.
   b. the Poles have great influence in American politics.
   c. many fine actors and actresses are Polish.
   d. people of Polish descent have become influential in American life.

2. Which of the following was not a reason for the Poles' success in America?
   a. The value they placed on financial independence.
   b. The value they placed on education.
   c. The value they placed on maintaining their ethnic "neighborhoods."
   d. The value they placed on hard work.

3. We can conclude from this passage that
   a. the Poles are masters at planning military strategy.
   b. the Poles are the most industrious of the Europeans who immigrated to America.
   c. the Poles have contributed greatly in the growth of America.
   d. the Poles are usually artistically inclined.

4. The author cites Count Pulaski and General Kosciuszko to show
   a. that the Poles have been involved in the development of America since the beginning of our nation.
   b. that Poles were involved in the Revolutionary War.
   c. how important the calvary was in the Revolutionary War.
   d. that Poles are brilliant military advisors.

5(a) As used in this passage, the word *idealist* means
   a. a person who believes in visions.
   b. a person who believes in beauty.
   c. a person who believes in absolute perfection.
   d. a person who believes in worthy humanitarian principles.

5(b) As used in this passage, the word *flamboyant* means
    a. lazy
    b. colorful
    c. quiet
    d. boring

5(c) As used in this passage, the word *terrain* means
    a. the surrounding trees
    b. the natural curvatures of the land
    c. the location
    d. the height

5(d) As used in this passage, the word *ethnic* means
    a. exclusive
    b. standard
    c. high-priced
    d. racially and culturally separated

PASSAGE 4-15

SUBJECT:
Roy Wilkins

In 1931, Roy Wilkins took a job as a secretary of the NAACP. This group was founded in 1909 by whites who sought to further integration of the races. Wilkins moved to New York. There he swiftly moved up in the offices of the National Association for the Advancement of Colored People. By 1934, Wilkins was editor of *The Crisis,* the NAACP journal, a top rank post. In 1949, Wilkins became head of internal affairs at the NAACP, and in 1955 he took the job of chief director. He held this post until he retired in 1977.

Wilkins was born in 1901. His parents had come to St. Louis to escape the impoverishment of Holly Springs, Mississippi. Because his mother died early, Roy was sent at the age of four to live with his aunt and uncle in St. Paul, Minnesota, and it was here that he learned to value hard work and commitment.

At college, Wilkins became interested in civil rights and journalism; after graduating with a diploma in social work, he went to work for a black newspaper in Kansas City. Wilkins wrote a column, urging blacks to unite themselves, to protest, and to exercise their civil rights; it was this column that made him a public figure, and it was this column that got him the attention of the NAACP and his first job with that group.

Black men were working by the thousands in the early thirties on flood control projects. Along the Mississippi, these men lived and worked under very primitive conditions. They were worked eighty hours a week, but their pay was often no more than ten cents an hour. Wilkins and another NAACP officer went to Mississippi and discovered these facts, which they published in *Mississippi River Slavery—1932.* The Senate inquiry that followed altered the conditions in these flood projects permanently.

During the great civil rights battles of the sixties, the NAACP was sometimes criticized for its moderate approach. Apparently some of the young radicals had forgotten Wilkins' early work. He also came under criticism for resisting the complete unification of all civil rights organizations into one body. But, to Wilkins' mind, such a course would have contradicted everything the NAACP had always stood for. Why should all blacks, with their varying hopes and goals, pretend to be all the same? Wilkins felt this might even create more stereotyped images of blacks.

Whatever criticism might have been leveled at Wilkins, history shows that during the almost fifty years he worked for the NAACP, blacks made their greatest advances in this country. In the 1920s, blacks were not even allowed in many public buildings, and lynchings were reported far too often. The NAACP led the fight that resulted in five Civil Rights Acts, the Voting Rights Acts, and the Fair Housing Act, as well as the public school desegregation laws.

▲ (477 WORDS) ▲

PASSAGE 4-15

Circle the correct answer:

1. The best title for this passage is
   a. Roy Wilkins, Civil Rights Leader
   b. Roy Wilkins
   c. Slavery on the Mississippi
   d. The NAACP

2. Which of the following statements about Roy Wilkins is not true?
   a. Roy Wilkins became a secretary of the NAACP.
   b. Wilkins became editor of *The Crisis* in 1955.
   c. Wilkins was born around the turn of the century.
   d. Wilkins led the NAACP for almost fifty years.

3. We can conclude from the passage that
   a. Wilkins left the NAACP disenchanted.
   b. Wilkins' college training was of little use to him as leader of the NAACP.
   c. Wilkins was more interested in his writing than in becoming the leader of the NAACP.
   d. Wilkins served as a moderating force in the civil rights movement.

4. The passage suggests that
   a. Wilkins saw the trap of unifying all civil rights movements under one organization.
   b. Wilkins realized that nonviolent protest would never solve the problems of blacks.
   c. Wilkins broke with the philosophy of liberal whites early in the 1920s.
   d. Wilkins' *greatest* achievement was helping the workers of the flood projects along the Mississippi.

5(a) As used in this passage, the word *impoverishment* means
   a. wealth
   b. poverty
   c. cruelty
   d. climate

5(b) As used in this passage, the work *primitive* means
- a. not evolved
- b. primordial
- c. crude
- d. remedial

5(c) As used in this passage, the word *altered* means
- a. changed
- b. helped continue
- c. left unchanged
- d. remotivated

5(d) As used in this passage, the work *moderate* means
- a. severe
- b. cowardly
- c. calmly reasonable
- d. unreliable

5(e) As used in this passage, the word *stereotyped* means
- a. frightening
- b. categorized
- c. obvious
- d. pleasant sounding

PASSAGE 4-16

SUBJECT:
Organic Foods

At a time when food prices are rising faster than ever before, it seems surprising that many consumers are willing to pay premium prices for "health" foods. In 1972 health foods—or natural or organic foods, for the terms are often used virtually interchangeably—accounted for $500 million in annual sales. Less than a decade later, the figure has changed to $3 billion.

The popularity of organic foods can be traced to many people's nostalgia for a simpler, more pioneerlike life-style. And many people believe that organic foods are safer than foods produced on a large scale by traditional methods. Many people also believe that these organic foods contain more and better nutrients than conventional food.

In fact, plants absorb all their food directly from the soil in inorganic form, no matter where the nutrients may originally have come from. Experiments in Michigan and in England that went on for twenty-five years were unable to find any difference in plants raised organically and plants raised with chemical fertilizers. Things that do affect nutrient content are climate, time of harvest, and genetics—but no difference results when plants are grown organically.

Neither are organically grown plants free from chemicals such as pesticides. Some pesticides leave traces in the soil for years; these traces may be absorbed by the plant that is "organically" grown. Rainfall may wash pesticides from neighboring farms onto "organic" fields, and sprays or other applications of chemicals may drift and cause the same problem.

Furthermore, all foods—whether grown conventionally or organically—may contain toxic substances to some degree; the Food and Drug Administration (FDA) maintains constant checks to ensure that these substances are kept at a harmless level, but aflatoxin (ă flū tŏx′ ĭn), a mold that causes cancer, may grow on corn or peanuts or be present in milk. Lead and arsenic (är′ sǝ nĭk) are sometimes present in bonemeal or seafood. And many vegetables contain poisonous compounds such as oxalic (ŏk′ sǝ lĭk) acid and nitrite (nī′ trāt) compounds. The point is that these may be present in a given food, no matter how the food was grown and cultivated. Toxic substances in food do not necessarily have to come from fertilizers or chemical sprays.

The government agencies may never totally regulate the organic food industry. Obviously, they keep watch over the presence of toxins or cancer-causing substances in food, but there is no way these agencies can protect the consumer against the largest fraud of all: substituting conventional foods for health foods and charging the customer a higher price. Because the two types of food are indistinguishable once they have left the farm, the FDA would have to watch the entire production of a plant, from the planting of the seed to the harvesting and processing before a food could be certified as organic. In our society, that's not going to happen for a long time. In the meantime, if you prefer organic foods, you should ask yourself if the psychological effect is worth the increase in your food bill every week.

▲ (497 WORDS) ▲

PASSAGE 4-16

Circle the correct answer:

1. This passage is mainly about
   a. the rise in demand for organic food in the last decade.
   b. how organic plants are grown.
   c. the toxic substances that are contained in both organically and inorganically grown food.
   d. the numerous fallacies that exist about organically grown foods.

2. The popularity of organic foods can be traced to all of the following except
   a. people's fear of vascular disease.
   b. people's nostalgia for a simpler life-style.
   c. people's belief that organic foods are safer.
   d. people's belief that organic foods are more nutritious.

3. We can conclude from the passage that
   a. there is some risk of toxic substances in all types of food grown in the earth.
   b. organic foods are more expensive because of the expense of growing them.
   c. though more expensive, organic foods are more nutritious.
   d. the FDA is more concerned with monitoring organically grown foods than inorganically grown foods.

4(a) The passage suggests that
   a. in the long run, organic foods are more dangerous than inorganic ones.
   b. the organic food industry is preying on the public's misconceptions about its product.
   c. organic foods can be dangerous because they aren't controlled by the FDA.
   d. higher food prices are a result of organic foods.

4(b) The author's tone is
   a. professional
   b. neutral
   c. negative
   d. positive

5(a) As used in this passage, the word *genetics* means
    a. descriptive of an entire group
    b. hereditary transmissions
    c. birth of anything
    d. ancestry

5(b) As used in this passage, the word *toxic* means
    a. nutritional
    b. beneficial
    c. caloric
    d. harmful

5(c) As used in this passage, the word *regulate* means
    a. own
    b. trust
    c. control
    d. defend

PASSAGE 4-17

SUBJECT:
Health Risks

Is ordinary, everyday living hazardous to your health? People are beginning to think so.

Since World War II, synthetic chemicals have spread throughout the human environment. Most of these are "convenience" chemicals; they preserve our food, color our hair, keep insects away. But they are new in our world and are still being tested to see if they increase the risks of living.

These preservatives, pesticides, colorings, and other chemicals are being tested in several ways. Laboratory tests can show if a chemical damages living cells immediately. Long-term studies of workers who make or contact a chemical regularly in their jobs may show if a particular chemical is harmful. Or a chemical can be tried on animals to determine whether it is harmful to humans and animals. So far, around thirty chemicals have been found to cause cancer in humans and animals. Under a law called the Delaney (də lān′ ē) Act, Congress must ban these chemicals immediately.

But the Delaney Act does not apply to chemicals that are clearly harmful as long as they do not produce cancer or as long as they are not in food. *Science* magazine estimates that of the 1,500 chemicals used to make pesticides, one-fourth possibly cause cancer, another one-third are clearly harmful, and only five are specifically restricted.

But there are enough natural poisons in food to make living risky enough. Aflatoxin (ăf lə tŏx′ ĭn) is a mold that occurs on corn, peanuts, and peanut butter; scientists say it definitely causes cancer. Potatoes and spinach contain a natural chemical that prevents the bones from absorbing the calcium (kăl′ sē əm) they need. Cabbage and cauliflower prevent the thyroid (thī′ roid) from obtaining the iodine (ī′ ə dīn) it needs and can thus produce goiters (goi′ tərz). Lettuce, spinach, tea, and leeks all have cancer-causing substances in them. Lima beans, yams, peas, apricots all have a chemical compound in them that is very similar to cyanide (sī′ ə nīd).

Potassium (pə tăs′ sē əm) 40 is a natural compound that exists freely in nature and that is radioactive. The body does not distinguish between radioactive potassium and other potassium. Any potassium is absorbed right into the muscle tissue with the other minerals. The more muscle you have, the more radioactive you are.

Along with the health hazards caused by chemicals in the environment, there are hazards caused by life-styles. Cigarettes may be linked with cancer and heart disease; smoking shortens your life by 2,250 days. Alcohol causes liver disease, so just average drinking will shorten your life by 130 days. Living in a polluted city shortens your life. Chest X rays can be dangerous, as is eating charcoal-broiled steaks. Living near a nuclear plant or living near a polyvinyl chloride (pŏl ē vī′ nəl klôr′ ĭd) plant increases your risk. Being overweight shortens your life expectancy by 1,300 days, and becoming a miner is risky because of cave-ins and black lung disease; even staying single is dangerous, too. On the average, unmarried men live 3,500 fewer days than married men.

It is impossible to exist in this world and avoid risks; although everything is not hazardous to your health; so many things are that it is impossible to avoid danger altogether.

▲ (509 WORDS) ▲

PASSAGE 4-17

Circle the correct answer:

1. The purpose of this passage is to
   a. discuss the man-made and natural hazards to our health in our everyday life.
   b. to compare man-made cancer-causing agents and natural cancer-causing agents.
   c. defend the use of man-made chemicals.
   d. refute the idea that everyday life is dangerous to our health.

2. According to the passage, which of the following statements is not true?
   a. The human body knows the difference between radioactive potassium and ordinary potassium.
   b. The Delaney Act applies only to cancer-causing chemicals or to chemicals found in food.
   c. Aflatoxins are molds found on corn, peanuts, and peanut butter.
   d. Chest X rays and eating charcoal-broiled steaks are both dangerous to humans.

3. We can conclude from the passage that
   a. cancer-causing agents occur only in food.
   b. the Delaney Act is not sufficient to control dangerous chemicals.
   c. potassium should be avoided in the human diet.
   d. vegetables should be avoided because they are cancer-causing.

4. The passage suggests that
   a. the cancer-causing agents in vegetables are absorbed by the plants from fertilizers in the soil.
   b. it is safer to live near a polyvinyl chloride plant than to live near a nuclear plant.

    c. even without man-made chemicals, man's health is in danger from natural substances.
    d. cigarette smoking is more dangerous to your health than remaining single.

5(a) As used in this passage, the word *hazardous* means
    a. important
    b. conducive
    c. beneficial
    d. dangerous

5(b) As used in this passage, the word *pesticides* means
    a. fertilizers
    b. preservatives
    c. hair dyes
    d. insect poisons

5(c) As used in this passage, the word *ban* means
    a. promote
    b. restrict
    c. produce
    d. encourage

5(d) As used in this passage, the word *distinguish* means
    a. differentiate
    b. duplicate
    c. rely
    d. avoid

PASSAGE 4-18   SUBJECT:
Nineteenth- and Twentieth-Century Eating Habits

In the nineteenth century, the working class made great advances in the quality of its food and diet. Bread was no longer "the staff of life"; higher wages, greater agricultural production, and the importation of cheap meat and grain, particularly in England and America, allowed a much greater variety of food. The average working man could afford meat and vegetables every day. Bacon, eggs, and fish were becoming common; puddings and tarts were favorite desserts. Margarine was invented in 1870, and the lower classes happily used this as a substitute for butter. As people moved into towns and away from the country, where fresh produce had been available, canned and potted food took the place of produce and provided them foods many had never seen before.

In upper-class Victorian houses, by 1865 or so, the variety of foods was enormous. A lavish and elaborate breakfast would be followed by midmorning tea or wine with biscuits; the midday meals were varied and followed in midafternoon by tea and biscuits. Dinner was served later and later, as lunch became a more substantial meal later in the century. In the best homes, dinner was served in two courses: the first course was soup, then fish, then meats and six casseroles. The second course was two roasts, six vegetables, and two desserts. These dinners soon became extremely complicated and were often provided by a professional caterer, except in the homes of the very wealthy, who had enough servants to produce these extravaganzas (ĕk străv ə găn' zəz) themselves.

In America, early in this century, both upper-class and working-class households followed the English pattern. But working-class meals, particularly in rural homes, were changed by a very serious attempt to educate the housewife. Schools, the Department of Agriculture, and college extension courses urged the housewife to offer her family varied and balanced meals, and home canning and preserving offered the rural housewife a greater choice of foods, and the urban housewife benefited from healthy trade and markets. The "home-cooked meal" became not only a nostalgic ideal, but a practical and nutritious daily occurrence.

In the past two decades, though, a radically new practice has become commonplace. In Victorian times, restaurants were only for travelers or the wealthy, but Americans now spend one-third of their total food budget eating out in various types of restaurants and fast-food shops.

Perhaps the reason for this is that, compared to the early years of this century, the population has changed itself so dramatically. More housewives work, more people live alone for various reasons, and incomes are higher. For all of these reasons, people prefer to eat outside the home, either to save the time and energy that would have been spent on food preparation or simply to have a more enjoyable experience. Another reason for this trend is that the variety of restaurant services has increased, offering everything from takeout "fish-and-chips" to tacos, from steak to exotic ethnic foods.

As incomes have risen, the trend has always been toward more variety in foods and toward less labor on the part of the housewife.

▲ (509 WORDS) ▲

PASSAGE 4-18

Circle the correct answer:

1. This passage is mainly about
    a. the variety of foods eaten by the working class.
    b. the dietary habits of nineteenth-century Americans.
    c. how dietary habits developed in the nineteenth century and how they have changed in the twentieth century.
    d. the diets of upper-class Victorians.

2. As people moved into towns and away from the country,
    a. bacon, eggs, and fish became common in most homes.
    b. margarine came to be a substitute for butter.
    c. canned and potted foods took the place of produce.
    d. dinner became a three-course meal.

3. We can conclude from this passage that
    a. people ate more vegetables in the nineteenth century than we do today.
    b. dietary habits are greatly affected by income level.
    c. modern dietary habits are unhealthy.
    d. the upper-class considers the size of the evening meal as a status symbol.

4. The passage suggests that
    a. as America has modernized, so have our eating habits.
    b. prior to the nineteenth century, people ate only fresh foods.
    c. fast-food restaurants have taken the place of the extravagant feasts of the nineteenth century.
    d. the Women's Liberation Movement has affected America's dietary habits because women refuse to cook.

5(a) As used in this passage, the word *lavish* means
    a. extravagant
    b. torrent

    c. tasty
    d. catered

5(b) As used in this passage, the word *substantial* means
    a. unreal
    b. wealthy
    c. nutritional
    d. ample

5(c) As used in this passage, the word *extravaganzas* means
    a. elaborate meals
    b. charades
    c. useless affairs
    d. dances

5(d) As used in this passage, the word *nostalgic* means
    a. culinary
    b. longed for
    c. romantic
    d. unrealistic

PASSAGE 4-19   SUBJECT:
Agoraphobia (ăg ə rə fō′ bē ə)

Agoraphobia may be the world's most common, most misunderstood, and most often badly treated of all the phobias. Most of the phobias (fō′ bē əz) or irrational fears are fears of one specific object or situation. A person may be morbidly afraid of snakes or insects or even cats, or a person may have an irrational fear of high places or of eating in public. Agoraphobia is so different from these specific fears that some psychologists and psychiatrists argue that it should be classified separately—and treated differently—from any of the other phobias.

The Greek word *phobos* means "panic" or "flight"; *agora* means "place of assembly" or "meeting area." Thus agoraphobia refers to the fear of public places. Some doctors claim that agoraphobia is responsible for as many as 60 percent of all visits from patients with phobias. But figures and statistics about this disease are as misleading as they are difficult to obtain; because the sufferer from agoraphobia is often afraid to travel or even to leave home, many thousands of victims may never have sought treatment.

This "fear of open places" takes many forms. Patients with agoraphobia may fear traveling or fear being alone. Very frequently these fears are fears of "losing control" before a crowd of onlookers. Thus, the agoraphobic avoids shopping or standing in line at movie theaters. Quite often the fear takes the form of dreading some potential disaster: accident, death, madness, hurting or losing a family member. In fact, quite often the agoraphobic's (ăg ə rə fō′ bĭks) fear seems almost to be a fear of fear itself. Male agoraphobics, for example, often suffer from an irrational fear of losing confidence in themselves, of contracting disease, of losing their jobs, or of not being able to cope with their work.

It is important to distinguish here between rational and irrational fear. Any of these things that are the objects of the agoraphobic's fear would be at least an embarrassment, and many of them would, in fact, be disastrous. A sane person would do everything possible to avoid the loss of a loved one, for example. That all of us have a healthy interest in avoiding these disasters is one reason why diagnosing and treating agoraphobia is so difficult. But agoraphobia victims allow these fears to dominate all of their lives. Because they fear contracting a disease, for example, they may stay at home, miserable, when they really want the company of others.

In a study of 528 agoraphobics reported in a British journal in 1973, it was found that 91 percent of these victims were female. An overwhelming majority of the victims were married, and most first began to suffer from agoraphobia in their twenties and thirties. Almost all began to show the symptoms of agoraphobia shortly after a traumatic experience of some kind. Their mental illness may have been preceded by an illness, loss, or injury, the death of a parent, divorce, or other domestic stress.

It seems that quite often agoraphobics really do have a rational reason for their fears. The fear becomes an illness only when the fear becomes the most important element in the agoraphobic's life. Because it is a question of emphasis or balance rather than irrationality, agoraphobia is difficult to detect and difficult to treat.

▲ (541 WORDS) ▲

PASSAGE 4-19

Circle the correct answer:

1(a) The main purpose of this passage is to
   a. discuss human psychology.
   b. provide an introduction to agoraphobia.
   c. discuss rational and irrational fears.
   d. present current research findings about agoraphobia.

1(b) A good title for this passage might be
   a. What to Do if You're an Agoraphobic
   b. Fears: Rational and Irrational
   c. Phobia Treatment
   d. What Is Agoraphobia?

2(a) Male agoraphobics often suffer from irrational fear of
   a. losing their jobs.
   b. contracting diseases.
   c. losing confidence in themselves.
   d. all of the above.

2(b) A study of 528 agoraphobics in 1973 did not find that
   a. most of the victims had never had a traumatic experience.
   b. most of the victims were female.
   c. most of the victims were married.
   d. most of the victims first began to suffer from agoraphobia in their twenties and thirties.

3. We can conclude from the passage that
   a. most agoraphobics have experienced an occasional loss of control in public.
   b. agoraphobics are not treatable.
   c. the symptoms of agoraphobia vary from person to person.
   d. agoraphobics represent less than half of the phobia patients who seek help.

4. The passage suggests that
   a. agoraphobia is really an exaggeration of normal fears.

b. the fears of agoraphobics are mostly irrational.
   c. agoraphobia should be classified as a psychosis.
   d. agoraphobia is seldom curable.

5(a) As used in this passage, the word *phobias* means
   a. logical fears
   b. functional fears
   c. irrational fears
   d. behavioral fears

5(b) As used in this passage, the word *morbidly* means
   a. humorously
   b. unnaturally
   c. fatal
   d. slightly

5(c) As used in this passage, the word *traumatic* means
   a. psychologically damaging
   b. pleasant
   c. memorable
   d. unremembered

5(d) As used in this passage, the word *domestic* means
   a. powerful
   b. job-related
   c. internal
   d. home-related

PASSAGE 4-20   SUBJECT:
Adjusting to Cold Weather

Can the human body adjust itself for cold weather?

If you plan to go on a skiing trip or any sort of cold weather excursion, can you prepare yourself for the extreme cold you may face? Medical science disagrees about the body's ability to acclimate itself. Studies have shown that aborigines (ăb ə rĭj ə nēz) accustomed to extremes of temperatures can sleep on the cold ground with no bedding or in a very simple shelter in temperatures no other people, not even Eskimos, can withstand. Other scientists have studied the Korean pearl divers. Their investigations show that, as the women dive into the chilly water more, they shiver less. But no one will say for sure that this represents evidence that people ever really adjust to the cold.

It cannot be denied, though, that a person can gradually become more comfortable in cold weather. People considering a trip to an extremely cold climate should gradually acclimate themselves to the lower temperature, and thermostats at home and at work can be turned to the lower sixties to help make the change of climate less drastic.

Jogging outdoors is another way to become used to the cold; jogging is particularly useful as preparation for skiers because it builds endurance. But daily jogging is also a good way to increase exposure. Someone who jogs daily, not just once or twice a week, can make any adjustment to climate more easily, adjusting gradually as the seasons themselves change.

One caution concerns sickness: no one should leave for a skiing trip feeling exhausted or rundown. As vacations are often scheduled far in advance, the temptation is very strong to travel anyway, but sickness of any kind, particularly a fever, upsets the body's ability to cope with any change of climate.

Once the body has been prepared for the climate, outdoors people should focus their attention on their wardrobes. Basically, of course, an ideal winter wardrobe simply prevents the body temperature from dropping too low, for the muscles of the heart cease to contract properly below certain temperatures.

The best way to dress for winter is in several layers rather than by wearing one heavy item. Layers of clothing create dead space between the items of clothing. This traps air, thus acting as insulation. Wearing several thin layers of clothing also allows more range of movement than wearing bulky clothing.

Another advantage is that layers of clothing can be taken off as exercise raises the body temperature, allowing the outdoorsperson to remain comfortable. But remember that the skin temperature will lower rapidly after the exercise is finished, so it's best to put the discarded clothing back on quickly.

The most serious mistake is ignoring the special care needed for the head, hands, and feet. Heat loss is very rapid through the scalp and hair; in addition, the blood is somewhat cooled by the time it reaches the hands and feet, and the circulatory system is nearer the surface in these organs. Moreover, the hands and feet are sensitive; when they become chilled, a person feels cold all over.

The most common mistake is, according to John Baxter, who teaches skiing in Atlanta, wearing jeans in the winter. "Jeans are the worst thing a person can wear; they're stiff, heavy, and porous, and once jeans get wet from snow, they let cold air right in."

▲ (555 WORDS) ▲

PASSAGE 4-20

Circle the correct answer:

1. The main purpose of this passage is to
   a. discuss ways of preparing oneself for changes to colder climates.
   b. discuss the beneficial effects of jogging.
   c. offer data from several scientific investigations into climate adaptability.
   d. discuss the best manner of dress for colder climates.

2. Which of the following statements is not true?
   a. People can gradually become more comfortable in cold weather.
   b. Layered clothing is preferable to heavy, bulky clothing.
   c. Special care should be taken to correctly cover the hands, head, and feet.
   d. Jeans aren't good for colder climates because they aren't porous enough.

3. We can conclude from the passage that
   a. cold weather raises the body's natural resistance to infection.
   b. correct clothing is the only necessary precaution when a person is anticipating a change in climate.
   c. you should jog only if you are going skiing.
   d. the author believes we can prepare ourselves for cold weather, despite the disagreements among members of the medical profession.

4. The passage suggests that
   a. one of the biggest mistakes that people make when they exercise in the cold is putting back on wet layers of clothing.
   b. turning down our home thermostats will help conserve energy.
   c. most people have problems adjusting to climate changes because they don't prepare for it correctly.
   d. aborigines are healthier than Eskimos.

5(a) As used in this passage, the word *excursion* means
   a. trip
   b. trial
   c. illness
   d. exception

5(b) As used in this passage, the word *acclimate* means
   a. adopt
   b. adapt
   c. cure
   d. heal

5(c) As used in this passage, the word *drastic* means
   a. fatal
   b. effective
   c. severe
   d. efficient

5(d) As used in this passage, the word *discarded* means
   a. wet
   b. cold
   c. exercising
   d. removed

PASSAGE 4-21

SUBJECT: Elizabeth Blackwell

Elizabeth Blackwell, America's first woman doctor, has a background that in many ways pointed to the very exceptional life she was to live. Elizabeth was born in Bristol (brĭs′ tŭl), England, in 1821. Her father was a religious Dissenter, so his children had to be tutored at home. They were barred from attending English schools. Mr. Blackwell, a liberal and a farsighted man, insisted that both his sons and daughters be taught identical subjects.

The women in the Blackwell family were quite exceptional. One of Elizabeth's sisters became a newspaper correspondent; another became a teacher. Her sister Ellen was a writer and artist, and another sister, Emily, also became a doctor. Elizabeth's sisters-in-law were also pioneers. One brother married Lucy Stone, a women's rights activist, and another married Antoinette (ăn twä nĕt′) Brown, America's first woman minister.

The Blackwells moved to New York in 1832. After her father's death in 1838, Anna and the other Blackwell women opened a school. But after five years of teaching, Elizabeth decided she wanted to be a doctor.

None of the big medical schools would accept Elizabeth as a student. Finally, she was accepted at Geneva Medical College in New York State. What she didn't know was that the dean and students had voted to accept her application because they thought it was a practical joke. No woman except an immoral one would want to study anatomy, they thought; but Elizabeth finished her study at Geneva (jĭ nē′ və) and went on to serve as an intern in Paris.

Returning to New York, Elizabeth finally found rooms to rent so she could begin practicing medicine; but no patients wanted the care of a female physician. No hospital would hire her as a staff doctor, and she got a constant stream of hate mail; no decent woman tried to set herself up as a doctor.

To pass the time, Elizabeth prepared and delivered a series of lectures on the physical education of young girls. Some of Elizabeth's audience were aghast, but Elizabeth also had in her audience a large number of Quakers; these Quaker women were her first dozen patients. But people still thought of Elizabeth as a curiosity, not as a physician.

Desperate for an opportunity to practice her profession, Elizabeth opened a one-room clinic in Tompkins Square, one of New York's ghettos (gĕt′ ōz); no one came to the clinic for almost a month, even though a sign outside indicated that it was free. Finally, one patient, so near collapse that she could not climb the steps, came for treatment. She recovered, and told her friends how kind Dr. Blackwell had been. Word of mouth turned out to be Dr. Blackwell's greatest advertisement; she finally had a practice.

With the backing of her Quaker friends, Dr. Blackwell expanded her clinic into a real hospital. She eventually added a training school for nurses and a medical college for women; in 1857 she opened the first hospital for women, staffed by women.

Her struggle was not over, by any means; at least twice, Dr. Blackwell was forced to confront angry mobs at the steps of the hospital, gathered to avenge the death of a patient. Her own presence and the impeccable care that patients received at her hospital won Blackwell a reputation as a great doctor. Today her New York Infirmary is a skyscraper on Fifteenth Street, a testimony to Elizabeth Blackwell's dedication.

▲ (559 WORDS) ▲

PASSAGE 4-21

Circle the correct answer:

1. The main purpose of this passage is to
    a. discuss the Blackwell family's influence on American history.
    b. describe Elizabeth Blackwell's "free" clinic.
    c. provide a short biography of Elizabeth Blackwell.
    d. give information about the chauvinistic attitudes of the nineteenth century.

2. Which of the following statements is not true?
    a. Elizabeth Blackwell came to America in 1832.
    b. Elizabeth Blackwell studied at a Paris medical school first, then interned in New York.
    c. Elizabeth Blackwell opened the first hospital for women, staffed by women, in 1857.
    d. Elizabeth Blackwell's second office was opened at Tompkins Square.

3. We can conclude from the passage that
    a. because of her "free" practice, Elizabeth Blackwell died impoverished.
    b. Elizabeth Blackwell did not do well in her studies of anatomy.
    c. Elizabeth Blackwell considered French hospitals superior to those in America.
    d. chauvinism was the biggest obstacle Elizabeth Blackwell faced in her attempt to become a doctor.

4. The passage suggests that
    a. chauvinism in the nineteenth century was much stronger than it is in the twentieth century.
    b. Elizabeth Blackwell became despondent because of the hate mail she received.
    c. Elizabeth Blackwell felt intimidated by her male colleagues in medical school.
    d. Quakers only patronize women doctors.

5(a) As used in this passage, the work *tutored* means
   a. disciplined
   b. devout
   c. taught
   d. quiet

5(b) As used in this passage, the word *decent* means
   a. moral
   b. educated
   c. hardworking
   d. immoral

5(c) As used in this passage, the word *ghettos* means
   a. exclusive areas
   b. cities
   c. hospitals
   d. slums

5(d) As used in this passage, the word *confront* means
   a. stand up to
   b. greet
   c. lecture to
   d. restrain

5(e) As used in this passage, the word *impeccable* means
   a. psychological
   b. expensive
   c. flawless
   d. careless

PASSAGE 4-22   SUBJECT:
American Clerical Workers

Many—if not most—of the women who entered the labor force since 1950 entered secretary or clerk's positions. Secretarial workers are seldom represented by unions. Because most clerks are female, complaints about secretarial jobs and working conditions in them often involve claims of chauvinism (shō' vən iz əm) and sexual discrimination.

In Boston, one clerk claimed that she had to sew her boss's pants while he was still wearing them. Another secretary said she was forced to dress up as the company trademark, a bumble bee, and hand out ads on street corners.

One boss demanded that his secretary keep him supplied with carrots for his diet. Another insisted that his secretary coat the office plants with salad dressing to inspire them to grow. One boss fired an office worker when she refused to return a sandwich to the cafeteria for him—in the rain.

Most people estimate that 90 percent of the clerical workers in American offices are women. Because they are women, many think, male bosses just assume that the secretaries will make coffee and fetch lunch. Often, secretaries end up attending to very petty details. One Washington office worker says that she was required to order lunches for seven people from seven different offices for each of her boss's luncheon meetings. "It just seemed a waste of my time," she said.

In Atlanta, secretaries allege that their jobs go far beyond company business. Sometimes the boss's children have their college papers typed at the office; sometimes a secretary may have to deliver the boss's car to his service station; some secretaries type and write personal correspondence for their employers; many office workers water the plants and lie to the boss's clients. One secretary even planned her boss's daughter's wedding and kept records of all his club memberships—all on company time.

Not all secretaries mind this sort of thing. Some accept it as "just part of the job." Other office workers are organizing to protest against what they consider a lack of basic rights in the office. In Washington, a group called "Sixty Words per Minute" has formed to help federal office workers develop strategies for dealing with job harassment. In Boston, the group "Nine to Five" charges dues and uses bake sales to raise money. With their funds, the members use legal pressure to end harassment. They pressure companies to write job descriptions that define the responsibilities of secretaries. They file lawsuits forcing the federal government to investigate companies with federal contracts. Most importantly, "Nine to Five" has joined with a union, which can help them in their efforts to regulate policies concerning the office worker.

Not all of these women's complaints are trivial by any means. Their situation is basically that of any unprotected worker. "Sixty Words per Minute" members are surprised that Washington, with its enormous numbers of federal employees, isn't the "hotbed" of activity. "Perhaps federal employees . . . are frightened about their jobs," suggests one of the group's organizers. The Boston group says they are becoming familiar with what they call the "Friday Afternoon Firing": if a secretary refuses to do personal chores, she may be fired late Friday afternoon. "There is no warning . . . she is just told not to come in on Monday."

With no union, with no representative, and with no job description or standard dismissal procedure, the victim of a Friday Afternoon Firing has little recourse. The problems of this class of employees aren't insignificant matters: they are questions involving basic rights.

▲ (579 WORDS) ▲

PASSAGE 4-22

Circle the correct answer:

1(a) The main idea of this passage is that
  a. clerical workers comprise the majority of the current labor force.
  b. clerical workers are often mistreated by employers because they aren't unionized.
  c. clerical workers are often mistreated by their employers, but they are beginning to fight back by organizing.
  d. clerical workers in America are considered second-class citizens.

1(b) A good title for this passage might be
  a. Mistreated Secretaries Fight Back!
  b. Secretarial Work
  c. The Boss Is Always Boss
  d. America's Labor Force

2. Which of the following statements is true?
  a. Nearly 90 percent of the clerical workers in American offices are women.
  b. "Sixty Words per Minute" was founded to help state clerical employees.
  c. "Nine to Five" was organized by employers to protect their employees.
  d. Clerical workers must tolerate harassment because they aren't qualified for other jobs.

3. We can conclude from the passage that
  a. the majority of secretaries don't mind doing personal favors for employers.
  b. only secretaries involved in the Women's Liberation Movement complain about employers.
  c. clerical workers resent being treated like maids by their employers.
  d. secretaries aren't sensitive to the pressure their employers are under most of the time.

4. The passage suggests that
   a. clerical workers don't fully understand their roles in business.
   b. in some ways employers think of their secretaries as surrogate wives.
   c. secretaries expect preferential treatment from their employers.
   d. employers have too many things to do during the day to be bothered with minor details that can be assigned to a secretary.

5(a) As used in this passage, the word *chauvinism* means
   a. hatred
   b. impossible work assignments
   c. positive male attitudes
   d. negative male attitudes

5(b) As used in this passage, the word *trademark* means
   a. symbol
   b. seller
   c. pet
   d. name

5(c) As used in this passage, the word *fetch* means
   a. cook
   b. get
   c. buy
   d. prepare

5(d) As used in this passage, the word *petty* means
   a. damaging
   b. important
   c. unimportant
   d. difficult

5(e) As used in this passage, the word *strategies* means
   a. plans
   b. tricks
   c. clubs
   d. contracts

5(f) As used in this passage, the word *trivial* means
   a. real
   b. insignificant
   c. meaningful
   d. doubted

5(g) As used in this passage, the word *recourse* means
   a. protection
   b. claim
   c. unemployment benefits
   d. chance of making more money

PASSAGE 4-23

SUBJECT: Vegetarianism

Most Americans think of vegetarians as a minority, as food faddists. In fact, in this country people who include meat in their diets are the majority; but throughout the world, meat eaters are, and have been, the minority themselves. Though archaeologists can demonstrate that humans have kept animals for food for thousands of years, meat was generally for the rich; the poor in most countries are vegetarians. And the followers of many religions are also vegetarians. The Hindus, the Buddhists, the Sufis (soo͞' fēz), and other groups do not eat meat.

In fact, religion is a major reason still for choosing a vegetarian diet; many religions teach that eating meat weakens one's spirit. Adam and Eve were told to eat fruits and vegetables, according to Genesis. When Daniel was facing the lions, he followed a vegetarian diet, so he could remain pure.

Other vegetarians believe they are healthier than people who eat meat. Though this has never been scientifically proved, popular works on vegetarian diets often promise better health. There is evidence to show that vegetarians have greater stamina (stăm' ə nə), and many people on vegetarian diets live long lives.

Some people do not eat meat for economic reasons; meat is expensive and, in many parts of the world, very scarce. The most common reason for choosing a vegetarian diet, though, is the ethical one. Why do humans feel that they must kill other beings in order to eat well? Most vegetarians admit that they find eating the flesh of dead animals revolting. In fact, they refer to "flesh-eaters" as we might refer to cannibals and also use the zoo label "carnivore" (kär' nə vōr) interchangeably.

Because choice of diet is a cultural and ethical matter, not all vegetarian diets are alike. Ovo-vegetarians (ō' vō) eat vegetables, but will allow themselves eggs. The lactovegetarian (lăk' tō) eats vegetables mainly, but adds dairy foods such as milk and cheese. These two categories of vegetarians feel that eggs and dairy products are permissable; taking these products does no harm to the cow or chicken. Strict vegetarian ways are represented by the Vegan (vĕg' ən) Society, whose members prefer the label "vegan." Vegans live "on the products of the plant kingdom." Not only do vegans avoid meat; they also avoid eggs, honey, and milk in any form. They reason that it is as cruel to rob animals as it is to kill animals.

A vegetarian must be careful to maintain a balanced diet; and of course a carnivore—or omnivore (ŏm' nə vōr), really, because most people in America eat both meat and vegetables—must be equally careful. Excellent nutrition is important, whether for vegetarians or the rest of us (many people who eat meat assume their diet is nutritional for that reason alone). No one has ever been able to prove definitely that one diet is more beneficial than the other.

The most compelling argument in favor of vegetarianism, however, is vegetarianism's efficiency. The periodical *Scientific American* estimated in 1976 that there are enough plants to support several times the current world population; but if those plants are first fed to an animal to fatten it for slaughter, there is an 80 percent loss in efficiency by the time a human eats a pound of meat. Every human consumes 260 pounds of food annually to avoid starvation, and there are adequate food crops available to provide that 260 pounds for every one of us. The question is: Do we eat the plants, or do we eat the animal to which we feed them? And do we let someone else go hungry?

▲ (587 WORDS) ▲

PASSAGE 4-23

Circle the correct answer:

1. The purpose of this passage is to
   a. discuss vegetarianism as a fad.
   b. discuss the ethical reasons for becoming a vegetarian.
   c. discuss the disadvantages of eating meat.
   d. discuss the prevalence and advantages of vegetarianism.

2. According to the passage, which of the following statements is not true?
   a. Worldwide, meat-eaters are in the minority.
   b. There is some evidence that vegetarians have greater stamina than carnivores.
   c. All vegetarian diets are essentially alike.
   d. Ovo-vegetarians eat vegetables and eggs.

3. We can conclude from the passage that
   a. vegetarianism could help ease the world food shortage.
   b. lactovegetarians eat only vegetables.
   c. vegetarians are healthier than people who eat meat.
   d. most people don't eat meat for economic reasons.

4. The passage suggests that
   a. only poor people become vegetarians.
   b. most religions advocate vegetarianism.
   c. whether or not vegetarianism is better for the body is still debatable.
   d. vegetables aren't as nutritious as meat.

5(a) As used in this passage, the word *faddists* means
   a. opponents
   b. people attracted to what is currently fashionable

275

    c. fanatics
    d. "health-nuts"

5(b) As used in this passage, the word *stamina* means
    a. endurance
    b. pollen
    c. equilibrium
    d. appetites

5(c) As used in this passage, the work *ethical* means
    a. liberal
    b. financial
    c. immoral
    d. moral

5(d) As used in this passage, the word *cannibals* means
    a. animals that eat the flesh of other species.
    b. animals that eat only meat.
    c. animals that eat the flesh of their own species.
    d. animals that eat only raw meat.

5(e) As used in this passage, the word *omnivore* means
    a. eating only vegetables.
    b. eating only meat.
    c. eating both meat and vegetables.
    d. eating only dairy products.

5(f) As used in this passage, the word *compelling* means
    a. convincing
    b. damaging
    c. comforting
    d. irrational

PASSAGE 4-24

SUBJECT:
Andrei Gromyko
(ŏn drā´ grō mē´ kō)

Andrei Gromyko's career in the Soviet (sō´ vē ĕt) government has spanned well over twenty years. He is Russia's foreign minister, a post similar to our secretary of state. In his long career, he has sat across the treaty table from many famous American secretaries of state, such as Dulles (dŭl´ ləs), Rusk, Kissinger, and Vance. No other major foreign minister has lasted as long as Gromyko.

The press generally dislikes Gromyko, whom some of them call "Stoneface." He is not talkative when dealing with the media, a characteristic that enrages reporters. This is, however, a highly desirable trait for a diplomat who deals with government secrets. He may infuriate the press, but at the negotiation table Gromyko is very witty, friendly, even charming. But he can also be an iron-willed negotiator when he has to be. It is probably this iron will that has assured his survival as a major political figure in Russia and as a useful diplomat.

Gromyko comes from a peasant background. He was born in the huge agricultural region of the Byelorussia (byĕl ō rŭsh´ ə) in the west. He was interested at first in agriculture and in economics. He attended a huge Russian Institute of Agriculture at Minsk (mĭnsk), one of the largest cities in the Byelorussian area, and graduated with a degree in economics. He taught economics for a while, but became more and more interested in politics. Recognizing the better opportunities in the Foreign Office, he entered that branch of the Soviet government in 1939.

In 1940, Gromyko was sent to Washington, D.C., to serve in the embassy there. His solid competence and loyalty won Stalin's (stŏ´ lĭnz) confidence. Three years later, Stalin promoted Gromyko to ambassadorial rank at the age of thirty-four. This represented an incredible career step for a man so young. In fact, Gromyko served as the Soviet ambassador to both the United States and the United Kingdom during Stalin's period in office. His own abilities at diplomacy were often tested severely. Those were the years when Russia was America and Great Britain's most powerful ally in World War II.

As the war stretched on, Gromyko was trusted more and more. He was with Stalin at the Yalta conference, where the three superpowers of the United States, Britain, and Russia agreed on final strategies for winning the war. He adjusted quickly to the new relationships between these three powers after the end of the war. He was a vital member of the postwar conferences. He helped write the founding charter for the United Nations, and he was appointed as the first Soviet ambassador to the United Nations. Nikita Khrushchev (nĭ kē´ tə kroos´ chĕf), the Soviet premier famous for his explosive temper, recognized Gromyko's talents and services. It was he who appointed Gromyko foreign minister. At the time, he confided that he also liked Gromyko's background. It was quite similar to his own.

This combination of loyalty, competence, long service, and tight-lipped seriousness may make Gromyko sound dull, but he is far from dull. He developed a great taste for American and British culture during his years of service as ambassador; he became an expert on American and British affairs, from political and economic dealings down to the popular culture of both countries. Obviously, some of this knowledge was required for his position, but he pursues this knowledge with relish. He reads, speaks, and writes English quite well, and he delights in quoting Shakespeare and Robert Frost at well-timed moments. There is much more to this paradoxical man than we might guess from our occasional glimpses of him as a vague figure in the background at press conferences.

▲ (594 WORDS) ▲

PASSAGE 4-24

Circle the correct answer:

1. The main idea of the passage is
    a. to discuss the virtues of loyalty.
    b. to show Gromyko's relationships to the various premiers he has served.
    c. to trace Gromyko's rise to the position of foreign minister.
    d. to show Gromyko's adaptability to American and English culture.

2. During Stalin's period in office, Gromyko served as
    a. Consulate of the Russian Embassy.
    b. negotiator at the Yalta Conference.
    c. Soviet ambassador to the United Nations.
    d. Soviet ambassador to the United States and Great Britain.

3(a) Which of the following conclusions does this passage support?
    a. Gromyko separates his personal and public life.
    b. Gromyko prefers living in America to living in Russia.
    c. Gromyko is successful because he is always willing to compromise.
    d. Gromyko is often misrepresented by the press.

3(b) We can conclude from the passage that
    a. Gromyko has remained successful because he has proved adaptable to the ever-changing power structure in Russia.
    b. Gromyko will one day be premier of Russia.
    c. Gromyko was largely responsible for the success of the Yalta Conference.
    d. Gromyko is the second most powerful official in Russia.

4. The passage suggests
   a. that loyalty and competence are necessary for success in diplomatic circles.
   b. that Russia chooses only "stone-faced" diplomats to serve in the United Nations.
   c. that Gromyko has been made bitter by his long service.
   d. that Gromyko is more interested in art than in diplomacy.

5(a) As used in this passage, the word *trait* means
   a. characteristic
   b. fault
   c. temper
   d. look

5(b) As used in this passage, the word *competence* means
   a. sustenance
   b. sufficiency
   c. occupational ability
   d. adaptability

5(c) As used in this passage, the word *relish* means
   a. carelessness
   b. fervor
   c. boredom
   d. timidity

5(d) As used in this passage, the word *paradoxical* means
   a. simple
   b. puzzling
   c. ignorant
   d. friendly

5(e) As used in this passage, the word *vague* means
   a. solid
   b. clear
   c. ridiculous
   d. shadowy

PASSAGE 4-25

SUBJECT: Stress

There are basically two types of stress placed on human beings. One type of stress involves physical activity and its demands; the other type of stress is the result of mental and emotional demands. Stress from physical activity, if not carried too far, is actually beneficial. Exercise relaxes you and may help you forget about mental or emotional stress. But mental stress is almost always bad for you. If mental stress is unrelieved, it can actually cause diseases such as ulcers, migraine headaches, heart problems, or mental illness.

Whether physical or emotional in origin, stress causes the body to react in the same ways. In the first stage, your body prepares to meet the stress. The heartbeat and respiration rates increase, and the pupils of the eyes dilate; the blood sugar level increases, and the rate of perspiration speeds up, while digestion slows down as blood and muscular activity is diverted elsewhere. In the second stage, your body returns to normal and repairs any damage caused by the stressful situation. However, if stress continues, the body cannot repair itself, and the final stage, exhaustion, then begins. If this stage continues, if for example you are frustrated by your work and continue to be frustrated for a long time, physical or emotional damage will occur. These stages of stress reaction are always the same, whether the stress is caused by a cross-country run, a first date, buying a house, or narrowly missing an automobile accident.

Probably most harmful of all stresses is guilt; this common emotion is useful to have when it helps us realize that we have, in fact, committed some error, violated our own rules or social rules. If we did not feel guilt, we would never do anything except the things that brought us immediate pleasure—we'd never obey the law, work, exercise, or even study in school, unless we wanted to do so in the first place. As a person's conscience develops, guilt feelings become inevitable; guilt is the sorrow we experience when we know we have done something incorrect.

However, many of us as children learned rules that we no longer need: fat adults no longer should feel guilty about leaving a little food on the plate; a successful businessman need not feel guilty about spending a little too much money on a vacation, nor should he feel guilty that he can combine a business trip to the West Coast with some swimming and golf at an ocean resort. But many people do feel guilty over such apparently innocent actions. Excessive guilt can sour all of life and make life not worth living; guilt can cause self-hatred as well as other fears and anxieties that cause all life's successes to be bittersweet, at best.

Guilt and the worry that often accompanies this major stress are difficult to eradicate, but people subject to excessive guilt feelings should realize, as simple as it sounds, that no one is perfect. People cannot always be cheerful and helpful to everyone they meet. Another good lesson is that mistakes should be forgotten, not lingered over and brought out to examine periodically.

A life without stress, such as retirement with nothing to do, would be boring. Just as we need a little guilt—to keep us correct—and a little worry—to make us plan ahead—we need a little stress to stay interested in life. But when stress begins to bother you, change your routine. Take your mind off your worries with some physical activity, whether tennis, yoga, gardening, or meditation. Or talk your worries over with someone else; you may discover a solution you had overlooked before.

▲ (607 WORDS) ▲

PASSAGE 4-25

Circle the correct answer:

1. This passage is *mainly* about
   a. the most harmful of all stresses, guilt.
   b. physical activity and its demands on the body.
   c. the best ways to escape stress.
   d. using stress to your advantage.

2. According to the passage, which of the following statements is not true?
   a. Worry often accompanies guilt.
   b. Some of us feel guilty about very innocent actions.
   c. A person's respiration rate increases during a stressful situation.
   d. Guilt has no beneficial effects on man.

3. We can conclude from this passage that
   a. a stress-free life would be ideal.
   b. ulcers can only be caused by mental stress.
   c. guilt is often self-induced.
   d. worry is a more dangerous form of stress than is guilt.

4. The passage suggests that
   a. physical and mental stress in normal amounts are advantageous to man.
   b. worry often causes physical stress.
   c. physical stress can be more dangerous than mental stress.
   d. the body is ill-equipped to deal with stress.

5(a) As used in this passage, the word *beneficial* means
   a. helpful
   b. harmful
   c. ridiculous
   d. useless

5(b) As used in this passage, the word *origin* means
   a. amount

    b. cause
    c. belief
    d. central

5(c) As used in this passage, the word *dilate* means
    a. redden
    b. depress
    c. focus
    d. expand

5(d) As used in this passage, the word *diverted* means
    a. recreated
    b. ample
    c. turned
    d. burned

5(e) As used in this passage, the word *violated* means
    a. misunderstood
    b. broke
    c. made
    d. despised

5(f) As used in this passage, the word *inevitable* means
    a. inescapable
    b. different
    c. exhaustive
    d. unimportant

5(g) As used in this passage, the word *innocent* means
    a. tainted
    b. callous
    c. sophisticated
    d. simple

5(h) As used in this passage, the word *eradicate* means
    a. mask
    b. eliminate
    c. acquire
    d. deny

PASSAGE 4-26   SUBJECT:
Underground Homes

In the effort to save on housing costs, many people—designers, architects, and plain folks—are learning the benefits of underground life.

For centuries, the people in very hot climates such as the Australian desert, in the cold wastes in northern China, and in Russia have used varieties of underground homes as simple ways to stay comfortable. Until recently, though, no prospective homeowner in the Western world would have seriously considered living in the modern equivalent of a cave. The rising cost of heating and cooling the family home has changed our rather conservative attitudes about housing, though. A new home doesn't have to be a split-level, colonial, or ranch style to draw customers any longer, as long as that new home is cheaper to live in.

The main advantage of underground homes is a constant temperature. There are very few insulating materials more effective than plain old dirt. Eight inches of any commercial insulation available today will still allow almost seven times more heat loss than eight inches of soil piled against an outside wall.

In addition to the insulating properties of soil, the earth itself tends to stay at a constant temperature, and a home dug into the earth will share that constant temperature. The upper level of the earth's crust, the part most people consider "soil," has an average temperature of 50 degrees Fahrenheit (făr´ in hīt) the year round; at a certain depth, which varies from region to region, the temperature of the soil is always 50 degrees, whether there's a hot summer sun beating down or a raging winter snowstorm up above. And only a few feet down from the surface, less than ten feet, the average depth at which an underground home would lie, the earth is always more comfortable than the air above. In the summer, the ground is cooler, and, in the winter, the ground is warm.

This margin of comfort can be quite substantial. In Minneapolis (min ē ap´ ə ləs), a study of soil temperatures indicated that the ground was 47 degrees when the atmospheric temperature was 35 degrees below zero. When, in the summer, the atmospheric temperature was in the high nineties, the ground temperature was 51 degrees. An underground home in Minneapolis would be cool already in the summer; in the winter, it would be easier to heat with warm soil packed around it rather than subzero winds whistling around its corners.

There are several different approaches to constructing underground homes to take advantage of this energy efficiency. Some homes are built entirely underground, with nothing showing but a few air vents and an entry door or stairwell, but many people miss windows, so "berm" homes were developed. Berm homes are built into the side of a hill or into a sand dune, so that one side of the construction is left uncovered; the floor plan is generally arranged so that as many rooms as possible have access to views. Or sometimes the home is built with all rooms open into a central courtyard or atrium (ā′ trē əm); the soil is poured against the sides of the home and onto the roof, leaving the central area open to the sunlight and air.

Architects cannot agree on other advantages; underground homes will require much stronger roofs to support a soil layer, and drainage must be planned very carefully to ensure that ground water does not seep into the home. So, in some areas at least, underground homes may be more expensive to build. However, the cost of a properly designed underground home will be lower in the long run. There is no siding to repaint and replace, and there are very few windows to keep in good repair. And, of course, no shingles to replace—you can mow your roof.

▲ (619 WORDS) ▲

PASSAGE 4-26

Circle the correct answer:

1. The main idea of this passage is that
    a. most Americans aren't interested in living in underground homes.
    b. insulation is an important factor in building an underground home.
    c. underground home construction involves several engineering feats that are difficult and expensive.
    d. underground homes offer a reasonable alternative to traditional homes.

2. According to the passage, which of the following statements is not true?
    a. Underground homes are not new to other parts of the world.
    b. Soil temperature is greatly affected by atmospheric temperature.
    c. Underground homes benefit from the temperature of the soil that surrounds them.
    d. Stronger roofs are needed for underground homes because they must support a layer of soil.

3. We can conclude from the passage that
    a. underground homes are presently too expensive to construct to make them sensible for America.
    b. the temperature of 50 degrees Fahrenheit is considered "room temperature."
    c. the long-term expenses of underground homes are usually less than those for traditional homes.
    d. underground homes are currently only used in Minneapolis.

4. The passage suggests that
    a. underground homes may be the homes of the future because they are very energy-efficient.

b. commercial insulation is more effective than soil insulation, but the price of the commercial insulation limits its use.
   c. berm homes are less efficient than totally underground homes.
   d. no way has yet been found to keep ground water from seeping through the ceilings of underground homes.

5(a) As used in this passage, the word *prospective* means
   a. gambling
   b. abnormal
   c. possible
   d. insensate

5(b) As used in this passage, the word *equivalent* means
   a. equal
   b. unequal
   c. distinction
   d. dampness

5(c) As used in this passage, the word *conservative* means
   a. showy
   b. slovenly
   c. juvenile
   d. traditional

5(d) As used in this passage, the word *properties* means
   a. owners
   b. characteristics
   c. damage
   d. predictability

5(e) As used in this passage, the word *atmospheric* means
   a. mass
   b. spare
   c. air
   d. water

5(f) As used in this passage, the word *generally* means
   a. broadly
   b. usually
   c. necessarily
   d. narrowly

5(g) As used in this passage, the word *access* means
   a. quality
   b. entrance
   c. need
   d. availability

PASSAGE 4-27   SUBJECT: "Fish Sniffing"

Wine tasters and tea tasters you may have heard of. It's easy to believe that some company would employ a connoisseur (kŏn ə sûr′) of wines or teas to use his or her finely trained, discriminating palate to help grade and improve its products; occasionally, you might even see a television commercial in which a national authority on wines tells you that some inexpensive brand is just as tasty as some famous label. It might surprise you to know that there are also connoisseurs of rottenness and that, in fact, the best of these connoisseurs work for the federal government.

In Seattle and in New York, major ports where seafood is shipped into the country, the Food and Drug Administration (FDA) maintains labs to check the quality of imported fish. By federal law, any seafood imported into U.S. territory must be examined for freshness. Class I seafood or seafood products are completely fresh, and Class II is putrid; any shipment of seafood is allowed to exhibit percentages of Class II material in it, but too high a percentage of Class II seafood makes the whole shipment ineligible for sale. "Putrid" makes Class II sound worse than it is; fish classified this way are only slightly less fresh than fish in Class I.

It's Class III fish that are really foul; Class III exhibits all the signs of advanced decomposition, including the smell of ammonia. And all of this spot checking is performed by an FDA technician with a highly discriminating olfactory sense; all day long, this "sniffer" has to poke and sniff at frozen and raw seafood.

If chemists attempted an analysis of each sample chemically, it would simply take too long to do the inspection, so the FDA has selected and trained very sensitive sniffers to analyze fish samples with their sense of smell. A well-trained fish sniffer must be able to identify the fresh smells of hundreds of species of sea animals, as well as the distinct odor each species gives off when it has begun to decompose.

In addition to a sensitive nose, every fish sniffer who works for the Food and Drug Administration must be highly disciplined, for sniffers must undergo periodic examinations to make sure their exquisite, discriminating noses are not deteriorating—and in a job like this, it certainly happens. Of the hundreds of sniffers trained for these jobs, only a few have the discipline to withstand the pressure—let's face it; not many people want to roll out of bed every morning and know they are going to spend the day sniffing seafood that may be rotten. If a sniffer is easily distracted from work, forget it, too. Sorting fish involves remembering thousands of details of color, smell, and texture; and indulging in strong food or drink, even having a cigarette after lunch, may throw off a fish sniffer's sense of smell for an entire afternoon.

FDA sniffers cannot allow anything to interfere with their judgment because, in the absence of chemical evidence, a fish sniffer's judgment has the effect of law. If a fish sniffer says the fish is rotten, then it is rotten by law. The responsibility eventually overwhelms many of the apprentice sniffers, and they drop out of the training program, broken by the demands placed on them and their noses.

And the job is not getting any easier or simpler. Ocean pollution is complicating the sniffer's classification system by introducing the distinct smell of diesel oil to many of the samples. More and more strange species are being imported to satisfy the growing demand for seafood. Fish from the Indian Ocean, from Brazil, squid, octopus—the federal fish sniffer must identify and remember all these orders. A real stinker of a job, wouldn't you say?

▲ (621 WORDS) ▲

PASSAGE 4-27

Circle the correct answer:

1(a) The purpose of this passage is to
   a. discuss tea and wine tasting.
   b. describe the three classes of fish.
   c. describe the job of a "fish sniffer."
   d. show the problems pollution can cause.

1(b) A good title for this passage might be
   a. The FDA's Fish Classification System
   b. A Smelly Job
   c. Tea and Wine Tasting Around the World
   d. Pollution: A Smelly Problem

2. Decomposing fish are classified in
   a. Class I
   b. Class III
   c. Class II
   d. Class I or II

3. We can conclude from the passage that
   a. "fish sniffers" are underpaid.
   b. the FDA isn't overly concerned with controlling the quality of imported fish.
   c. "fish sniffers" are plentiful in the United States.
   d. "fish sniffers" are as expert at their jobs as wine and tea tasters are at their jobs.

4(a) The passage suggests that
   a. a lot of confidence is placed in the "fish sniffer's" ability.
   b. the FDA only controls the importation of fish.
   c. most "fish sniffers" aren't very disciplined.

287

d. pollution has helped the "sniffers" because it tends to make all rotten fish smell the same.

4(b) The author's tone is
   a. humorous
   b. sarcastic
   c. negative
   d. satirical

5(a) As used in this passage, the word *connoisseur* means
   a. buyer
   b. producer
   c. expert
   d. drinker

5(b) As used in this passage, the word *putrid* means
   a. pure
   b. fresher
   c. normal
   d. rotten

5(c) As used in this passage, the word *ineligible* means
   a. best
   b. not qualified
   c. destined
   d. worthy

5(d) As used in this passage, the word *foul* means
   a. fresh
   b. rotten
   c. chosen
   d. flavorful

5(e) As used in this passage, the word *decomposition* means
   a. growth
   b. suspension
   c. freezing
   d. decay

5(f) As used in this passage, the word *olfactory* means
   a. pertaining to the sense of taste.
   b. pertaining to the sense of sight.
   c. pertaining to the sense of smell.
   d. pertaining to the sense of feel.

5(g) As used in this passage, the word *periodic* means
   a. strenuous
   b. daily

c. occasional
   d. final

5(h) As used in this passage, the word *distracted* means
   a. diverted
   b. engrossed
   c. bored
   d. intimidated

PASSAGE 4-28

SUBJECT: Insurance Risks

Insurance companies have the reputation of being dull, boring firms. In some ways, insurance may be run by the dull statistics of actuaries. These men study life expectancies and accident and disease figures, along with occupational hazards, and help the company decide if it should insure you. Only 3 percent of the people who apply for life insurance are turned down. Actuaries may tell their company not to issue policies for steeplejacks, test pilots, nuclear plant technicians. An actuary knows, however, that "the law of large numbers" will protect the company.

If the company insured only five or six test pilots, they would be taking a very large risk indeed. But if they insure ten thousand test pilots, the odds are better; the company is protected by the law of large numbers. If at any given point one of the test pilots dies and the company has to pay the claim, there will be enough other test pilots paying for their own policies to let the company pay easily.

By spreading the risks this way, insurance companies are willing to take on almost any risk, to write a policy insuring against almost anything. One company, Travelers Insurance, insured the lives of the astronauts on the first moon landing mission; the company actually gave the astronauts better odds than NASA did. Another company will insure, for the same rate, any person, whether that person is a prizefighter, member of the police force, trapeze artist, or bomb squad member.

Insurance policies have been written on movie star's legs, on the expenses of moving neighbors of a nuclear plant in case of accident, on expensive cows to insure them against theft. The most recent form of insurance is liability insurance to protect a person who may be sued by someone he or she has damaged. Liability insurance often gets companies into colorful situations. One company paid to settle a claim caused by a "bleach fight" in the checkout line at a supermarket. Another company paid a claim to a voter whose finger was broken while shaking hands with a political candidate.

Many of the stranger policies are written by Lloyd's of London, which is really not a company at all, but a loose association of independent men who carefully calculate risk against gain. When Lloyd's issues a policy, it's almost as if a wealthy gentleman has just placed a large wager that the policy will not be forced to pay out its claim.

Lloyd's began in the seventeenth century as a coffee house that had many ships' captains as clients. Gradually, wealthy men came there to strike bargains on these ships and their goods, and slowly Lloyd's became the place to go to have a ship insured. Members of Lloyd's, who still sit at tables resembling the booths of a coffee house, pass sheets of paper describing the risks of a certain policy from booth to booth. Each member who wishes to share in the policy—and the profits, should no claim be made—adds his initials under the description; thus, an insurer is referred to as an "underwriter."

Each Lloyd's underwriter must have $225,000 instantly available to pay claims on policies. Each underwriter must back his policies with everything he owns, so members spread their risks by taking small shares in hundreds of policies at one time.

When something is insured by Lloyd's, it is generally assumed that the policy is safe. The company earned its reputation in 1906 when it promptly paid millions of dollars in claims against its San Francisco earthquake policy. Since then, Lloyd's and the law of large numbers have insured the *Titanic,* the moon buggy, the world's fairs, supertankers, and jet aircraft. What could be safer—or duller—than insurance?

▲ (625 WORDS) ▲

PASSAGE 4-28

Circle the correct answer:

1. The purpose of this passage is to
   a. explain the job of an insurance actuary.
   b. discuss the risks insurance companies take and how they protect themselves against losses.
   c. provide a short history of Lloyd's of London.
   d. define the different types of insurance.

2(a) Liability insurance protects you against
   a. accidental death.
   b. occupational hazards.
   c. suits arising from damages you cause to others.
   d. all of the above.

2(b) According to the passage, which of the following statements is not true?
   a. An "underwriter" is an insurer.
   b. Lloyd's of London began in the 1600s.
   c. Insurance companies spread the risks among their policyholders.
   d. Travelers Insurance Company insures prizefighters, members of the police force, and bomb squad members.

3(a) We can conclude from this passage that
   a. the members of Lloyd's of London participate in writing policies in order to make money.
   b. Lloyd's of London has lost more money than it has made in recent years.
   c. Lloyd's of London's last claim was the 1906 San Francisco earthquake.
   d. Lloyd's of London made money by insuring the *Titanic.*

3(b) Which of the following conclusions does the passage support?
   a. There are many things that insurance companies will not insure under any circumstances.
   b. In reality, the policyholders of an insurance company end up paying for the company's losses.
   c. The more people a company insures, the greater its chances of loss become.
   d. Insurance companies make very little money on high risk insurance policies.

4. The passage suggests that
   a. insurance companies insure only low-risk clients.
   b. occupational claims against insurance companies are more numerous than personal claims.
   c. most members of a police force are unable to get insurance.
   d. insurance is basically a business of "educated gambling."

5(a) As used in this passage, the word *actuaries* means
   a. people who program computers
   b. policyholders
   c. insurees
   d. people who study risk factors

5(b) As used in this passage, the word *liability* means
   a. financial responsibility
   b. moral responsibility
   c. physical responsibility
   d. psychological responsibility

5(c) As used in this passage, the word *colorful* means
   a. tinted
   b. pale
   c. unusual
   d. bright

PASSAGE 4-29

SUBJECT:
Galileo (găl ə lā′ ō)

In 1979 the Catholic Church finally forgave Galileo for claiming that the Earth and other planets revolved around the sun. In 1633 the examiners at the Minerva (mĭ nûr′ və) Church in Rome had found Galileo guilty of <u>heresy</u>, spreading false beliefs.

Galileo was sixty-eight years old at the time of his trial and was ill. After two days of continuous questioning and the threat of torture, Galileo confessed to heresy and kneeled before the examiners, saying for all to hear that his theories had been wrong. The judges could have had Galileo burned at the stake for his beliefs, but because he had confessed, they were <u>lenient</u> with the astronomer. They sentenced him to an unlimited term in prison, but quickly changed the sentence to house arrest in his own home, effectively ending Galileo's teaching career.

For years Galileo had believed that the earlier theory, that the stars revolved around the Earth, was incorrect, but he kept quiet out of respect for the Church. He had never finished his university studies in mathematics because he had run out of money, but his brilliant work as a student allowed him to teach. He proved the <u>uniform</u> effect of gravity in a series of brilliant calculations, for example (not by dropping a feather and a cannonball from the Leaning Tower of Pisa (pē′ zə), his home city, as is commonly thought).

In 1606, though, Galileo learned of the invention of the telescope; he redesigned and improved his own telescope in one day. Using the telescope to test his mathematical calculations, he also discovered Jupiter's moons, the features of Earth's moon, and the structure of the Milky Way. But while watching the movement of sunspots, he became convinced, once and for all, that the earlier astronomer, Copernicus (kə pûr′ nĭ kŭs), was right: the Earth and other planets <u>orbited</u> around the sun. The Earth was one of many planets, and not the center of the universe. Galileo began to press for permission from the Church to write about his "theories of the world," and in 1624 he received permission.

His greatest book, contrasting the two systems, was written and published eight years later. *Dialogue Concerning the Two World Systems* was quickly seen as a <u>landmark</u> scientific work, both for its ideas and for its fine writing. But the Church meantime had its own problems with the Protestant Reformation. Church leaders now considered Galileo's work dangerous and revolutionary. A "document" was found that contradicted the permission Galileo thought he had obtained to write about his theories. Galileo was then arrested and placed before the Inquisition.

After the trial and Galileo's confession, he remained on his country estate near Florence. He could not teach, but Galileo continued to write and to conduct mathematical and scientific experiments to test his calculations and observations. His work was summed up in *Dialogue Concerning Two New Sciences,* which was smuggled out of Florence and published in Holland. Galileo died in 1642, blind and still imprisoned in his own home. He remained convinced that he had always been right.

The Church, 346 years later, finally agreed that he had been correct. The findings of the judges at Galileo's trial were not reversed, even though their precise finding had been that the astronomer was "vehemently suspect of heresy." The findings of any inquisition, even the Galileo court—as well as the notorious Spanish Inquisition—must be allowed to stand, at least partly because their findings often resulted in death sentences for people accused of heresy. But in 1979, Pope John Paul addressed the August Pontifical (pŏn′ tĭ′ fĭ kəl) Science Academy in the Vatican and offered apology to Galileo: "The greatness of Galileo, like that of Einstein (in′ stin′), is known to all. But the former had to suffer greatly, we cannot hide it, from Church institutions and men."

▲ (624 WORDS) ▲

PASSAGE 4-29

Circle the correct answer:

1. The purpose of this passage is to
   a. discuss why the Catholic Church persecuted Galileo.
   b. provide a short biography of Galileo.
   c. discuss the two theories of the solar system.
   d. show how science has progressed over the last three hundred years.

2(a) Galileo was
   a. a college graduate.
   b. finally put to death in 1642.
   c. dedicated to teaching and researching.
   d. violently opposed to the Catholic Church.

2(b) According to the passage, which of the following statements is not true?
   a. Galileo redesigned the telescope in 1609.
   b. Galileo did not receive the harshest punishment he could have received.
   c. Galileo felt that, although the Earth revolved around the sun, it was still the center of the universe.
   d. Galileo's observations included views on Jupiter's moons and the Milky Way.

3. We can conclude from the passage that
   a. Galileo was held prisoner in his home for nine years.
   b. the Catholic Church has not accepted Galileo's theory of the solar system.

c. Galileo invented the telescope.
   d. the Protestants conducted the Inquisition.

4(a) The passage suggests that
   a. the Catholic Church still believes the Earth is the center of the universe.
   b. Galileo's theory has been proved incorrect in modern times.
   c. the Inquisition seldom dealt harshly with people who came before it.
   d. the Catholic Church was more concerned with maintaining the status quo in the 1700s than the truth about Galileo's theory.

4(b) The author's tone is
   a. negative
   b. objective
   c. sarcastic
   d. satirical

5(a) As used in this passage, the word *heresy* means
   a. false beliefs
   b. spying
   c. regicide
   d. immorality

5(b) As used in this passage, the word *lenient* means
   a. stricter
   b. less harsh
   c. confused
   d. frustrated

5(c) As used in this passage, the word *uniform* means
   a. arbitrary
   b. consistent
   c. ridiculous
   d. fatalistic

5(d) As used in this passage, the word *orbited* means
   a. stood
   b. stationed
   c. circled
   d. collided

5(e) As used in this passage, the word *landmark* means
   a. superficial
   b. useless
   c. highly important
   d. fixed

5(f) As used in this passage, the word *vehemently* means
   a. morally

    b. plainly
    c. slightly
    (d.) strongly

5(g) As used in this passage, the word *notorious* means
    a. friendly
    b. benevolent
    c. fair
    (d.) ill-reputed

PASSAGE 4-30   SUBJECT:
Muhammad Ali (mə hŏm′ ad ō lē′)

In modern boxing, there have been four very popular heavyweight champions. There is Joe Lewis, whose speciality seemed to be the dramatic knockout. Max Baer (băr), who had a terrific punch, grew lax in training, a common fault. Rocky Marciano (mâr cē ăn′ ō) was an awesome puncher. Marciano retired in 1955, and for almost ten years the popularity and the earning power of boxing declined. A bored public was now drawn away to the newer pleasures of TV and pro football.

But in 1964, the fourth man, Muhammad Ali, gained national attention by fighting Sonny Liston for the title. Ali's name was then Cassius (kăsh′ əs) Clay, but he had already developed the hysteric, self-promoting antics that made him the best-known champion in history. He raged against Liston in newspaper and television interviews. He visited Liston's training camp and taunted the champion, challenging him to fight; Ali had to be restrained at the prefight weigh-in, when he charged at the glowering, scowling Liston. In the seventh round of the fight, Liston never left his corner; then the newly crowned champion astonished reporters the next day by announcing his name change and declaring his Black Muslim religion.

Few people realize, because Ali's method seems so effortless, how lengthy and how difficult his work and training to be world champion were. No one is a natural-born fighter; though Muhammad may come as close to being a natural as anyone ever has, he has trained since before the age of twelve. He trained at a Louisville police gym, sparring, working on both light and heavy bags, skipping rope, doing his roadwork before school. He won the flyweight class in the local Golden Gloves tournament, entered Amateur Athletic Union (AAU) tournaments, and finally, at eighteen, won the National A.A.U. championship. In 1960 he won a gold medal at Rome in the Olympics.

A long string of bouts led up to the Liston fight, too. Ali turned professional and first fought professionally on October 29, 1960, fighting in Louisville and winning by a decision in six rounds. Five straight knockouts followed, until Ali was traveling, and his fights were becoming more and more important. In Las Vegas he fought Duke Sabedong (săb′ə dŏng). The fight itself was unimportant. Ali beat Sabedong easily— but while promoting the fight, Ali appeared on a local TV show with Gorgeous George, the infamously flamboyant wrestler whose sequins and curly blond hair would hold attention anywhere. Ali was impressed. His first impressive opponent was Archie Moore, and Ali began his antics, prophesying in verse that "Archie Moore will fall in four."

Ali then used the press and his "loudmouth" antics to improve the quality of his opponents. Constantly challenging Liston in the press, he worked his way up to the champion by fighting Charlie Powell, Doug Jones, and Henry Cooper before finally meeting Liston in Miami in 1964.

Since then Ali has used the boxing ring as a base from which to spread the Muslim (mūz' ləm) gospel and continued his use of the media to publicize his antics, focusing attention on boxing and on Ali. He has become a very political fighter, one who has become identified with some of the major issues of our time, particularly when he refused to be drafted into the U.S. Army. (His religion is against that sort of violence.) But with his controversial behavior, he has helped boxing regain its central place in American sports, in fact giving boxing greater legitimacy than it had ever enjoyed before. And Ali was the first to become a real "world" champion. His bouts in Manila, Zaire (zī' îr), and San Juan (wŏn) show that his popularity is, if anything, even greater outside the United States. But his showmanship, profitable though it may be, should never be allowed to outshine his skills, training, and endurance.

▲ (624 WORDS) ▲

PASSAGE 4-30

Circle the correct answer:

1(a) A good title for this passage might be
   a. A History of Boxing
   b. Four Great Heavyweights
   c. The World of Boxing
   d. Muhammad Ali, World Champion

1(b) This passage is mainly about
   a. Ali's personality as compared to the other three great champions.
   b. Ali's vocal antics.
   c. Ali's boxing career.
   d. four great heavyweights.

2. Which of the following was not one of Ali's opponents between 1960 and 1964?
   a. Charlie Powell
   b. Archie Moore
   c. Henry Cooper
   d. Joe Frazier

3. We can conclude from this passage that
   a. Ali's vocal antics in and out of the ring eventually diminished his popularity.
   b. Muhammad Ali is the greatest of the four great heavyweight champions.
   c. Ali brought a "flair" to boxing that it had never had before.
   d. the other three champions eventually lost the title because they became lax in their training.

4(a) The passage suggests that
   a. Gorgeous George taught Ali how to get the public's attention through boisterous behavior.
   b. Ali's "personality" in the ring was largely calculated to draw attention to boxing and himself.
   c. Ali used his vocal antics to fight emotional insecurity before his fights.
   d. Ali's behavior kept him from becoming the truly "great" champion like Lewis or Marciano.

4(b) The author's tone is
   a. condemning
   b. journalistic
   c. admiring
   d. obstinate

5(a) As used in this passage, the word *antics* means
   a. fears
   b. actions
   c. boxing
   d. wrestling

5(b) As used in this passage, the word *taunted* means
   a. mocked
   b. congratulated
   c. frightened
   d. embraced

5(c) As used in this passage, the word *infamously* means
   a. not popular
   b. grossly shocking
   c. barely
   d. elaborately

PASSAGE 4-31

SUBJECT:
Batteries

Mankind has known for thousands of years that energy can be made by chemical actions. In the late 1700s, an Italian scientist named Volta (vōl' tə) found a new way to make electricity. Volta found that when a moist cloth is placed between different metals, an electric current is formed.

Volta used different metals in succession, finding that the amount of current produced varied, depending on the combination of metals. Volta also experimented with other chemical solutions, which he used to wet the cloth between the two metals.

The first electric cell, or battery, grew from his experiments. This battery, called a galvane (găl' văn) cell, used copper and zinc as the two metals. The moistening solution is hydrochloric (hī drə klō' rĭk) acid. In the galvane cell, electricity is produced when a stream of electrons leaves the zinc. Exactly one and a half volts is produced, until the zinc is used up.

The batteries powering most radios and flashlights today are developments of another early electric cell called the Leclanché (lə klŏn' shā) cell. The Leclanché cell improved upon the galvane battery by using cheaper materials. In the Leclanché cell, a rod of pressed carbon and a rod of zinc are encased in ammonium chloride; as the zinc electrode rod was used up, it could be replaced, and water could be added to the ammonium chloride at any time, so the battery never needed charging. The electricity was produced, as in the galvane cell, by the consumption of the zinc rod.

Leclanché cells were very useful and were once used by the millions to power telephones and doorbells; when a system required more power than one cell could produce, Leclanché cells could be connected in line to create more power. The modern "dry" battery is called this to distinguish it from the "wet" Leclanché cell; the modern battery is simply a sealed, disposable Leclanché cell, using a dry medium between the two metals.

People today tend to think of themselves as the inventors of electricity, but archaeologists have made a startling discovery that may change our ideas. In Iraq (ĭ răk'), archaeologists found two-thousand-year-old copper tubes with iron rods inside. Other copper tubes were later found near the Tigris (tī' grĭs) River. These long, neatly made copper tubes look much like early electrical cells. After checking the residues in the tubes, scientists decided that vinegar had been the medium separating the iron and the copper. When vinegar was poured in the tubes, each container produced one-half of a volt for eighteen days. Possibly these electric cells were used for healing rituals or for religious purposes.

Today researchers are looking into using our most common element, water, to make electricity. Besides efforts being made to use the waves and tides to turn generators, scientists hope to perfect a water cell.

We have long known that two electrodes dipped in water will separate it into hydrogen and oxygen. This process, called hydrolysis (hī drŏ′ lə sĭs), is used to purify metals such as aluminum. Today scientists are trying to reverse this process. After hydrolysis has occurred, the electrodes can be left in the separated gases. After a moment, the oxygen and hydrogen begin to recombine to form water again. And the movement of the gases creates an electrical current. This process is much more efficient than any previously known process that could be contained in a battery. The electrodes are not used up, and heat is produced as a by-product. If the heat could be used to generate even more currents, we would have found a cheap renewable source of electricity.

The batteries used until now have been very primitive. In fact, we only recently learned precisely how primitive our electrical cells were. Volta was simply reinventing something known thousands of years ago. But if reverse-hydrolysis batteries can be perfected, we may finally and actually be able to make machines and appliances that "run on water"—indirectly, at least.

▲ (640 WORDS) ▲

PASSAGE 4-31

Circle the correct answer:

1. The main purpose of this passage is to
    a. provide a short biography of Volta.
    b. discuss the history and current state of the art of battery design.
    c. discuss the history of batteries.
    d. discuss ways batteries can replace the use of oil in electricity production.

2. The Leclanché battery
    a. was a "dry" cell battery.
    b. introduced the galvane cell.
    c. used carbon and zinc as electrodes.
    d. used copper and zinc as electrodes.

3. We can conclude from the passage that
    a. ammonium chloride *only* dissolves zinc.
    b. hydrochloric acid is the best moistening solution to use in a battery.
    c. Volta invented the battery.
    d. the modern dry cell battery is not significantly different from the Leclanché battery.

4(a) The passage suggests that
    a. vinegar is a better moistening medium than acid.

b. "dry" cell batteries are more efficient than "wet" cell batteries.
   c. modern batteries are almost as primitive as ancient batteries.
   d. modern batteries are less expensive to produce than the older Volta-type battery.

4(b) The author mentions the discovery of batteries by archaeologists in Iraq to
   a. show how advanced Iraqi civilization is.
   b. show how little real progress has been made on batteries.
   c. ridicule Volta for claiming to have invented the battery.
   d. demonstrate that Eastern culture is more advanced than Western culture.

5(a) As used in this passage, the word *succession* means
   a. sequence
   b. corrosion
   c. danger
   d. analysis

5(b) As used in this passage, the word *encased* means
   a. corroded
   b. saturated
   c. joined
   d. enclosed

5(c) As used in this passage, the word *consumption* means
   a. explosion
   b. heating up
   c. using up
   d. lighting up

5(d) As used in this passage, the word *disposable* means
   a. encased
   b. discardable
   c. powerful
   d. electrical

5(e) As used in this passage, the word *medium* means
   a. conveyance
   b. average
   c. method
   d. common

5(f) As used in this passage, the word *primitive* means
   a. unoriginal
   b. callous
   c. crude
   d. unsuccessful

PASSAGE 4-32

SUBJECT:
The Television Industry

During the last ten years, the television industry has seen changes in equipment and its use that would have been incredible in 1948, the year that broadcasting began. For example, one out of five homes in America with TV sets also subscribes to a pay-TV hookup, usually a cable TV hookup that draws in as many as twenty or twenty-five channels, often channels with quite special functions. Some run only old movies from the 1940s, others run only sports programs, and others run constant news or weather updates. In addition, 1.6 million homes subscribe to pay channels that run recent movies, theatrical features, and sports specials, often for a fee added to the monthly cost of a cable installation.

Many homes now contain "do it yourself" television. Video (vĭ′ dē ō) cassette recorders are now being produced in quantity, making them cheaper and within the range of many middle-class family budgets. Often these recorders are cheaper than the price of a second set, and many buyers are using them almost as a second set. These recorders are most often used to record a show that was broadcast at an inconvenient time or at a time when the majority of the family voted to watch something else; the interested viewer can see his or her show alone later, when the recorder replays it over the family set. With commercial recordings easily available, viewers can quickly build themselves a library of their favorite movies or Super Bowls, and with the addition of a fairly inexpensive video camera, home movies for television are a possibility. Many homes now also contain video games that use the family set for projection and display. These games include blackjack, pinball, tennis, Ping-Pong, and military strategy games, as well as many others; but not many people realize that some of these games are so complicated that they are virtually small computers.

The future of television, however, seems even more incredible. Already available in Europe are two-way televisions that permit the viewer to push buttons and answer questions the program has asked. Imagine the meaning of this for mass education by television and for our elections, polls, or referenda. Sets are sold now, though at very high prices for most budgets, that project the image onto 45-inch to 84-inch screens. These are used mainly in commercial establishments now. Their price will probably fall into a more reasonable range once enough sets are produced. Also available, in Europe at least, are televisions that allow you to watch two programs at once, by projecting the second channel onto only a corner of the screen, allowing you to keep an eye on some continuing event such as a sports program, while watching another show.

Also planned for production in the immediate future are new round antennae. These will provide much clearer, sharper pictures than were ever possible before.

New sets may also have stereo sound built into them, and networks may soon start broadcasting their sound this way. Viewers may also be able to use a new computer system that will allow them to tune in an instant, continual, news summary. Another possibility is the adaptation of satellite communications antennae for home use. These dishlike antennae could be aimed to receive signals from any of the dozens of communications satellites now in orbit, giving every home access to any TV program broadcast anywhere in the world.

But a newly developed glass filament called an optical fiber has the most promise for the future of television. These tiny "wires" use laser light to carry huge numbers of channels of information. One hookup for a home could carry phone lines, cable television, even computer links. The family set could then be used for regular viewing, pay-TV channels, remote banking, and for lessons, recipes, and traffic and weather reports. The family set could even be used to view goods in a supermarket miles away, place an order for the groceries, and transfer the funds from the family bank account to the supermarket's. Daily newspaper delivery might be in the form of a constant scan of ever-changing headlines on one channel or even on several. The future uses of television look limitless.

▲ (691 WORDS) ▲

PASSAGE 4-32

Circle the correct answer:

1. The main purpose of this passage is to
   a. compare American and European television services.
   b. show how the computer has revolutionized television.
   c. describe cable television services.
   d. discuss the current and future uses of television.

2(a) Which of the following is a service offered to viewers in Europe, but not to viewers in America?
   a. videotape recorders
   b. 45-inch to 84-inch screens
   c. two-way televisions
   d. videotape games

2(b) Which of the following are features that may be offered via television of the future?
   a. daily newspaper delivery
   b. traffic and weather reports
   c. remote banking
   d. all of the above

304

3(a) We can conclude from the passage that
   a. videotape recorders are still too highly priced to be available to the average American.
   b. the computer age has been particularly influential on the television industry.
   c. dishlike antennae will make pay television obsolete.
   d. larger screened televisions offer a better picture than conventional television sets.

3(b) Which of the following conclusions does the passage support?
   a. Optical fibers are more efficient than current wiring apparatuses.
   b. Optical fibers are currently too expensive to use commercially.
   c. The use of optical fibers would impair the efficiency of phone lines or cable television hookups.
   d. Optical fiber cables would, unfortunately, prevent the use of videotape recorders and videotape games.

4. The passage suggests that
   a. cable television is already used in most American homes.
   b. television will eventually expand to the point that regular network programs will disappear from use.
   c. in several ways Europe is further advanced in the services that television offers the viewer than is America.
   d. as the supply of large screened televisions increases, the price will rise proportionately.

5(a) As used in this passage, the word *inconvenient* means
   a. inopportune
   b. beneficial
   c. unrealistic
   d. embarrassing

5(b) As used in this passage, the word *commercial* means
   a. advertising
   b. industry-produced
   c. color
   d. standard

5(c) As used in this passage, the word *mass* means
   a. solid
   b. selective
   c. widespread
   d. exclusive

5(d) As used in this passage, the word *adaptation* means
   a. confiscation
   b. technology
   c. manifestation
   d. application

5(e) As used in this passage, the word *remote* means
   a. timely
   b. impossible
   c. slight
   d. distant

5(f) As used in this passage, the word *scan* means
   a. display
   b. error
   c. analysis
   d. misrepresentation

PASSAGE 4-33

SUBJECT:
Confucius (kən fyoo′ shəs)

No teacher or thinker ever had as great an effect on a culture as Confucius has had on that of China. For twenty-five centuries, the central characteristic of Chinese culture has been its reliance on Confucius' teachings. At first ignored when Confucius was alive, Confucianism finally spread throughout China to Korea, Japan, and Vietnam. Three hundred years after his death, Confucius was declared the official creator of the creed of China. His books became the basis of all Chinese education. He singlehandedly forged the many different cultures of the China of his day into the one culture that has flourished longer than any other culture on earth. Even the peasants who cannot understand philosophical works acknowledge Confucius as "supreme master."

Confucius was born in Shantung (shăn′ tŭng′) province in 551 B.C.; his original name was Chiu (choo′), the Chinese word for hill, so named because of a prominent bump on Confucius' head. Confucius was raised by his mother because his father died when the boy was only three. As a child, Confucius enjoyed taking part in ceremonies and rituals; even his playing as a child consisted of pretending to perform ceremonies.

Such a serious boy did not remain a child long. When he was fifteen, Confucius decided to become a scholar, so he found a job as a secretary in a ceremonial temple. Confucius attended every ceremony and asked questions about each ritual. He became an expert on rituals and began to attract followers of his own.

Confucius' study of ritual is one element of his thought that makes him difficult for Western minds to understand. In the age when Confucius lived, the old social order was being destroyed. In his own province, Confucius saw the old rulers losing control over rebellious dukes, each of whom claimed to own a section of the province. The poor people were suffering from hunger and war because government had become ineffective.

Confucius felt that the leaders of his day were neglecting the ancient ceremonies, performing them incorrectly or performing ceremonies that they had no right to perform. This was a symbol of the leaders' disrespect for authority. If only people learned to love each other and to respect authority, a perfect social order would result. Confucius felt that the social rituals of public worship and festivities illustrated a sense of propriety, that all things were in order.

At the age of fifty, Confucius was given a chance to translate his teachings into action, when he was made secretary of justice. He performed these duties admirably, and five years later was named prime minister.

Confucius had served only a few years, however, when he realized that social and economic conditions were not improving. He resigned his post and wandered through

China for fourteen years, searching for the ideal ruler in whose service his theories could be put into practice. As Confucius and his group of disciples traveled throughout China, many rulers offered Confucius government positions, but these offers never met his standards. When he was sixty-eight, Confucius returned to his home and spent the next five years teaching his philosophy.

The "great teacher" had a greater effect on education in his lifetime than he had on politics. Education had, before Confucius' time, been reserved for only the rich and aristocratic. The rich students studied the "six arts" of ritual, music, archery, history, chariot driving, and mathematics, all to learn how to rule themselves and others. But Confucius transferred education from the temple to the marketplace. In his lifetime, he taught over three thousand pupils from all over China. Confucius' popularization of the six arts helped produce a unified culture for China.

During this period, Confucius edited the classics for reference in his teaching, and he also produced a volume of his own, the *Chun* (cho͝on) *Chiu,* a history of his own province. His disciples gathered Confucius' sayings into the *Lun Yu* (lo͝on yü), which became more popular than any of the classics. When Confucius died in 479 B.C. at the age of seventy-two, he was buried in his home province. His disciples followed the ancient rituals of mourning, residing in huts beside the grave for three years. For twenty-five centuries, buildings at the grave site have been added to, until it has some of the most magnificent buildings and gardens in China.

▲ (714 WORDS) ▲

PASSAGE 4-33

Circle the correct answer:

1. The main purpose of this passage is to
   a. discuss Chinese culture.
   b. provide a short biography of Confucius.
   c. illustrate Confucius' influence on politics.
   d. illustrate Confucius' influence on social change.

2(a) Which of the following is not included in the "six arts"?
   a. music
   b. history
   c. art
   d. archery

2(b) According to the passage, which of the following statements is not true?
   a. Confucianism has spread to Korea, Japan, and Vietnam.
   b. Confucius died at the age of sixty-eight.

    c. Confucius began his development as a scholar by becoming a secretary.
    d. Confucius' greatest contribution was in the field of education.

3(a) We can conclude from the passage that
    a. Confucius sided with the rebellious dukes against the established order.
    b. Confucius tried to start a revolution in China.
    c. Confucius was influential only among the rich.
    d. Confucius was popular with the poor and uneducated.

3(b) Which of the following conclusions does the passage support?
    a. Confucius helped bring education to the common man.
    b. Confucius did not believe in teaching the "six arts."
    c. Confucius catered only to aristocratic students.
    d. Confucius added an additional "art" to the "six arts."

4. The passage suggests that
    a. Confucius didn't believe in respecting authority.
    b. Chinese culture is still based on Confucius' teachings.
    c. Confucius' teachings did not survive him.
    d. Confucius is best remembered for his religious teachings.

5(a) As used in this passage, the word *reliance* means
    a. refutation
    b. misinterpretations
    c. dependence
    d. policy

5(b) As used in this passage, the word *creed* means
    a. government
    b. beliefs
    c. religion
    d. society

5(c) As used in this passage, the word *forged* means
    a. scattered
    b. divided
    c. segmented
    d. shaped

5(d) As used in this passage, the word *flourished* means
    a. thrived
    b. began
    c. repressed
    d. socialized

5(e) As used in this passage, the word *prominent* means
    a. malignant
    b. noticeable

    c. normal
    d. unsightly

5(f) As used in this passage, the word *propriety* means
    a. religion
    b. frustration
    c. conformity
    d. irreverence

5(g) As used in this passage, the word *aristocratic* means
    a. upper class
    b. uneducated
    c. popular
    d. poor

PASSAGE 4-34

SUBJECT:
Black Tuesday

The 1920s in America was a decade of almost perfect prosperity. During this period, the number of cars on the road doubled, then doubled again. At the beginning of the decade, there were fewer than one hundred millionaires in America; by 1929, there were more than five hundred people worth at least a million. As the average American rushed to buy new appliances and cars, the economy grew to meet this demand, but by 1929, it was clear that the average family had bought all it could afford, at least for a while. No more factories planned expansions or purchases of new equipment, and warehouses began to fill up with unsold goods.

Everything began to slow down except the stock market in New York. Many of the new millionaires had made their fortune playing the stock market, and stories of successful players made the rounds quickly. Nurses were supposed to be getting rich investing on tips they received from rich patients; shoeshine boys were asking their Wall Street customers for advice and were supposed to be secretly worth hundreds of thousands of dollars; butlers who overheard conversations were gathering in millions, according to the stories.

And there were people who were making $50,000 a day in stocks. The prices of stocks seemed to be rising, no matter what happened in the country's businesses. Almost anyone who purchased any stock at any price could maintain the stock for a while and then resell it a few days later to someone else looking for the same immediate, unwarranted profit. And probably most temptingly, you didn't have to have enormous piles of capital to get into this game; banks and stockbrokers would loan investors up to 90 percent of the purchase price of any stock. For $100, you could buy $1,000 in stock, then sell it a week later, as prices doubled and quadrupled, so savings accounts all over the country were emptied as people rushed to put their money into the stock market.

Between August and September of 1929, the stock market increased in value almost 500 percent. One broker describes the market in 1929 as a "colossal suction pump," sucking money out of America and Europe. Only a few investors imagined the market would collapse; they knew the market was not worth all the capital that had been invested in it. People were rushing to buy stock in companies about which they knew little or nothing, simply trusting that the price would rise.

One economist, Roger Babson, finally predicted, on September 5, that prices had to fall. Thousands of investors rushed to sell their stock while prices remained high, and by October 3, prices were indeed falling. On October 19, some stocks dropped $40 in value in only two hours, and investors all over America and Europe who had invested their capital in the market experienced their initial panic. If the value of a stock falls below the value at which you purchased it, you lose money; if you bought the stock with borrowed capital and it falls very far, you end up owing huge sums of money for the rest of your life. On yachts, in luxurious "customer's rooms" on Wall Street, in average homes in America, people were trying to sell their stock before they lost everything. Such enormous numbers of sellers lowered confidence in the market even further, and prices began dropping faster than ever.

Banks and brokers made a heroic effort to shore up the sagging market by buying major stocks in batches of ten thousand shares at a clip, but even this demonstration of confidence didn't help. On Monday, October 28, the market lost $14 billion in value. By Tuesday the twenty-ninth, nobody would buy stock in anything; the small investors were all wiped out, and the rich stood by helplessly and watched their fortunes disappear as the values of stocks <u>plummeted</u>. AT&T dropped $28 a share; Allied Chemicals dropped $35 a share. General Electric stock dropped one dollar every ten seconds in the first six minutes the market was open. In all, the market lost $10 billion in value in that single day, more than twice the amount of capital available in the entire country then; on "Black Tuesday," the stock market had vacuumed all the capital out of the country, and the Great Depression was about to begin.

▲ (724 WORDS) ▲

PASSAGE 4-34

Circle the correct answer:

1. The purpose of this passage is to
   a. describe the events that led up to Black Tuesday.
   b. discuss the workings of the stock market.
   c. describe the economy of the 1920s.
   d. discuss several methods of making money in the stock market.

2. According to the passage, which of the following statements is not true?
   a. In 1920 there were over five hundred millionaires in the United States.
   b. Most everyone was successful in the precrash stock market of the twenties.
   c. Some people were making fifty thousand dollars a day in the stock market.
   d. The prediction of an impending market collapse came in early fall of 1929.

3(a) We can conclude from the passage that
   a. only average Americans were wiped out by the market collapse.
   b. the average American made millions in the stock market during the twenties.
   c. most servants made a great deal of money in the market.
   d. many people went heavily into debt to invest in the market.

3(b) Which of the following conclusions does the passage support?
   a. The market failed because prices on stock were illegal.
   b. The market failed because of drastically inflated prices on stock.

312

    c. The market failed because several large companies went bankrupt.
    d. The market failed because people stopped buying appliances.

4(a) The passage suggests that
    a. most people knew the rising prices of stock couldn't continue.
    b. few people really believed the market could collapse.
    c. careful investors weren't hurt by the market's collapse.
    d. most rich people continued to buy stock even after prices started to drop.

4(b) The author's tone is
    a. skeptical
    b. sarcastic
    c. objective
    d. negative

5(a) As used in this passage, the word *prosperity* means
    a. honesty
    b. failure
    c. success
    d. poverty

5(b) As used in this passage, the word *unwarranted* means
    a. unsafe
    b. earned
    c. deserved
    d. undeserved

5(c) As used in this passage, the word *capital* means
    a. money
    b. interest
    c. investors
    d. credit

5(d) As used in this passage, the word *colossal* means
    a. small
    b. beneficial
    c. market
    d. gigantic

5(e) As used in this passage, the word *initial* means
    a. mild
    b. first
    c. last
    d. worst

5(f) As used in this passage, the word *plummeted* means
    a. rose
    b. steadied
    c. dropped drastically
    d. were resold

PASSAGE 4-35

SUBJECT:
Wood Burning

Early in the history of the nation, America was so heavily forested that a squirrel could travel from Maine to the Mississippi River by hopping from one tree limb to another, never having to touch the ground. Three centuries of cutting for timber, for firewood, and to clear land for farming have taken a toll of America's forests. But many people are surprised to learn that one-third of all the land in America is still classified as forest land. Even America's most densely populated strip, the section of land between Boston and Washington, is half woods.

One hundred years ago, wood supplied almost all of America's energy; then wood fuel was gradually displaced by cheaper fuels like coal and oil. Now, as these fuels increase in price, Americans are turning back to firewood to heat their homes and even to operate factories. Wood now supplies us with 3 percent of our heating and energy—nuclear energy only supplies 6 percent—and officials project that wood may eventually supply as much as 10 percent of all the nation's energy. Some parts of the country, in fact, already use much more wood now; northern New England, with its heavy forests and its tradition of country living, already uses wood as a primary source of heat in 20 percent, and as a secondary source of heat in 30 percent, of the homes there.

Many industries are turning to wood as an energy source simply because it's much cheaper than other available fuels. With only minor adjustments, most oil, coal, or gas boilers can be modified to burn wood. Pulp and paper mills have led the changeover to wood, using wood for almost half the energy required to power their operations, but many other industries are following. The city power company in Burlington, Vermont, converted an old coal boiler to wood in 1977; since then, its cost has decreased by half. The power company, encouraged by this, recently converted their second boiler. They are planning to build a giant generator completely powered by wood from a nearby stand of trees. Officials say that modern forestry management will make the timber supply last forever.

Forest managers are enthusiastic, for industrial burners can use waste or residual wood, the materials loggers previously had left in the forest or thrown away after sawing timber into boards. In some logging operations, 60 percent of the wood is left behind as waste, but now sawdust, bark, trimmed limbs, stumps, and all can be put to use. In addition, clearing the land so thoroughly will allow faster replanting than has ever been possible before. And the new trees developed in the last few years will grow faster than the older trees they replace. Wood's greatest advantage is that it is so renewable.

Wood has always been in demand as a source of heat for homes, but that demand is increasing rapidly now. Twenty million existing homes have fireplaces in them. In

1978 two million woodburning stoves were delivered to individuals trying to escape the high price of home heating oil while at the same time enjoying the beauty of a wood fire burning quietly in the family room or den.

All this demand for wood worries environmentalists, despite the fact that modern forestry management allows land to be recovered with trees rapidly. They fear, first of all, that the demand for wood fuel, combined with the demand for wood building products, will cause wilderness areas to become glorified "tree farms." And increased demand for timber may initiate cutting in areas that are not being managed by forestry officials, for the legitimate demand for wood as a heat and energy source is further boosted by its use in decorative, "leisure" fires in homes where other heat is available.

This demand has already created a new class of criminal—the timber rustler. Though it's a simple matter to obtain a permit to cut wood on public land, many people don't bother to get their permit. They may wind up cutting trees in timberland that isn't being managed. In the Northwest, thieves are "rustling" 600- to 700-year-old cedar and fir trees to be cut into shingles and flooring. In the East, valuable walnut trees are being stolen to cut into furniture. Forestry officials worry that these trees are becoming rare—and every acre given over to growing firewood or timber may mean that these trees will become even rarer in the future.

▲ (765 WORDS) ▲

PASSAGE 4-35

Circle the correct answer:

1(a) The main idea of this passage is that
    a. wood once supplied all of our energy needs.
    b. the use of wood for heating homes and supplying energy for industries is becoming common again.
    c. industries are starting to use woodburning generators to save money.
    d. the current demands for wood to be burned in fireplaces worries environmentalists.

1(b) A good title for this passage might be
    a. Wood Stoves: A Threat to the Environment
    b. Using Wood to Save Money
    c. The Renewed Demand for Wood
    d. Converting Wood to Synthetic Fuel

2(a) Timber rustlers
    a. are destroying 600- to 700-year-old cedar and fir trees.
    b. work for the federal government.

c. consider walnut trees invaluable.
   d. are often hired by furniture manufacturers.

2(b) According to the passage, which of the following statements is not true?
   a. Of the homes in New England, 80 percent are heated by wood fireplaces.
   b. Of the homes in New England, 20 percent use wood as a secondary heat source.
   c. Of the homes in New England, 20 percent use wood as a primary heat source.
   d. Of the homes in New England, 30 percent use wood as a primary heat source.

3. We can conclude from the passage that
   a. industries want to change to burning wood so their profits will double.
   b. the conversion from oil-burning to woodburning boilers is a complicated and expensive process.
   c. wood is more expensive than coal as a fuel.
   d. woodburning boilers and generators can help industries save money.

4. The passage suggests that
   a. wood provides more even heating than does coal or oil.
   b. the major advantage of wood as a fuel is that the supply can last forever.
   c. as is true of oil, there is a finite amount of wood on the earth.
   d. burning wood endangers surrounding areas because of air pollution.

5(a) As used in this passage, the word *classified* means
   a. destroyed
   b. worthless
   c. secret
   d. categorized

5(b) As used in this passage, the word *densely* means
   a. uniquely
   b. ethnically
   c. sparsely
   d. heavily

5(c) As used in this passage, the word *converted* means
   a. retained
   b. changed
   c. maintained
   d. destroyed

5(d) As used in this passage, the word *environmentalists* means
   a. merchants
   b. lumber dealers
   c. conservationists
   d. criminals

5(e) As used in this passage, the word *initiate* means
   a. end

b. begin
   c. continue
   d. threaten

5(f) As used in this passage, the word *legitimate* means
   a. alien
   b. financial
   c. reasonable
   d. frightening

PASSAGE 4-36 SUBJECT: Thomas A. Edison

In 1879, Thomas A. Edison invented the first useful and cheap electrical light. That bare statement of fact does little to emphasize what a profound change Edison's invention has caused in our lives. Forget the small electric devices and machines that make our lives more interesting or easier. Stereos, televisions, hair dryers, and electric can openers are insignificant beside the electric light. Since the beginning of time, all human action had stopped when night fell except for the little social interaction that could occur around a campfire or fireplace. Even candles and oil lamps could provide light only for social activities; no serious work could go on by candlelight.

Edison's invention may be the primary distinction of the modern age. We have all-night stores, bars, and nightclubs. Our factories work throughout the night. Electricity has changed everything about the modern age, how we work, how we fight, communicate, or learn; but that one first change, the transformation of the dark of night, was all-important.

When he began working on the electric light, Edison had already invented the telephone transmitter, the microphone, and the phonograph, as well as the electric stock ticker, the electric vote recorder, and an improved telegraph system. Electric arc lights were already in use in European cities, but they were expensive and dangerous. As usual, Edison began his experiments with a year of study before his fifty-person team at his "invention factory" in Menlo (měn' lō) Park, New Jersey, began working with him.

Edison was a very practical man. Like most geniuses before him, he was self-taught, and he learned and experimented by trial and error. Edison wasted no time, though; he always carefully read the reports on previous research to make sure that he didn't repeat the work of other men. Possibly because of this habit, many of Edison's inventions and patents are refinements of the basic work of other inventors. Edison liked to brag that he had a practical streak that other inventors lacked. He could take almost any basic design or machine and quickly see ways it could be made more efficient or built more simply. He could see the practical, business use of almost any pure experiment or theory. His systematic, businesslike approach to invention and his personal direction of his fifty assistants produced thousands of lucrative patents for him at his Menlo Park labs.

Once Edison began to pursue an idea, his approach was always the same. After reviewing previous research, he would draw three-dimensional sketches of the problem. If he couldn't "picture" the problem in this way, he couldn't work on the problem.

Then began trial-and-error experiments. Each possible solution was tried until one worked; then the solution was refined until it was useful. All this was always guided by Edison's practicality. Untrained in mathematics and with no faith in untested theories, Edison used his amazing mind to find shortcuts that were perfectly obvious—once he had pointed them out. He once asked a mathematical physicist to help him figure the volume of a pear-shaped glass bulb. Upton, the physicist, worked for hours tracing the shape of the bulb on graph paper and creating complicated mathematical equations. Exasperated, Edison filled the bulb with water, then poured its contents into a standard measuring beaker, finding the correct volume in a few seconds. Upton never knew if Edison really wanted to know the volume or if he just wanted to test Upton.

Once Edison began earnestly pursuing the problem of efficient electric lights, other lifelong habits aided him. As he was almost deaf, his concentration was seldom interrupted by distractions of any kind; Edison could concentrate all his mental energy on a complicated problem for hours, even days. In addition, Edison required less sleep than other people. He could work on a problem nonstop for four days and never sleep; even on the fifth day he could take catnaps and refresh himself as much as other people with eight hours of sleep.

Theorists of that period said that Edison's experiments with the invention of practical electric light were impossible, but Edison ignored theorists. He simply worked hard and long and used his research lab to multiply his own efforts by fifty. He constructed over 3,000 theories and tested each one until he found a filament that would not burn itself out, as the arc light did. Then he experimented more and discovered that these filaments, inside a vacuum bulb, lasted long enough to be practical and cheap. Then, as was his custom, he called his own news conference and explained his invention to the newspapers. After he patented the electric light bulb, he refined electric power lines and generators until the electric power business was practical—and, by the way, his.

Edison once said, "Discovery is not invention . . . a discovery is more or less in the nature of an accident." He would have preferred to be called a discoverer. He learned how to make useful "accidents" happen.

▲ (824 WORDS) ▲

PASSAGE 4-36

Circle the correct answer:

1(a) The purpose of this passage is to
    a. discuss Edison's amazing scientific career.
    b. discuss Edison's invention of the electric light bulb.
    c. discuss the process used by inventors.
    d. discuss Edison's practicality in his approach to his inventions.

1(b) A good title for this passage might be
   a. Edison and the Light Bulb
   b. Thomas A. Edison: Practical Mind
   c. How Do Inventors Work?
   d. Edison's Career

2. According to the passage, Edison
   a. seldom tried experiments more than once.
   b. never used trial and error in his experiments.
   c. used trial and error to find the correct method for his inventions.
   d. primarily duplicated the experiments of other men.

3(a) We can conclude from the passage that
   a. Edison's electric light bulb was quite different from electric arc lights.
   b. Edison relied heavily on the design of electric arc lights for his design.
   c. Edison never found a practical way to build his light bulbs.
   d. electric arc lights were superior to Edison's light bulb.

3(b) Which of the following conclusions does the passage support?
   a. Edison stole his ideas from previous men's research.
   b. Edison relied heavily on theory in his designs.
   c. Edison was limited by his lack of education.
   d. Edison's lack of formal training in several areas often worked to his advantage.

4. The passage suggests that
   a. Edison died at an early age because of his poor physical condition.
   b. Edison always announced his inventions to the press because he was afraid his ideas would be stolen.
   c. Edison's invention literally changed the future of civilization.
   d. Edison worked entirely alone on all of his inventions.

5(a) As used in this passage, the word *profound* means
   a. insignificant
   b. important
   c. minimal
   d. negative

5(b) As used in this passage, the word *interaction* means
   a. communication
   b. chaos
   c. isolation
   d. loneliness

5(c) As used in this passage, the word *transformation* means
   a. benefit
   b. dread

c. continuation
   d. change

5(d) As used in this passage, the word *systematic* means
   a. unorganized
   b. haphazard
   c. organized
   d. theoretical

5(e) As used in this passage, the word *lucrative* means
   a. worthless
   b. unprofitable
   c. useless
   d. profitable

5(f) As used in this passage, the word *exasperated* means
   a. frustrated
   b. impressed
   c. confused
   d. tired

5(g) As used in this passage, the word *earnestly* means
   a. hopelessly
   b. seriously
   c. helpfully
   d. happily

PASSAGE 4-37   SUBJECT:
Okefenokee Swamp (ō kə fə nō′ kē)

Southern Georgia offers a little-known, and certainly unusual, vacation possibility. A few people each year are allowed to take overnight canoe trips into the Okefenokee Swamp.

The Okefenokee is one of the last wilderness areas left in the southern United States. As it is a wildlife refuge, it has been left untouched since the early 1900s, except for a few trails around its edge. The swamp is located south of Waycross, Georgia, on the Georgia-Florida border.

At one time, dozens of these huge swamps spread across the south, but drainage projects and timber harvests of the valuable cypress trees gradually reduced their size and number. Because the swamps, along with their distinctive wildlife, were disappearing, federal officials decided to save the Okefenokee. Now it is one of the last natural habitats for alligators and certain species of snakes. The alligators are very lively in the summer and spring, but during the fall and winter they are only seen sunning themselves on banks and logs, trying to stay warm.

The swamp is a winter home for many different migratory birds, such as ducks, sandhill cranes, and other birds that have flown in from the north, a common sight from fall until March. The winter is also the time to see the swamp's distinctive otter species, for they are more likely to be visible when the alligators are cold. In fact, winter is probably the best season for visiting the Okefenokee for several reasons. From April to October, the mosquitoes become a serious problem any time after sundown; the Okefenokee is a perfect hatching ground for them, and the infrequent human visitors seem to attract them. Deerflies, which can deliver a very painful bite, are common around the edges of the swamp in the summer, but disappear once you travel deeper into the wilderness. The summer is, of course, the active season for the "gators," too. They are no real danger as long as humans keep a reasonable distance and leave the alligator nests alone. Swimming is not permitted for equally obvious reasons, and pets are not permitted in the swamp. Alligators, it seems, are particularly fond of nice, tame, tender dogs.

Anyone may arrange reservations on a first-come basis by contacting the refuge manager in Waycross. The minimum size of a canoeing party is two people in a single canoe; no one is permitted into the Okefenokee alone. No more than twenty people in ten canoes are permitted in one party. Each person must register before venturing into the swamp and must have a life preserver. Each canoe must contain a compass and a signal light for use in emergencies, and each party must set out before 10 A.M. to make sure that the next overnight stop can be reached.

There are seven individual canoe routes in the Okefenokee, allowing excursions ranging in length from two days to a week; each trail is limited to one party daily, so vacationers will be virtually alone. Most people taking these canoe trips never see another party for the entire length of their adventure.

The Okefenokee itself is entirely flat; there is no moving water to speak of, so you must be prepared to paddle the entire distance from one overnight campsite to another. There is very little dry land in the swamp, so some of the overnight stops are fourteen-by-twenty wooden platforms. Imagine camping at night on a tiny wooden platform, with absolute darkness and absolute stillness all around—except for the occasional roar of a bull alligator lurking in the swamp. Even on those few overnight stops that are on dry land, canoeists should remain alert. As there are so few areas of dry land in the Okefenokee, these islands are likely to be occupied already by one or more alligators before your arrival.

Other areas where the land is almost out of the water are referred to as "prairies." These are areas where the thick, dark cypress forest is replaced by open spaces with low plant growth, and the water is very shallow here. Canoeists must be careful in the prairies to avoid overexposure to the sun and wind.

During most of the year, temperatures in the Okefenokee are mild. But from June through September, the temperature almost never drops below 90 degrees. The humidity is almost 100 percent during the summer months, and it rains almost every afternoon. Campers must be very wary of the lightning that accompanies these showers. The winter has the most hospitable climate, for most of the temperatures are in the fifties and sixties. Fishermen like to visit the Okefenokee in early spring and late fall to avoid the extreme temperatures and to catch the bass when they are moving about.

A rugged vacation, at best, but certainly not the usual family outing, a trip through the Okefenokee must be well planned and carefully prepared for. It may turn out to be a test rather than relaxation.

▲ (822 WORDS) ▲

PASSAGE 4-37

Circle the correct answer:

1(a) This passage is mainly about
    a. the Okefenokee Swamp as a vacation possibility.
    b. the need for wildlife refuges.
    c. survival in the swamp.
    d. the behavior of alligators in the wild.

1(b) A good title for this passage might be
    a. Watch Out for the Alligators!
    b. How to Stay Alive in the Swamp

c. Save the Wildlife!
   d. Vacationing in the Okefenokee Swamp

2. Summer vacationing in the Okefenokee Swamp is not affected by
   a. mosquitoes
   b. deerflies
   c. migratory birds
   d. alligators

3(a) We can conclude from the passage that
   a. alligators keep the Okefenokee Swamp from becoming a refuge for migratory birds.
   b. many of the species of wildlife in the Okefenokee Swamp are not found anywhere else in the United States.
   c. the Okefenokee Swamp was saved because it has no cypress trees.
   d. drainage projects will eventually require the federal government to move the wildlife refuge elsewhere.

3(b) Which of the following conclusions does the passage support?
   a. There are occasionally dangerous rapids in the swamp.
   b. Canoes must be propelled by paddles because there is not any current.
   c. Alligators live only in salt water.
   d. Swimming is not allowed in the Okefenokee Swamp because of the swift currents.

4. The passage suggests that
   a. the Okefenokee Swamp can be very expensive to the vacationer.
   b. only young people should consider vacationing in the Okefenokee Swamp.
   c. park rangers patrol the canoe routes to watch over the vacationers.
   d. people who don't enjoy the "rough and ready" outdoors life may not enjoy vacationing in the Okefenokee Swamp.

5(a) As used in this passage, the word *refuge* means
   a. experiment
   b. zoo
   c. garbage
   d. protective area

5(b) As used in this passage, the word *distinctive* means
   a. particular kind of
   b. common
   c. flesh-eating
   d. bizarre

5(c) As used in this passage, the word *habitats* means
   a. normal environments
   b. traditions
   c. sources
   d. experiments

5(d) As used in this passage, the word *excursions* means
   a. raids
   b. groups
   c. chores
   d. journeys

5(e) As used in this passage, the word *wary* means
   a. comforted
   b. alarmed
   c. frightened
   d. cautious

5(f) As used in this passage, the word *hospitable* means
   a. hostile
   b. dry
   c. welcoming
   d. frightening

DIAGNOSTIC POSTTEST

DIRECTIONS: Wait until your instructor has reviewed the posttest with you and has indicated how your answers are to be recorded. During the test, be sure to read each paragraph carefully and to check your answer on each item by referring to the paragraph and by eliminating the other choices as possible answers before moving on to the next paragraph.

OPTIONAL STUDENT ANSWER SHEET

Circle the correct answer:

PARAGRAPH 1-1
1. a. b. c. d.
2. a. b. c. d.
3. a. b. c. d.
4. a. b. c. d.
5. a. b. c. d.

PARAGRAPH 1-2
1. a. b. c. d.
2. a. b. c. d.
3. a. b. c. d.
4. a. b. c. d.
5. a. b. c. d.

PARAGRAPH 2-1
1. a. b. c. d.
2. a. b. c. d.
3. a. b. c. d.
4. a. b. c. d.
5. a. b. c. d.

PARAGRAPH 2-2
1. a. b. c. d.
2. a. b. c. d.
3. a. b. c. d.
4. a. b. c. d.
5. a. b. c. d.

PARAGRAPH 3-1
1. a. b. c. d.
2. a. b. c. d.
3. a. b. c. d.
4. a. b. c. d.
5. a. b. c. d.

PARAGRAPH 3-2
1. a. b. c. d.
2. a. b. c. d.
3. a. b. c. d.
4. a. b. c. d.
5. a. b. c. d.

PARAGRAPH 4-1
1. a. b. c. d.
2. a. b. c. d.
3. a. b. c. d.
4. a. b. c. d.
5. a. b. c. d.

PARAGRAPH 4-2
1. a. b. c. d.
2. a. b. c. d.
3. a. b. c. d.
4. a. b. c. d.
5. a. b. c. d.

PARAGRAPH 4-3
1. a. b. c. d.
2. a. b. c. d.
3. a. b. c. d.
4. a. b. c. d.
5. a. b. c. d.

PARAGRAPH 4-4
1. a. b. c. d.
2. a. b. c. d.
3. a. b. c. d.
4. a. b. c. d.
5. a. b. c. d.

PARAGRAPH 1-1

SUBJECT:
Tires

In the past, almost all tires were of bias-ply design, meaning that layers of nylon, rayon, or polyester (pŏl′ ē ĕs′ tər) were applied in crisscross fashion from one edge of the tire, around the tread surface, to the other rim edge. This design gives strength to the tire body. A belted-bias tire is made in the same way, but before the tread is applied, belts of nylon, rayon, polyester, fiberglass, or steel are added, which encircle the circumference of the tire. This lessens flex, keeping the tread firmly in place, and the belts make the tire strong and resistant to punctures and cuts. Radial tires have bodies made of cords that run straight up and over in hoop-fashion from one rim edge to the other, and they are encircled with two or more belts under the tread. This gives a very flexible sidewall for quick steering and comfort and a very strong tread area. Radial tires are much more expensive, but they usually last longer because the tread is so stable.

▲ (168 WORDS) ▲

PARAGRAPH 1-1

Circle the correct answer:

1. The purpose of this paragraph is to
    a. describe the different types of tires.
    b. describe radial tires.
    c. discuss the history of the tire.
    d. discuss the use of synthetics in tire production.

2. Radial tires are
    a. inflexible.
    b. more expensive than other tires.
    c. crisscrossed with synthetic fibers.
    d. always steel-belted.

3. We can conclude from the paragraph that
    a. bias-ply tires are no longer used on cars.
    b. radial tires are used only on sports cars.

c. few real improvements have been made in tire design over the years.
   d. the major function of "belting" a tire is to provide strength to the tire.

4. The paragraph suggests that
   a. few Americans can afford radials.
   b. belted-bias tires are more comfortable than radials.
   c. radials are the best tires available.
   d. fiberglass is a better belting material than polyester.

5. As used in this paragraph, the word *circumference* means
   a. inside
   b. portion
   c. side
   d. perimeter

GO ON TO THE NEXT PAGE ──────────────────────▶

PARAGRAPH 1-2

SUBJECT:
Ice Cream

The historical origins of the ice cream that young and old alike adore are shrouded in mystery. Before this popular dessert was invented, Marco Polo (môr′ kō pō′ lō) had returned from the Orient with a recipe for sherbet. Hundreds of years earlier, the Roman emperor Nero (nē′ rō) had snow and ice rushed to Rome from the mountains by special teams of runners. He flavored the ice with fruit juices. Ice creams like the modern variety were probably invented in Italy, and it quickly became an expensive treat for the very rich. King Charles I of England bragged of his secret recipe for ice cream; Henry II of France served a different flavor to his court each day for a month to mark his marriage. In America, Thomas Jefferson also bragged of his secret flavors. George Washington, according to a merchant's books, spent almost $200 on ice cream in 1790. And Dolly Madison served ice cream at her husband's Second Inaugural at the White House. It was pointedly evident that the cream was from the president's cows; the fruit, from the White House garden. Not until the nineteenth century, when ice could be kept because of the use of insulated icehouses and a hand-cranked ice-cream freezer was invented, were the lower classes able to afford ice cream.

▲ (212 WORDS) ▲

PARAGRAPH 1-2

Circle the correct answer:

1. The purpose of this paragraph is to
    a. prove that ice cream came from the Orient.
    b. discuss the history of ice cream in America.
    c. discuss the history of ice cream.
    d. compare ice cream and sherbet.

2. According to the paragraph, which of the following statements is not true?
    a. Marco Polo brought the recipe for sherbet from the Orient.
    b. The Roman emperor Nero enjoyed ice and fruit juices.
    c. Henry II of France served ice cream to celebrate his marriage.
    d. Ice creams like the modern variety were probably invented in France.

3. We can conclude from the paragraph that
   a. Nero got his idea for ice and fruit juices from the Orient.
   b. many famous people tried to make the public believe that they could make ice creams that no one else could.
   c. ice cream is no longer popular in France and England.
   d. ice cream making was refined in Italy after being introduced in the Orient.

4. The paragraph suggests that
   a. the lower classes could enjoy ice cream in the late nineteenth century because they could make it instead of buying it.
   b. after the lower classes could afford ice cream, the rich lost interest in the treat.
   c. ice cream was introduced in America before it was known in France or England.
   d. sherbet and ice cream are exactly the same thing.

5. As used in this paragraph, the word *evident* means
   a. incredible
   b. apparent
   c. hidden
   d. rumored

GO ON TO THE NEXT PAGE ──────────────▶

PARAGRAPH 2-1

SUBJECT: Brick

Brick has long been a useful building material, usually because of its permanence and ability to stand up to wear without costly painting or other care. Now brick is being ordered for many new homes because of its insulating properties; brick has "thermal inertia." Unlike lighter products like wood, brick absorbs, stores, and releases heat slowly. On a hot summer day, brick walls will heat more slowly than wood or stucco (stŭk′ ō). On cold winter days, brick walls, once heated from the inside out, delay the loss to the outside greatly and need less fuel for the maintenance of room temperatures. Besides their traditional use in walls, bricks are handy as solar collectors, once again because of their thermal inertia. A Trombe (trömb) wall is a layer of brick and glass separated by insulated air space; sunlight magnified by glass heats the brick, and the heated air can be drawn off and circulated. With brick and careful planning, the very walls of homes can become heating units.

▲ (164 WORDS) ▲

PARAGRAPH 2-1

Circle the correct answer:

1. This paragraph is mainly about
    a. the permanence and durability of brick.
    b. the insulating properties of brick.
    c. the inadequacies of wood and stucco.
    d. the Trombe wall.

2. According to the paragraph, which of the following statements is not true?
    a. Brick is very durable and permanent.
    b. Brick has "thermal inertia."
    c. A Trombe wall consists of two layers of brick separated by an air space.
    d. Brick can be used as a solar collector.

3. We can conclude from the paragraph that
    a. Trombe walls are used to provide a type of solar heat.
    b. wood and stucco absorb too much moisture to provide good insulation.

333

    c. brick has become very expensive recently.
    d. the best construction design for homes uses both brick and either wood or stucco.

4. The paragraph suggests that
    a. brick needs painting only occasionally.
    b. brick insulates better in the winter than in the summer.
    c. brick is a cheap building material.
    d. the future will probably see a lot of brick-constructed homes.

5. As used in this paragraph, the word *thermal* means
    a. heat
    b. transparent
    c. draft
    d. varying

GO ON TO THE NEXT PAGE ─────────────────────▶

PARAGRAPH 2-2

SUBJECT:
Leisure Studies

One of the most popular fields of study for college students these days is leisure studies. The names of the courses, "Introduction to Sport" or "The Philosophy of Sport," conjure up scenes of college students idly talking of Frisbees and sleeping on the grass. But leisure studies is a deadly serious field: students learn how to run the sports programs of big city park departments, how to manage a ski resort or a vacation hotel. The students learn how to organize a teenage soccer league where little or no interest exists in the sport, how to teach and keep beginners interested, and how to keep track of admissions money. To do all these things, they must take courses in psychology and business management along with those in leisure. As people grow more involved in sports activities, in vacations, and in trips, the job outlook for leisure majors is quite good; but can you imagine trying to explain to your parents that you're spending their tuition money studying leisure?

▲ (168 WORDS) ▲

PARAGRAPH 2-2

Circle the correct answer:

1. The main idea of this paragraph is that
   a. college is becoming too easy.
   b. academic classes are incorporated into the leisure studies program.
   c. leisure studies students learn to run city park departments.
   d. leisure studies is actually a serious field of study.

2. According to the paragraph, which of the following statements is not true?
   a. Leisure studies students are actually physical education majors.
   b. Leisure studies includes the study of business management.
   c. The need for leisure studies majors is increasing.
   d. Leisure studies is one of the most popular fields of study today.

3. We can conclude from the paragraph that
   a. it is easy to get a degree in leisure studies.
   b. leisure studies is not highly regarded by other students at most colleges.

c. leisure studies trains students to "manage" people's free time.
   d. leisure studies majors need not be physically fit.

4. The paragraph suggests that
   a. leisure studies programs are quite expensive.
   b. many parents feel college should be difficult and "serious."
   c. there are few jobs available to current leisure studies majors.
   d. few major colleges now offer programs in leisure studies.

5. As used in this paragraph, the word *conjure* means
   a. distinguish
   b. divert
   c. call forth
   d. break

GO ON TO THE NEXT PAGE ─────────────────────────────▶

PARAGRAPH 3-1   SUBJECT:
Guernica (gwâr′ nĭ kə)

The city of Guernica, destroyed in 1937, has become a symbol of the effects of all-out modern war. The entire population of the city died, between 1,000 and 2,000 people. The bombing took place on a market day, and no one knows how many people were in the city. Of course, even figures like these shrink beside casualty counts from later battles and bombings of World War II, but when Guernica was attacked, it was the first time bombers had been sent out to destroy a whole town. Guernica also lives on in memory because Picasso (pi ka′ so) immortalized the moment of the bombing in his painting *Guernica* and because correspondents described the scene to newspapers all over the world even while Guernica was still burning. Though the Germans bombed the town at the request of Spanish officials, for rebel bands were using the town to rest, and captured German papers show that the town burned mainly because of wind conditions, Guernica is still viewed by most as a preview of the horror and destruction visited on entire civilian populations during any major war.

▲ (182 WORDS) ▲

PARAGRAPH 3-1

Circle the correct answer:

1. This paragraph is mainly about
    a. Picasso's painting of Guernica.
    b. Guernica's unique place in history.
    c. the cruelty of the Germans during World War II.
    d. the effects of the media on history.

2. According to the paragraph, which of the following statements is not true?
    a. Guernica was destroyed in 1937.
    b. Guernica was bombed at the request of Spanish officials.
    c. Picasso went to Guernica to paint his picture of the town's destruction.
    d. Rebel armies were using Guernica as a regrouping and resting place.

3. We can conclude from the paragraph that
    a. the media played a large part in making Guernica a "symbol."

    b. the precise number of people killed at Guernica is known.
    c. Guernica was destroyed by nuclear weapons.
    d. the Germans were justified in destroying Guernica.

4. The paragraph suggests that
    a. the Germans had no idea how powerful their weapons were.
    b. Guernica was the first battle in World War II.
    c. the news media knew in advance about the impending attack on Guernica.
    d. the fire that destroyed the town of Guernica was made worse by the wind.

5. As used in this paragraph, the word *immortalized* means
    a. preserved
    b. canonized
    c. distorted
    d. polluted

GO ON TO THE NEXT PAGE ────────────────────▶

PARAGRAPH 3-2   SUBJECT:
Cellulose (sĕl′ yə lōs)

The diet sensation of the 1980s may be the addition of fiber—"roughage" it was called a few years ago—to the diet. Fiber <u>advocates</u> add bran, fruits, vegetables, and coarse, unrefined bread to their menus, on the theory that dietary fiber, the portion of plants that is unaffected by the chemical action of the human stomach, is beneficial to humans. Actually, these people may have been obtaining more dietary fiber from their diets than they thought: cellulose from wood or cotton has been used in ice cream to keep it from freezing, in salad dressings and whipped cream as a stabilizer, and in liquid and powdered egg substitutes. Cellulose is regularly added to certain frozen foods to help "glue" the pieces together, and it's added to chocolate milk to thicken the mixture and keep the flavoring from settling. Because cellulose has no taste or odor—and usually no color—it is added to many flour products to "stretch" the flour and to lower the calories in, say, a slice of bread. And now these manufacturers can advertise their products as "high-fiber" foods, as well.

▲ (185 WORDS) ▲

PARAGRAPH 3-2

Circle the correct answer:

1. The main idea of this paragraph is that
    a. fiber has a beneficial effect on health.
    b. fiber is not new to Americans' diets.
    c. cellulose helps keep foods from spoiling.
    d. cellulose is now used in dietetic foods.

2. Cellulose
    a. promotes freezing.
    b. dilutes liquids.
    c. is used as a stabilizer.
    d. raises the calorie count in bread.

3. We can conclude from the paragraph that
    a. some high-fiber diet advocates know little about their present diet.

b. high-fiber diets are not beneficial to man.
   c. dietary fiber disrupts normal digestion.
   d. dietary fiber can cause cancer.

4. The paragraph suggests that
   a. cellulose is used to tint clear liquids.
   b. cellulose is used to cover the foul odor of some types of food.
   c. cellulose sweetens the taste of milk.
   d. manufacturers are "cashing in" on the high-fiber diet fad without having to change their product.

5. As used in this paragraph, the word *advocates* means
   a. supporters
   b. critics
   c. scientists
   d. diets

GO ON TO THE NEXT PAGE ─────────────▶

PARAGRAPH 4-1

SUBJECT:
Coca-Cola

People who lived in towns and cities could easily refresh themselves in the hot summers just before the turn of the century. Coca-Cola had been invented in Atlanta in the 1890s, and it was for sale at thousands of drugstores and candy store soda fountains all over America. But people who lived in the country couldn't easily go into town every time they wanted a Coca-Cola or a flavored soda water. So Joe Biedenharn (bī' děn hōrn), a Vicksburg, Mississippi, candy store owner, decided soda should be taken out of the cities and into the country, where most Americans lived. He began to fill 10½-ounce, wire-stoppered bottles with Coca-Cola, shipping them by wagon and boat to the small towns along the Mississippi River. His business grew quickly; the bottled coke was so popular that Biedenharn was forced to move his bottling plant to a larger building. Ironically, the first bottling operation was viewed as a curiosity by the Coca-Cola Company. Biedenharn sent them his first two cases; he was politely thanked and then just as politely ignored.

▲ (171 WORDS) ▲

PARAGRAPH 4-1

Circle the correct answer:

1. The purpose of this paragraph is to
    a. discuss the introduction of bottled Coca-Cola.
    b. discuss the history of Coca-Cola.
    c. show the Coca-Cola Company's lack of concern for rural customers.
    d. provide a short biography of Joe Biedenharn.

2. According to the paragraph, which of the following statements is not true?
    a. Coca-Cola was invented in Atlanta in the 1890s.
    b. Joe Biedenharn first shipped his bottled Coca-Cola to Vicksburg, Mississippi.
    c. The first bottled Coca-Colas used wire stoppers.
    d. Joe Biedenharn was a candy store owner.

3. We can conclude from the paragraph that
    a. the Coca-Cola Company stole Joe Biedenharn's idea.

b. Joe Biedenharn finally went bankrupt because of poor management at his plant.
   c. Joe Biedenharn eventually sold his business.
   d. Joe Biedenharn's bottling business was very successful.

4. The paragraph suggests that
   a. most of Coca-Cola's customers lived in the Mississippi River Valley.
   b. the wire-stoppered bottles didn't preserve the Coca-Cola well.
   c. at the time Biedenharn started his bottling operation, Coca-Cola was serving only a small part of the population.
   d. Biedenharn didn't serve Coca-Cola in his candy store.

5. As used in this paragraph, the word *curiosity* means
   a. disaster
   b. conscience
   c. threat
   d. novelty

GO ON TO THE NEXT PAGE ────────────────────────▶

PARAGRAPH 4-2   SUBJECT:
English Educational System

In the English educational system, students take three very important examinations. The first is the eleven-plus, which is taken at the age of eleven or a little past. At one time the ability or aptitude shown on the eleven-plus would have determined if a child stayed in school. Now, however, all children continue in "comprehensive" schools, and the eleven-plus determines which courses of study the child will follow. At the age of fifteen or sixteen, the student is tested for the Ordinary Level of the General Certificate of Education. This examination covers a wide range of subjects; once students have passed this exam, they are allowed to specialize, so that two-thirds or more of their courses will be in physics, chemistry, classical languages, or whatever they wish to study at greater length. The final examination, at eighteen, covers only the content of the special subjects. Even at the universities, students study only in their concentrated area, and very few students ever venture outside that subject again; in a real sense, the English boy or girl is a specialist from the age of fifteen.

▲ (183 WORDS) ▲

PARAGRAPH 4-2

Circle the correct answer:

1. The purpose of this paragraph is to
   a. show why most English students are "specialists."
   b. show the superiority of the English educational system.
   c. discuss the inequalities of the English educational system.
   d. describe the three tests that the English educational system is based on.

2. The exam for the Ordinary Level of the General Certificate of Education is administered at the age of
   a. fifteen
   b. eighteen
   c. eleven
   d. thirteen

3. We may conclude from the paragraph that
   a. the exam that is taken at age eighteen is easier than the other two exams.

    b. failure on the eleven-plus exam excludes a student from further schooling.
    c. higher education is much narrower in scope in England than in America.
    d. physics and chemistry are the two most popular courses of study.

4. The paragraph suggests that
    a. most people in England are college educated.
    b. schooling is very closely controlled in England.
    c. the failure rate on the eleven-plus exam is quite high.
    d. England's structured educational system has reduced the illiteracy rate in that country dramatically.

5. As used in this paragraph, the word *content* means
    a. difficulties
    b. framework
    c. material
    d. pleasure

GO ON TO THE NEXT PAGE ⟶

PARAGRAPH 4-3   SUBJECT:
Office of Strategic Services

During World War II, spying against the enemy was performed by the Office of Strategic Services (OSS). The OSS was formed and run by General "Wild Bill" Donovan, who assembled an army of spies for the job. Many of Donovan's spies went on to become famous in public life after the war. Some were German prisoners of war who, it turned out, were anti-Hitler and had been forced into the German army; and some were refugees from Germany who had come to America in the thirties. These agents were given authentic clothing, identity papers—usually counterfeited by OSS engravers—and cover stories about their pasts, which each agent had to memorize down to the smallest detail. German counterintelligence agents questioned suspected spies about very small details of life in Germany, such as the cost of bus tickets in small German towns the spy knew. These spies were influential in the conduct of the war: one group, just outside Berlin, kept the Allies posted on German production plants; another pinpointed the site of rocket development in Germany. The OSS was the beginning of America's intelligence agencies that operate today.

▲ (188 WORDS) ▲

PARAGRAPH 4-3

Circle the correct answer:

1. This paragraph is mainly about
    a. Germans who later became famous in public life.
    b. General "Wild Bill" Donovan's life.
    c. the OSS's function in World War II.
    d. German counterintelligence operations.

2. The OSS provided the German refugees who became spies with
    a. cover stories about their past.
    b. identity papers.
    c. authentic clothing.
    d. all of the above.

3. We can conclude from the paragraph that
    a. General Donovan was killed during World War II.

b. some of the German spies helped the United States because of their hatred for Hitler.
   c. the OSS was later disbanded by Congress.
   d. the German spies returned to Germany after the war.

4. The paragraph suggests that
   a. German counterintelligence agents suspected that Germans were being used by the United States.
   b. the German spies destroyed the rocket development site they discovered.
   c. many of the German spies were members of the United States Armed Forces.
   d. few of the German spies got out of Nazi (nŏt′ zē) Germany alive.

5. As used in this paragraph, the word *authentic* means
   a. expensive
   b. genuine
   c. fake
   d. dark

GO ON TO THE NEXT PAGE ⟶

PARAGRAPH 4-4

SUBJECT:
Smithsonian Institution

The largest museum in the world is in Washington, D.C., on the National Mall. The Smithsonian Institution completely fills thirteen large buildings—and the Washington Zoo. Even with all this room, 95 percent of its collection is always in storage, loaned to other towns, or in traveling exhibits. No one knows why James Smithson, who died in Italy in 1829, left his entire wealth—almost $500,000—to found the museum. He was a scientist himself, but he had never even seen America. But the money was shipped, 105 bags of gold, in 1838, and the U.S. government built and began to run this mammoth museum. The daily business of the museum is run by its secretary, but the Board of Regents is made up of the chief justice, the vice-president, six congressmen, and nine private citizens. Over the years, the collection has grown to include more than 78 million items, including the buildings themselves—fine architecture and the scene of a great deal of history—as well as the tomb of Smithson himself. The donor's body was brought to the Smithsonian from Genoa (jĕn′ ō ɔ) in 1904, escorted by Alexander Graham Bell. Never before have a private gift and government funding built a museum to rival this one.

▲ (202 WORDS) ▲

PARAGRAPH 4-4

Circle the correct answer:

1. The purpose of this paragraph is to
   a. describe the administrative structure of the Smithsonian Institution.
   b. provide a short biography of James Smithson.
   c. describe the Smithsonian building.
   d. provide a short history of the Smithsonian Institution.

2. According to the paragraph, which of the following statements is not true?
   a. The Smithsonian Institution's collection consists of over 78 million items.
   b. There are seventeen members on the Board of Regents for the Smithsonian Institution.
   c. The Smithsonian Institution is the largest museum in the world.
   d. James Smithson was born in Italy.

3. We can conclude from the paragraph that
   a. Smithson's original donation still supports the Smithsonian Institution.
   b. the Smithsonian Institution is considered an important governmental agency.
   c. Smithson's relatives serve on the Board of Regents.
   d. many of the items in the museum are worthless.

4. The paragraph suggests that
   a. Smithson must have had some unknown affinity for America.
   b. the Italian government participates in the administration of the Smithsonian Institution.
   c. the vice-president is chairman of the Board of Regents.
   d. Alexander Graham Bell knew Smithson personally.

5. As used in this paragraph, the word *rival* means
   a. challenge
   b. compete with
   c. defy
   d. approach

STOP ▲

You have now completed the diagnostic test. Await further instructions from the teacher.

STUDENT SCORE SHEET

QUESTION NUMBER

	1	2	3	4	5	TOTAL
Paragraph 1-1						
Paragraph 1-2						
Paragraph 2-1						
Paragraph 2-2						
Paragraph 3-1						
Paragraph 3-2						
Paragraph 4-1						
Paragraph 4-2						
Paragraph 4-3						
Paragraph 4-4						
Totals						

STUDENT PROGRESS CHART

Record your progress by placing an *X* in the box beneath each item you answered incorrectly for a particular passage. Total your number of *incorrect* answers, and record them in the box marked TOTAL.

	#1	#2	#3	#4	#5	TOTAL
Passage 1-1						
Passage 1-2						
Passage 1-3						
Passage 1-4						
Passage 1-5						
Passage 1-6						
Passage 1-7						
Passage 1-8						
Passage 1-9						
Passage 1-10						
Passage 1-11						
Passage 1-12						
Passage 1-13						
Passage 1-14						
Passage 1-15						
Passage 1-16						

Passage 1-17						
Passage 1-18						
Passage 1-19						
Passage 1-20						
Totals for All Passages						
Passage 2-1						
Passage 2-2						
Passage 2-3						
Passage 2-4						
Passage 2-5						
Passage 2-6						
Passage 2-7						
Passage 2-8						
Passage 2-9						
Passage 2-10						
Passage 2-11						
Passage 2-12						
Passage 2-13						

Passage 2-14						
Passage 2-15						
Passage 2-16						
Passage 2-17						
Passage 2-18						
Passage 2-19						
Passage 2-20						
Totals for All Passages						
Passage 3-1						
Passage 3-2						
Passage 3-3						
Passage 3-4						
Passage 3-5						
Passage 3-6						
Passage 3-7						
Passage 3-8						
Passage 3-9						
Passage 3-10						

Passage 3-11						
Passage 3-12						
Passage 3-13						
Passage 3-14						
Passage 3-15						
Passage 3-16						
Passage 3-17						
Passage 3-18						
Passage 3-19						
Passage 3-20						
Totals for All Passages						
Passage 4-1						
Passage 4-2						
Passage 4-3						
Passage 4-4						
Passage 4-5						
Passage 4-6						
Passage 4-7						

Passage 4-8						
Passage 4-9						
Passage 4-10						
Passage 4-11						
Passage 4-12						
Passage 4-13						
Passage 4-14						
Passage 4-15						
Passage 4-16						
Passage 4-17						
Passage 4-18						
Passage 4-19						
Passage 4-20						
Passage 4-21						
Passage 4-22						
Passage 4-23						
Passage 4-24						
Passage 4-25						

Passage 4-26						
Passage 4-27						
Passage 4-28						
Passage 4-29						
Passage 4-30						
Passage 4-31						
Passage 4-32						
Passage 4-33						
Passage 4-34						
Passage 4-35						
Passage 4-36						
Passage 4-37						
Totals for All Passages						
Grand Totals All Sections						